4: CYBERNETICS: A New Management Tool.

CYBERNETICS AND SYSTEMS SERIES

Editor in Chief

J. ROSE

Director–General,
World Organisation of General Systems and Cybernetics

Already Published

1. Philosophical Foundation of Cybernetics
2. Fuzzy Systems
3. Artificial Intelligence
5. Economic Cybernetics
6. Cybernetics and Society
11. Computers and Cybernetics

Other Titles in Preparation

7. Models and Modelling of Systems
8. Automation and Cybernetics
9. Medical Cybernetics
10. General System Theory
12. Neurocybernetics
13. Metamodels and Metasystems.

CYBERNETICS:
A New Management Tool

Dr. Barry Clemson, PhD

Director, MAXIMUS, Technical Consultants

ABACUS

PRESS

First published in 1984 by

ABACUS PRESS

Abacus House, Tunbridge Wells, Kent, TN4 0HU

Printed by Chanctonbury Press Ltd,

British Library Cataloguing in Publication Data

Clemson, Barry
CYBERNETICS: A New Management Tool
1. Cybernetics 2.Management
I. Title
658.4'03 HD38

ISBN 0 85626 166 1

DEDICATION

To Rochelle,
one of the world's
most talented
(not to mention, lovely)
cyberneticians and
my preferred partner
in all sorts of
Enterprises.

SERIES PREFACE

The inter- and trans-disciplinary sciences of cybernetics and systems have made tremendous advances in the last two decades. Hundreds of books have been published dealing with various aspects of these sciences. In addition, a variety of specialist journals and voluminous post-conference reports have appeared, and learned societies, national and international, established. These substantial advances reflect the course of the Second Industrial Revolution, otherwise known as the Cybernetics Revolution.

In order to extend the readership from experts to the public at large and acquaint readers with up-to-date advances in these sciences which are rapidly achieving tremendous importance and which impinge upon many aspects of our life and society, it was considered essential to produce a series of concise and readable monographs, each concerned with one particular aspect. The twelve topics constituting the first series are as follows (in alphabetical order).

Artificial Intelligence, Automation and Cybernetics, Computers and Cybernetics, Cybernetics and Society, Economic Cybernetics, Fuzzy Systems, General Systems Theory, Medical Cybernetics, Metamodels and Metasystems, Neuro-cybernetics, Organizational Cybernetics: A Metascience for Management, Philosophical Foundations of Cybernetics.

The authors are experts in their particular fields and of great repute. The emphasis is on intelligible presentation without excess mathematics and abstract matter. It is hoped each monograph will become standard reading matter at academic institutions and also be of interest to the general public. In this age of enormous scientific advances and of uncertainty concerning the welfare of societies and the very future of mankind, it is vital to obtain a sound insight into the issues involved, to help us to understand the present and face the future with greater confidence.

J. ROSE
Blackburn

PREFACE

Management has long been recognized as more art than science. The notion of 'a metascience for management' which this book expounds, is at least audacious and perhaps outrageous. However, management, like all other human activities, is constrained by natural law. This book is about co-operating with the natural order of things rather than continuously bloodying our heads on stone walls. Perhaps an example will help make the point. Physics is the relevant science for bridge building, but the design of bridges is still very much an art. The laws of physics can't tell you what type of bridge to build, but physics does let you calculate the required sizes for the girders. And physics is necessary to avoid building in natural frequencies that will cause the bridge to shake itself apart — as occasionally happened in the past. Similarly, Management Cybernetics establishes the fundamental principles and provides limits on what is and is not possible for organizations.

Cybernetics and its sibling system sciences are still in their infancy as sciences go. Many scientists would thereby argue that my subtitle is pretentious and premature, that we do not yet (and perhaps never will) have a science for management. Our science certainly looks puny relative to problems such as war/peace, poverty, racism, inhuman working conditions and institutions whose primary purpose seems to be their own comfort. However, our present medieval practices in management make the readily available science look pretty good.

I make the claim to 'science' with considerable trepidation because most works with the words 'science' and 'management' in the title are neither scientific nor good management. Perhaps the kindest thing that can be said about most books that talk about science and management is that they offer prescriptions for managerial behavior and/or solutions to some of the standard problems that managers face. This book, on the other hand, offers no prescriptions for proper behavior and few ready made solutions. *Cybernetics: A New Management Tool* does two primary things. First,

it introduces a framework for thinking about organizations and management, i.e. it provides a set of natural laws, theorems, and principles which specify the limits for organizations in much the way that physics describes the limits for bridge building. Second, the book provides practical assistance in problem solving and organizational design. Several methods of great power and generality are presented, along with examples of their previous use and guidelines for their application. These methods have been tested in many different types of organizations.
bridge building. Second, the book provides practical assistance in problem solving and organizational design. Several methods of great power and generality are presented, along with examples of their previous use and guidelines for their application. These methods have been tested in many different types of organizations.

The book was commissioned as an introduction to Stafford Beer's management cybernetics. Stafford Beer has written six large books and roughly two hundred papers on management cybernetics. The criticisms, commentary, and applications by others run to many times the size of Beer's own considerable output. It was therefore clear from the beginning that ruthless selectivity would be required. My guidelines (clear in retrospect if not before) were:

*concepts: Select the minimum set of basic concepts necessary to provide an outline of cybernetics. These concepts are summarized in chapter eight, both in a glossary and as a set of 'laws'.

*methods: The methods selected for discussion meet several criteria. First, they are immediately useful to managers without elaborate preparation or extended technical study. Second, the methods are useful in those managerial situations of greatest uncertainty, i.e. when the relevant problem definition is unclear. Ackoff suggests these are the situations which require 'mess management'. Third, the methods are applicable to both problem solving and design situations. Fourth, the methods use the basic principles of cybernetics.

*non-mathematical: The book is entirely non-mathematical. This is not because mathematics are unimportant, because there are many crucial problems that require the use of statistics, linear programming, etc. However, this book was commissioned as an introduction and *if the problem is adequately formulated* it is relatively easy to select the requisite technical expertise. The obverse is anything but true: high powered technical expertise applied to the wrong problem is always expensive and sometimes disastrous. Those readers interested in the technical aspects of management cybernetics will want to consult Stafford Beer's writing and the extensive literature that derived from it.

My primary debt is to Stafford Beer. His books and papers have been my companions for almost two decades. And the many hours of discussion with Stafford, including hundreds of shared stories, taught me a great deal about the messy human side of management cybernetics.

Two novices at cybernetics (but not in much else), Karen Harlan and Deborah Castonquay, proved invaluable in finding passages that were ambiguous, unclear or simply incomprehensible. John Hayman wrote the most abrasive and helpful criticisms imaginable. David Beatty pointed out the absolute necessity for chapter seven which (Damnit, Dave!) almost killed me before it was finally subdued. And Shelley Clemson convinced me I was truly on the right track when we successfully taught this stuff in rural Maine. Thanks to all this superb help, the book seems to occasionally approach scientific grace, i.e. to be simple, true and beautiful. I happily claim sole responsibility for the remaining complexities, errors, and ugliness.

B. Clemson
University of Maine

CONTENTS

Chapter 1

THE HUMAN OBSERVER

The characteristics of the manager obviously influence the organization managed. Chapter One shows that this phenomenon is a particular example of the more general (and unavoidable) interaction between reality and some observing system.

Managers have some choice in *how* they choose to perceive their organizations and in *what* they choose to perceive about those organizations. Again, this is shown to be an example of the general phenomenon that faces one in defining a system for study or manipulation.

The alternatives open to a manager are partly a matter of the 'objective givens' of the situation, but they are also partly a matter of the choices (whether conscious or not) that the manager makes about how to perceive his/her organization. In the long run, those choices are absolutely fundamental in shaping the organization and in determining the alternatives the manager will and will not have available to him/her.

INTRODUCTION

Our *way* of thinking obviously affects what we do. However, the extent to which our thought patterns influence our actions is not so obvious. Not only *what* we think, but *how* we think and the very categories and concepts we use to think *with* all have a profound influence on our behavior. The practical manager, teacher, or doctor may feel that consideration of these matters is at best an interesting but esoteric pursuit without practical import. This section will attempt to demonstrate that the practical payoff for consideration of our ways of thinking can be very high indeed.

FOUR SCENARIOS

To set the stage I will briefly sketch out four different scenarios depicting the same managerial situation with four different twists. Relatively small differences in the manager's approach end up creating very different situations. The setting is a human service agency, but the precise nature of the agency (e.g. a school, hospital, employment agency) has been deliberately left vague so that the reader might imagine that the scenarios describe his/her own type of agency. The background is the same for all four scenarios.

Joan's selection as the administrator didn't surprise anyone, least of all Joan herself. After all, Joan was not only a local person, but also a personable, highly motivated, highly competent go-getter with all the right family connections. In addition, she was very active in community affairs including active membership in the biggest church in town, and had a long history with the local girls club culminating last year with coaching their field hockey team to an unbeaten season.

It was clear to Joan before she ever set foot in her new office that the new job would be a challenge. As a well connected local resident, Joan was all too keenly aware of the degree of citizen dissatisfaction that had built up around her staff and their performance. This was a relatively new phenomenon for Pleasantville. Pleasantville, a town of 25,000 with a mixed economy of light industry and agricultural products, had generally escaped the turmoil that swept through its larger neighbors in the last few decades. Now though, as Joan contemplated beginning her new job, it was clear that there were serious problems of public disaffection and that there were real organizational problems at the foot of this disaffection.

The community had changed in the last ten years so that the clientele had new needs, many of which clearly weren't being met. The staff had suffered considerable turnover in recent years, and there was a clear reluctance on the part of many to extend themselves on behalf of their clients. This manifested itself perhaps most clearly in the staff's tendency to work to the letter of the law in such matters as the hours spent on the job and unwillingness to participate in peripheral but important matters such as social events involving other staff and/or clients.

a. The first year: scenario one

It was clear to Joan that restoration of public confidence was an absolute necessity or her budget was going to be cut radically. And there was only one way to restore public confidence: they had to dramatically improve the service they were providing. Joan's first staff meeting included a presentation laying out the need for improved service and Joan's impassioned declaration that she was there to see to it that the staff had the wherewithal to provide that improved service.

During the following month Joan instituted a series of measures designed to ensure that the staff was really trying: a sign-in and sign-out form recorded the arrival and departure times of the staff, community reactions to the staff's performance was solicited, Joan spent a great deal of her time visiting the staff on the job, and a comprehensive staff evaluation procedure was devised.

By the end of the third month Joan had identified two staff members as glaringly inadequate and had begun the tedious, red-tape laden process for getting rid of them. The rest of the staff was more alert and busy than they had been for several years. It was clear to all concerned that new life had been instilled in the organization.

After six months on the job, Joan was working long hours and her staff was learning how to work with her. There was no longer a problem with tardiness and early departures, but sick days seemed to be increasing. The staff's relationship to Joan was always courteous and seemingly cooperative, but her proposed improvements seemed increasingly to run into a sort of passive defiance—there was never any overt resistance, somehow new initiatives got done (if at all) 'to the letter of the law' and never in the spirit of the law. The two inadequate staff members were, if anything, performing worse all the time — Joan's documented case against them was being nicely built by the very low level of their own performance.

By the end of that first year, Joan knew that her staff had improved its performance over the previous year. There was, however, a nagging doubt in Joan's mind. The last four months she had been increasingly consumed with checking on the staff. And the staff was increasingly withdrawn and defiant — and not so passively defiant as they had been at midyear. The number of resignations and requests for transfers was even higher than it had been in the two previous years. Joan consoled herself that the turnover represented getting rid of the deadwood and that change always involved some casualties. But she couldn't help wondering how they were to meet the human needs of their clients when the level of initiative, trust, and cooperation among the staff seemed so low.

b. The first year: scenario two

It was clear to Joan that either public confidence would be somehow restored or her budget would suffer large cuts. And there was really only one way to restore public confidence: they had to dramatically improve the service they were providing. Joan's first staff meeting included a presentation of her feelings that they needed to improve service, that they in fact had the ability to do so, and that she saw her job as one of facilitating the staff in doing their jobs.

During the next month Joan spent an enormous amount of time talking with individual staff members and small groups of staff. Most of the conversations began with Joan asking them what they thought needed to be done to improve things. The staff had a large number of fairly minor complaints, such as a shortage of proper writing paper and pens and pencils. Joan made a real effort to deal with these complaints as rapidly as possible and in some cases was able to remedy them completely. In other cases she fell into the habit of letting the relevant staff members know what she had tried and that it hadn't worked. In one or two cases the staff members then suggested strategies Joan hadn't thought of.

As Joan assessed her first month on the job she realized that she had developed a good working relationship with her staff, but that the only things she had actually done in any concrete sense were quite trivial: get more paper and pencils, eliminate one particularly onerous bit of paperwork, and rough out (an as yet not implemented) plan for cutting down on the practice of citizen complaints going to higherups without ever involving the person against whom the complaint is directed.

By the end of her third month, Joan and the staff were still trying to work out the bugs in the new process for handling complaints. The spirit behind the new procedures was that all complaints were initially directed to the person being complained about. In theory, none of the higher ups were supposed to deal with a complaint until after the citizen had at least tried to resolve the problem directly with the responsible staff member. Joan and her superiors were finding that while this sounded like a very good idea, the public was accustomed to a sympathetic ear at the top and were frequently irritated by the suggestion that they try talking to the responsible staff member first. Nevertheless, Joan decided that the issue was important to her staff and that she should persevere for the time being.

At the end of six months Joan, her staff, and the public seemed to be getting accustomed to working with each other. The number of citizen complaints that came directly to Joan had decreased dramatically and those that did come to her generally involved a real disagreement between a citizen and some member of the staff. In these cases Joan would hold a meeting with the relevant staff member and the citizen and was sometimes able to resolve the matter to the satisfaction of all concerned, but more often found herself supporting the staff against some unreasonable complaint. In a few cases the complaints pointed up real problems with their organization and Joan was still grappling with ways of resolving these. There were aspects of the community's needs that the organization should have been handling that somehow they couldn't seem to deal with. Joan, not quite knowing what else to do, began to meet with a select group of staff members to discuss these problems that they couldn't seem to resolve. These meetings consumed a lot of time and energy and involved very complex discussions without getting much of anywhere. The difficulty seemed to be that the problems fell between various individual's responsibilities.

By the end of the first year, staff morale was the highest it had been in several years, there were very few resignations, no requests for transfers, and people were putting in far more than the required number of hours. On the other hand, there was a nagging sense of inadequacy being expressed by a large minority of the staff because those clients with particularly difficult problems were not being dealt with to the staff's satisfaction. Joan strongly agreed with this position. Their discussions of these problems during the preceding months had sort of dribbled off into nothing because the conversations kept circling the issue of organizational structure without any way of dealing with it and therefore no way of deciding how to deal with client problems that fell between the cracks.

c. The first year: scenario three

It was clear to Joan that, unless public confidence was rapidly restored, the budget was going to be slashed. And there was really only one way to improve the public's confidence in them: they had to radically improve the service they provided. Joan's first meeting with her staff included her presentation of the urgent necessity for improvement, her honest admission that she, as a brand new administrator didn't have the answers, and finally her confidence that working together they could make the necessary improvements. A series of meetings with the various departments followed, each focusing on the question of how to improve their overall performance.

At the end of the first month it was clear that the staff, while demoralized from struggling with a long series of unresolved issues, was basically very talented and capable. Further, many of the problems facing the organization involved issues of coordination of services across departmental lines. It seemed that certain organizational changes were required to achieve the necessary integration of services.

By the end of the third month, Joan and the staff had worked out a series of measures that, when implemented, should resolve most of the glaring difficulties in providing client service. Unfortunately these measures involved certain changes in the way Joan's organization related to the larger system. But, since Joan's superiors had been extremely supportive so far, Joan was optimistic that the necessary adjustments could be worked out — they were after all very minor. Accordingly, Joan prepared a beautifully worked out presentation that candidly outlined the deficiencies in client service to date, showed how the problems arose through lack of any integrative mechanism for their various services, and showed how the new measures would achieve that integration of services. The presentations seemed to be an enormous success. Joan was warmly congratulated by her superior and a long discussion followed about the details of implementation. During this discussion, certain difficulties emerged because there were a few implications of the proposed change at the superior's level that Joan had no way of knowing about in advance. However, the superior's enthusiasm was a good sign and Joan left, much encouraged, with her boss's promise to get back to her within the week with a definite yes or no to the proposal.

Ten days later Joan hadn't yet gotten her definite yes or no and didn't feel it was wise to raise the issue because most of the higher ups seemed to be embroiled in dealing with a political issue raised by a prominent citizen.

Six weeks after Joan's initial presentation, she finally got together with her boss and they again discussed the proposal. Most of the changes were acceptable, but one had some political implications that were worrisome and Joan's boss wondered if they might do without it. Unfortunately, from Joan's perspective, this was the centerpiece of the proposal: it involved increasing the staff's discretionary powers to cut across departmental lines when the client's needs demanded it. The higher ups were worried about accountability and clear lines of authority. Joan and her staff went back to the drawing boards.

After six months on the job, Joan was ready to try to integrate services again. Another presentation to her boss was again received enthusiastically and another spirited discussion followed. This time the staff's discretionary powers to cut across departmental lines was surrounded by a whole system of paper work designed to ensure that the higher ups knew what was going on, that there was an identifiable individual who was responsible and that there was little possibility of a public relations or legal difficulty arising. A week later Joan had permission for the new system.

By the end of the year Joan had seen some fine examples of interdepartmental cooperation that dealt, in a truly outstanding way, with some very difficult problems. As she thought back over the last six months, though, Joan realized that most of these examples of integrative efforts had occurred shortly after the new system was put into effect, and that there was quite a lot of complaining about the amount of red tape required to make it all work. In recent months there were very few examples of interdepartmental cooperation and Joan wondered if maybe the staff had 'solved' the paperwork problems by the simple expedient of ignoring those problems that required an integrative approach. The year ended with Joan spending a lot of time wondering why it was so difficult to make even simple changes in the way they operated.

d. The first year: scenario four

It was absolutely clear to Joan that her budget would be shredded unless she and the staff managed to restore public confidence in the organization. And, in the long run, there was only one way to do that: they had to dramatically improve their service. Joan's first staff meeting included a presentation in which she tried to get across her feelings of urgency about improving their performance, her faith that working together they could do it and her confidence that while she didn't have specific solutions yet, she did have some powerful methods for attacking such a problem.

The next month was largely taken up with meetings with various groups and individuals from the staff. Most of these meetings dealt with two separate questions:

1. What sort of problems do you think we have or what sort of changes would help you?
2. What sort of outputs does the larger system absolutely require of us, or, what are the constraints on us that we can't get away from?

By the end of the month a fairly coherent picture had emerged. The major shortcomings in providing service all involved client problems that involved more than one department. There were currently no good ways to integrate services across several departments. Secondly, the constraints on the organization seemed to be of three general types: 1. legally, they had to meet certain broadly defined criteria, 2. their higher ups were very sensitive to citizen complaints (therefore these had to be minimized) and to certain quantitative measures of their client service (although they were pretty cynical about the validity of these measures), 3. there was a loosely defined but important 'ethos' or set of professional norms that determined whether one was perceived as a proper professional or not.

At the end of that first month, Joan held a long staff meeting in which she discussed these notions. She argued that 1. the staff was individually extremely competent, 2. there were certain problems (e.g. those requiring integration of several departments) for which the organization was structurally incompetent (and this was no reflection on anyone), and finally that the constraints they had identified also defined the areas in which they could unilaterally make some changes. The last point is tantamount to saying that once you truly understand the constraints placed upon you by the larger system, then in other matters you can do anything you like. Organizationally, then, if the outputs are maintained, the organization could rearrange itself in any way it wished. There followed a period of further meetings with various groups and individuals on the general topic of 1. what do we really want to be accomplishing, 2. how could we do that? 3. to what extent are we doing things based on historical precedents that no longer make sense? Many of these meetings went round and round with no sense of getting anywhere.

By the end of her first six months on the job, Joan was getting some pretty clear ideas about all three of the questions. The next job was to translate these ideas into structural and programmatic form that the staff would buy.

By the end of the first year, Joan and her staff had implemented a flexible structure that seemed to be accomplishing several things:

1. It took advantage of the unique strengths and interests of the staff.
2. It maintained the critical outputs to the rest of the system at a high level.
3. It routinely handled the run of the mill needs of their clients, and
4. It provided for a wide variety of special responses to difficult client needs by giving the staff enormous discretionary power in these cases.

As Joan reflected over the last two months since beginning implementation of the new plan, she felt a mixed sense of enormous pride in her staff's dedication and competency and, on the other hand, considerable anxiety over the frequent appearance of what seemed to be barely controlled chaos as some of the more creative staff members tackled particularly difficult problems. She consoled herself in those times with the thought that she would rather be hanged for attempting a good job than for ignoring the very real human needs that they were ostensibly set up to deal with.

These four scenarios featured very different persona in the role of Joan, the new administrator. The different persona, naturally enough, elicited very different responses from the rest of the system, including particularly the staff and superiors. By the end of the first year, the situation described in the four scenarios had gone in four different directions and we might say that we ended with four quite different situations even though they all started out the same (except for the persona of Joan). The usual 'scientific' explanation of this sort of phenomenon is that human perception is distorted, partial, or strongly influenced by our biases and ideology There is a strong (even if usually unstated) implication that a truly objective view would eliminate these differences. To make the point in its most crass form, if we could somehow create four identical situations and put four different (but truly 'objective') persons into those situations in the role of Joan, they would then all perceive the situation the same and presumably react the same. Thus, at the end of the year, the four scenarios would all read the same. We might characterize this point of view as the naive view of scientific or objective truth.

THE CYBERNETICS OF OBSERVING

Cybernetics holds quite a different view. Whereas traditonal science assumes that in most cases the reality observed is (or can be made) independent of the observer, cybernetics asserts that the observation is very generally dependent upon the observer, and that the process of observing typically influences the reality observed, and that objectivity in the naive sense is a pernicious myth. Perhaps some concrete examples will help make the point. To begin with, here are four summary examples based upon the scenarios given above:

1. A boss holding a McGregor Theory X view point (i.e. workers are lazy and irresponsible) will find plenty of evidence to reinforce that view and will behave in such a way as to generate lazy and irresponsible workers (i.e. he/she will mistrust the workers and will spend much time checking up on them). In short, this type of boss will create the situation that is expected.
2. A boss holding a McGregor Theory Y view of workers (i.e. workers are responsible and enjoy challenges) will find plenty of evidence to reinforce that view, will behave in a way to elicit responsible workers, and in general will tend to create the situation expected.
3. The boss who thinks that improvements require action from those above will find that in fact nothing can be done because all the power is in the superiors' hands.
4. The boss who 'knows' that his department has walls or boundaries around it and that the rest of the world notices only his outputs, can do anything he/she wants to with the internal structure provided only that those outputs are maintained.

Next, it may be helpful to see some examples from the 'hard' sciences. To simplify our task somewhat, suppose we wanted to obtain the objective truth about something so simple as a pencil. We could assemble a team of physicists, chemists, etc. and ask them to ascertain the objective reality of that object consisting of wood, glue, graphite, clay, metal and rubber called a pencil. They might begin with the list of variables that they could measure, e.g. hardness, ductility, conductivity, bending strength, tensile strength, compressibility, reflective index, resistance to moisture penetration (by the paint and by the glue), resistance to swelling, rot, mold, bacterial or viral contamination, resistance to temperature changes — the list gets very long in simply characterizing the object in terms of its gross physical characteristics.

We might also inquire after the pencil's micro-characteristics on the level of its atoms and molecules: precise chemical composition (including the various isotopes of carbon, silicon, etc.), adsorbed gases, trace elements, irregularities in structure, precise structure of the wood cells and their arrangements, etc.

If all of the above was accomplished, we might want to investigate the relationship between the pencil and human beings: it is, variously, a writing instrument with certain pleasing (or not) characteristics of size, shape, texture, appearance, and smell; a chewing instrument (for dogs, babies, and temporarily stymied authors); a sword (for unruly seventh graders engaging in pencil fights); a cheap billboard, a makeshift dowel rod, and so on.

It may be theoretically possible to obtain a complete knowledge of that pencil, but I suspect that I can think of aspects of it to measure faster than the team of scientists can actually carry out the measurements — without even using the fact that many of our more sophisticated measurements in physics generally suggest new, previously unthought of measures. So it seems that we are always going to be stuck with partial knowledge, even about relatively simple objects. Whatever we 'know' about a pencil will be some small selection of the potentially knowable.

To continue with the hard sciences, lets think about the question of the 'objectivity' of a given observation. Any observation involves a relationship between the measuring instrument and the phenomenon to be measured. In the simplest case this involves, for instance, laying a ruler on an object to be measured. Even in this case there are numerous conventions to be observed, e.g. position your eye on a line perpendicular to the part of the ruler to be read. The relationship between the ruler and the object measured is then the one that we call 'length'. In more complicated cases, the relationship between the instrument and the object is often somewhat obscure, but always critical. The next few paragraphs present more complicated examples.

The cell pathologist examining a tissue sample with a microscope has, in addition, to the microscope (whose proper use requires that a whole series of conventions be followed), a whole set of cognitive structures which permit him/her to interpret the view in the microscope. The untrained observer simply sees a chaotic jumble of shapes and colors which are meaningless even when healthy and diseased tissues are juxtaposed for easy observation. This observation involves, at a minimum, the cell, the procedures for preparing it (which always change it to some degree), the conventions for using the microscope, and the cognitive structures in the observer's head.

The physicist or chemist using a mass spectrometer analyzes his sample by shooting charged particles of it through a strong magnetic field. The particles can be sorted according to their weight (among other things). The results of such an exercise are usually recorded on a moving strip of paper upon which an electrically controlled pen makes jiggly marks. The scientist then takes long strips of such paper and measures the height of the various peaks and the distance between them. Given a little mathematics, the atomic mass of the various constituents of the sample can then be determined. These observations involve the physical characteristics of atoms and magnetic fields as *interpreted* through the jiggly lines on a strip of paper. Worse yet, the lines on the paper are the mass spectrometer's *interpretation* (via banks of electronic components) of what is going on inside itself. Unfortunately, the mass spectrometer is unable to tell the difference between legitimate signals and various kinds of noise that arise in its components. The scientist then is faced with the task of deciding which of the multitude of zig-zag peaks and valleys produced by the spectrometer are meaningful and which are not.

The relationship between the ruler and the object measured is relatively clear. The relationship between the instrument (i.e. the microscope, tissue slide, and the pathologist's eye/brain) and the healthiness of the unstained cell is anything but clear. Similarly, the relationship between the instrument of the physicist (i.e. the mass spectrometer plus the eye/hand/brain) and the material sampled is extremely complex. What is 'objective' about these processes is that, given a *great* deal of care, a given result can be independently duplicated. Kenneth Boulding points out that this sort of objectivity is meaningful only for relatively common events — any event that is sufficiently rare simply can't be dealt with because it is not replicatable by these methods.

Light passing through pinholes will provide one final example from physics. Given two pinholes, one behind the other, light goes through the holes as if it were a stream of bullets — it gets through the second hole only if it is lined up with the stream. However, if the holes are sufficiently small, the first hole will scatter the light as if it were a wave instead of little bullets, and a fraction of the light will go through the second hole. Physicists (after some struggle) have learned to think of light as consisting of discrete little particles and *also* as consisting of continuous waves, like a vibrating string. The nature of light thus seems to depend upon the size of holes you use to measure it.

These considerations of physics lend support to the following conclusions:

1. Our knowledge is always partial.
2. Such partial knowledge as we can achieve depends upon our establishing some relationship between a measuring 'instrument' and reality.
3. The relationship between the measuring instrument and reality always depends upon characteristics of the person(s) doing the measuring.
4. In many of the measurements (or observations) science makes, the process of carrying out the observations actually changes the thing observed.

We scientists have not generally paid much attention to these considerations until quite recently.

THE HUMAN REALITY

Cyberneticians have been concerned with the observer-observation interaction.* One of the sorts of questions they have asked is how the characteristics of the human critter have affected our perceptions and understanding of our world. Warren McCulloch[1] put it this way (and devoted his life to trying to find an answer); 'What is the nature of a number that man may know it, and the nature of a man that he may know a number?' Heinz von Foerster[2] is another one who has been concerned with the nature of the human apparatus for perception and the way in which it influences our view of our world. One of von Foerster's favorite points is that the human nervous system deals in undifferentiated electrical impulses. The differences between sensations of mild and intense pain are simply the frequency of nerve impulses. The differences between pleasure and pain are simply different patterns of impulses. The nervous system has no way of distinguishing the various sensations except in terms of the patterns of impulse arrival. All of our perceived world is built out of these undifferentiated electrical impulses. We literally construct our own reality out of an undifferentiated flow of identical electrical pulses. The patterns we perceive as our reality (e.g. cup, tree, square, circle, dancing, talking, mating, running, etc.) are either genetically programmed into us (as the sociobiologists argue) and therefore determined by the process of evolution and not really under our control *or* are created by each of us in a process of socially conditioned learning that eventuates in most of us sharing most aspects of our understanding of reality (as the cybernetician argues).

The extent to which our 'reality' is objectively true and out there, or merely our own creation, is an open question (and one that is perhaps not ultimately answerable). What seems clear at this point is that 1. there is a 'reality' out there (e.g. speeding Mack trucks have the same effect on careless pedestrians whether we believe in them or not) and 2. the nature of that reality for us, (which is after all the reality that counts) is partially created by our own nature as observing systems.

As soon as we truly internalize the idea that our reality is partially our own creation, a number of very practical results obtain. To begin with, let's go back to the four scenarios in the beginning of this chapter: there were four different administrators attempting to deal with the same situation and they, based on different perceptions of the situation, ended up with very different results:

a. The first case was a McGregor theory X type leader and she (through her theory X leadership) generated a theory X staff.

b. The second case was a McGregor theory Y type leader who, through theory Y leadership, generated a theory Y staff along with its attendant problems.

The third case began with the perception on the administrator's part that change within her unit required change and permission from the higher levels in the organization. Given strong support from the higher levels, Joan actually managed to make some changes, but somehow they didn't seem the change the actual problems they had set out to deal with in the first place.

d. The last case began with the administrator's perception that her unit was, in large measure, an isolated 'black box' and that so long as the proper outputs were given to the larger system they could internally do whatever they decided to do. As we saw, this approach had its own unique problems.

These four administrators had four very different perceptions of the situation, acted in very different ways (based on those perceptions), and ended up by creating very different organizations. The point is that administrators have some choice over which aspects of their situation to emphasize and that these matters are seldom clear cut. There was no 'right' solution to the case posed at the beginning of this chapter, as there is seldom, if ever, only one 'right' solution to dealing with any administrative situation. Our choice of action needs to be based on some combination of 'objective' analysis of the situation and our understanding of the consequences of our premises. This last point seems very strange to those of us schooled in western rationality, but again the four cases illustrate the point: the premises chosen by the administrator at the beginning strongly influence the resulting 'reality' of the situation.

The university's division of reality into disciplines provides another good example of the practical implications. Suppose that a school or hospital administrator sets out to hire a consultant because he/she feels that the organization's productivity is lower that it should be. To overstate the case only a little, to choose any given consultant is to also automatically define the problem and imply a particular type of solution. For instance, the following consultants each have characteristic problem definitions/solutions:

a. Dr. Psychologist: the problem is one of individual characteristics and individual motivations. If you get the right people and set up the proper system of rewards, productivity will improve.

b. Dr. Sociologist: the problem is one of group norms and roles. The group norms prescribe the amount that is to be produced and each individual, other than for a few deviants, follows those norms. Work with the group leaders to find ways to increase the level of productivity norms.

c. Dr. Macro Economist: the problem is clearly that you are operating with all sorts of outmoded technologies and methods. If you were not protected from competition you would have gone bankrupt long ago. The solution is obviously to set up a competitive situation. We will get the government to change the tax structure so that citizens have a voucher system whereby they can use any school (or hospital) they wish and the schools (or hospitals) will have to compete for clients.

d. Dr. Micro Economist: the problem is obviously one of lack of payoff for the worker — it makes no difference to the worker's pay if he/she works very well or very poorly. It is necessary to have clearly defined measures of output and a salary scale tied to that output.

e. Dr. Operations Researcher: 'the problem is obviously that you haven't specified your payoff function. If you will be specific about what consititues success, we will show you how to optimize that one measure'.

I could go on (there are for instance, several varieties of psychologist, the political scientists, and the 'systems approach' folks). The special educators provide a deliciously tempting target because of their self-righteousness and obvious blindness to the social system of the school that their proposals all unknowingly attempt to change. The point is that despite the ease of ridiculing the disciplines, they are *all* right. Each of the disciplines has its own way of looking at the world and each thereby perceives a different reality. The problem comes in only when we get trapped into the common game of trying to determine which of these views is the 'correct' one for the *truth* is that they are all 'correct' and all partial (which is to say all are defective). I might just add, lest there be engineers or natural scientists who are feeling smug about this narrative, that they are in the same boat with the rest of us, as my examples from the natural sciences have tried to make clear. And if any doubts remain, think about the results when our administrator looking for a consultant hires Dr. Aerospace Engineer: the problem is defined more or less in terms of getting the right components arranged in the right order (i.e. do a big PERT or other flow chart and manage *that*). The managerial results of following the aerospace engineer's advice have varied from nil to disaster, depending it seems upon the vigor with which the PERT imperatives were pursued.

The managerial lesson in all this is that one must be very careful in hiring a consultant, because most consultants have defined the problem in advance and have the solution ready in advance. This is fine if you are sure you, as the manager, know what the real problem is and what sort of solution you want. The difficulty comes in because figuring out what problem to attack is often the hardest part. If this were not true, our social institutions would not be in such a mess.

A SYSTEM IS A SYSTEM IS A .....

All of us (and scientists rather explicitly) proceed to define more or less explicit systems. As individuals, we deal with our family, employer, government, town, etc., etc. Normally we don't bother to make the boundaries between 'our' system and the rest of the universe explicit (even scientists don't usually do this). However, depending upon what we include in or exclude from our definition of the particular system, we have more or less possibilities for change, flexibility, growth, stability, etc. The next few paragraphs look at a few examples (we will proceed from the very concrete to the very soft).

The physical object that constitutes a pendulum might be considered as any of a large number of systems. For instance, we might define the following three systems:

1. mass, velocity, and position of the pendulum bob.
2. length of the arm, gravitational field, and period of the pendulum.
3. cost in dollars, accuracy in keeping time, and aesthetic quality of its appearance.

The physicist is fond of system two and includes it in most elementary physics texts precisely because it permits a simple, deterministic description of the pendulum behavior. Among other advantages, this definition of the system facilitates construction of pendulums for specific purposes, e.g. clocks and metronomes. System one seems like a nice simple way to describe a pendulum but in fact does not permit a description of the pendulum behavior except in terms of a lengthy table that shows the velocity and position at each moment. Nor does system one permit easy construction of various pendulums with different characteristics. The third system definition is worthless to the physicist or engineer but may be just what you or I need to choose a metronome.

Science has always counted it a great success when they succeed in finding a system definition, like that of the pendulum definition number two above, that permits a simple description of system behavior and manipulation of the system (e.g. prediction or construction of systems with desired characteristics). It would not be stretching things very much to say that the central activity of science is the search for systems that permit this sort of description and manipulation.

Consider again the various consultants we discussed above. One, perhaps the *basic*, difference between these folks is that they have radically different definitions of the system. For instance:

1. Psychologist's system: the variables defining this system are individual characteristics and system rewards and penalties for the individual. Also considered are the relationships (transactions) between *pairs* of individuals.
2. Sociologist's system: the variables considered include the characteristics of groups and roles within those groups. This includes group norms and relationships between pairs of groups.
3. Macro economist: cost of materials, labor and capital; amount of competition; and efficiency of the operation.
4. Micro economist: the utility function for the individual, the measures of production, and the payoffs for the individual.

5. Operations research: the objective function (i.e. the criteria of success), the components of the system, the inter-relationships among the components, and the scheduling of interactions among those components.

The mere list of the variables that these various types of scientist consider, reveals why they can't talk to each other — each of them is examining a 'system' that is radically different from the system examined by any other. The reality being studied is quite literally different for each of these specialists. Not surprisingly, the 'truths' about the situation and the ways of manipulating the situation turn out to be quite different.

We can examine the implicit systems in the four scenarios that opened the chapter: Scanning the scenarios for the variables considered yields the following lists:

1. McGregor theory X system: system performance, time spent on the job, community reaction to staff performance, staff evaluation (including identification of incompetents), supervision of staff.
2. McGregor theory Y system: system performance, staff perceptions of needed improvements, quality of working relationships, directing of citizen complaints to the lowest practicable level, problems that fall between the organizational cracks.
3. The 'change requires higher level system involvement' system: system performance, staff perception of how to improve performance, coordination of services across departmental lines, changes required in the system levels above, superiors' willingness to make changes in their operations, staff discretionary authority, red tape.
4. The 'black box' system: system performance, staff perceptions of problems and needed changes, outputs the larger system requires from the black box, integration of services, organizational structure, the mission of the unit, alternative ways of structuring the unit internally.

The list of variables, again, reveals that these four managers had very different definitions of the system they were in charge of. One of the advantages of being thus explicit about the variables that make up a system, is that one begins to get a pretty good sense about the sort of system manipulation a given system definition will, or will not, support. So long as the system definition is merely implicit, it is very hard to get any handle on whether or not the variables being considered will permit manipulation of the aspects of the situation that are of crucial interest.

CONCLUSION

This chapter has used examples from management, the natural sciences, and the social sciences to illustrate the point that we, as observing systems, influence our own reality. The practical aspects of this are perhaps best dealt with in terms of the way managers go about defining the system that they lead. There are perhaps two fundamental aspects of defining the system that every manager should give attention to: choosing the set of variables that define the system as a thing, and choosing basic premises or beliefs about the way the system operates. Unfortunately these two are not cleanly separate. The four scenarios earlier in this chapter illustrated the effect of four administrators who differed both in their choice of variables and in their premises about the way the system worked. The examples from the natural sciences illustrated the effect of choice of variables.

There are two major lessons to be drawn from all this

1. The choice of variables that define the system is critical in determining what the system is, what its behavior will be (and whether or not that behavior will be comprehensible) and what can and can't be done about, or to, that system. Unfortunately there is no simple formula for choosing the 'right' set.
2. The choice of premises about how the system works is crucial in two respects: in the case of social systems, those premises will partially determine how the system actually does work and those premises influence the variables thought to be important in defining what the system is. We know enough about human behavior to know *some* of the consequences of particular choices of premises, e.g. McGregor's theory X and theory Y are both self fulfilling prophecies. Unfortunately, again, there is no simple formula for choosing the right premises. Some of our most distinguished and most experienced scientists in this area (Waddington[3], Ackoff[4], Beer[5]) insist that the biggest gains in practical situations are likely to arise from seriously questioning the most obvious and certain of the 'facts'.

I might summarize both of these points by saying that the nature of reality depends partially (and unavoidably so) upon the nature of the observing system. Further, since the observing system is part of reality, the nature of the observing system depends upon the nature of reality. Thus the whole process of 'knowing' or 'understanding' nature is circular, and there are unavoidable limits in the extent to which we can get out of this problem.

The argument culminating in the last paragraph is perhaps the most scientifically controversial point in all of cybernetics. I am obviously convinced the cyberneticians are in the right, but the reader should be warned that in many quarters the debate is raging still. The interested reader might consult Stephen Toulmin[6], Stephen Brush[7], and Thomas Kuhn[8] for the philosophy of science arguments. The papers of Heinz von Foerster[9] and his colleagues present the major arguments from the standpoint of cybernetics.

Notes

*Other scientists have, of course, also been interested in these questions. The Heisenberg Uncertainty Principle is perhaps the best known example of the point.

CHAPTER ONE REFERENCES

1. Warren McCulloch, 'Recollections of the Many Sources of Cybernetics' *Cybernetics Forum* **VI**, No.2, 5-16 (Summer, 1974), page 5.
2. See Heinz von Foerster under the topic of perception in the *Collected Works of the Biological Computer Laboratory* edited by Kenneth L. Wilson (Illinois Blueprint Corp., Peoria, Illinois, 1976) (microfiche).
3. Conrad Waddington, letter 'Operation Research' in *Science* **183**, No. 4130, 1141 (March 22, 1974).
4. Russell L. Ackoff, *The Art of Problem Solving,* Wiley-Interscience, New York, 1978) especially chapter one.
5. Stafford Beer, *Platform for Change* (Wiley, London, 1975) and *Decision and Control* (Wiley, London, 1966) especially part one.
6. Stephen Toulmin, *Foresight and Understanding: an Inquiry into the Aims of Science* (Harper and Row, New York, 1961).
7. Stephen G. Brush, 'Should the History of Science be Rated 'X'?' *Science* **183,** No. 4130, 1164-1172 (March 22, 1974).
8. Thomas Kuhn, *The Structure of Scientific Revolutions* (The University of Chicago Press, Chicago, 1962).
9. See the *Collected Works of the Biological Computer Laboratory* edited by Kenneth L. Wilson (Illinois Blueprint Corporation, Peoria, Illinois, 1976) (microfiche)

Chapter 2

THE ORIGIN AND NATURE OF CYBERNETIC LAWS

In one sense there is very little new about cybernetics. The interaction between the observer and reality (discussed in chapter one) has been recognized by physicists, social scientists, and philosophers. Most of the insights (or 'laws') discussed in this chapter were also drawn from other sciences (e.g., electronics, information theory, general systems theory).

In another sense, cybernetics is quite novel. Cybernetics has taken insights from these various other sciences, generalized them, and integrated them into a powerful framework for dealing with complex, dynamic, probabilistic systems.

The present chapter articulates and discusses some of the basic concepts and principles of cybernetics. The self-organizing system law asserts that truly complex systems largely organize themselves. The feedback law shows how phenomena with circular causality behave as if they had goals of their own. The law of requisite variety gives a fundamental limit to the regulation achievable by any given control system. Taken together, these three laws provide a compelling explanation for much organizational behavior that is usually attributed to incompetence, fear of change, or evil motives. These three laws provide both limits and guidance for any attempt at organizational change.

INTRODUCTION

Chapter one gave arguments to show the role of the observer. In particular, that chapter advanced the argument that managers can choose to define their system in many different ways and that their choice of system definition strongly influences the policies and actions that are or are not possible. The narrative has so far not provided much help in choosing a useful definition. That task is begun by the present chapter which sets out to provide some of the major outlines of the world view or paradigm for cybernetics.

THE BIRTH OF CYBERNETICS

Norbert Wiener[1], who is generally accorded the title of the father of cybernetics, defined it as 'the science of effective communication and control in man and the machine'. Wiener took the word cybernetics from the Greek word for steersman or governor. This definition has never helped me much and I prefer Stafford Beer's[2], which says 'cybernetics is the science of effective organization'. When Beer[3] says this, he is thinking of systems with the following characteristics:

-**complex**, i.e. they have more relevant detail than the given observer can possibly cope with.

-**dynamic**, i.e. they are changing in their behavior or structure or both.

-**probabilistic**, i.e. there are important elements whose behavior is at least partly random.

-**integral**, i.e. they act in some important sense as a unity.

-**open**, i.e. they are embedded in an environment which affects them and which they affect.

Thus cybernetics studies the difference between effective and ineffective modes/structures/methods of organization in certain classes of systems. Another way of saying it is that cybernetics is concerned with the general patterns, laws and principles of behavior that characterize complex, dynamic, probabilistic, integral, and open systems. Cybernetics thus studies, for example, brains, ecologies, groups, organizations, factories, etc. The emphasis is always to find those general principles that apply to all such systems. Management cybernetics, on the other hand, is the applied science that uses cybernetics as its starting point to deal with organizations.

It may also help in understanding cybernetics to see the relationship of it to the other sciences. This 'history' attempts to put cybernetics in the context of the other sciences by characterizing the system types or the types of questions each addresses. The four categories of science[4] are listed in the order in which they got started, but all are still very much with us and important today. The history of science that follows is absurdly short and simple and, strictly speaking, probably not totally accurate. However, it seems to convey a fairly fundamental truth and this truth perhaps justifies the violence that is done to the details.

The first simplification is to talk about only four aspects of reality: matter, energy, information, and the observer. Matter and energy are clearly recognized as fundamental aspects of reality, and in the last few decades cybernetics has made a strong case for information as a third fundamental aspect of nature. The justification for the observer is to get the human being into the picture because (as shown in chapter one) our peculiarities are important in determining the 'truths' we wrest out of mother nature.

1. Organized Simplicity

Classical physics and biology studied the (mostly) deterministic systems that could be explained in terms of the characteristics of the parts or described and classified natural phenomena (e.g. star charts or biological taxonomies).

ORGANIZED SIMPLICITY
classical physics and biology

matter energy

2. Disorganized Complexity

The statistical sciences, beginning with statistical mechanics, studied the patterns resulting from the essentially random 'behavior' of large numbers of 'atomistic' parts in some system (e.g. gas atoms, voters, genes). Einstein's famous equation, $E=mc^2$, showed the relationship between matter and energy, thereby linking the two aspects (matter and energy) that were previously considered as immutably separate.

DISORGANIZED COMPLEXITY
statistical sciences

matter energy

3. Organized Complexity

Cybernetics and general systems theory are concerned with systems, usually involving both deterministic and random elements, which are resistant to the methods of both the first two sciences, i.e. examining characteristics of the parts or statistical averages. Cybernetics has also emphasized the relationship between information and matter/energy, i.e. information negative entropy, thereby linking all three basic aspects of reality.

ORGANIZED COMPLEXITY
cybernetics and general systems theory

matter energy information

4. Relativistic Organized Complexity

Second order cybernetics is concerned with the nature of the observer as that observer interacts with a system-being-observed. The activity of observing, in general, has some influence on the observed system (this might be termed a generalized Heisenberg effect). Further, the nature of the observer partially determines what the resulting observation will be. Second order cybernetics might be termed the cybernetics of observing systems.

Second order cybernetics thus links up the three basic aspects of reality (matter, energy, and information) and the observer (or the observing system to be perfectly general about it). Second order cybernetics has demonstrated that the nature of our reality is unavoidably tied up with our nature as observing systems. If we had some other nature (or, as we are doing to some extent, if we change our nature, for example through a change in values or instrumentation) then our reality will be different.

RELATIVISTIC ORGANIZED COMPLEXITY
second order cybernetics

matter

the observing system — energy

information

Cybernetics has built upon and in some respects extended the rest of science.

FEEDBACK

Perhaps the key notion in cybernetics is that of circular causality. Science has traditionally thought in terms of a given phenomenon having a cause or causes. A given cause might have a more fundamental cause and so on. Causes and effects were thought of as A causes B, B causes C, C causes D, and so on for as far as you might want to trace it. This sort of chain can be diagrammed as follows A→B→C→D. Only in the 1940's did science begin to consider cause-effect relationships that were circular, i.e. A causes B and B causes A or in diagram form: A B. The problem with a circular situation is that it is very messy and difficult to deal with compared to a nice linear chain. Examples of circular causality include those marital spats that seem to start over nothing and escalate into a brawl, arms races, feuds, mutual infatuations, and generally any of those processes that we refer to as a vicious cycle. As cybernetics began to understand the importance of these circular processes, it gradually became clear that the relationship between the elements might well be more important than the nature of the elements themselves in determining overall system behavior. In particular, several sorts of system behavior that were previously considered anomalous by science, became understandable.

Circular causal processes are generally called feedback. There is a language problem here because 'feedback' in popular usage has come to mean one person's response to another person's action or performance, i.e. an instructor provides 'feedback' to the student on the student's performance. This popular usage of 'feedback' is a severe distortion of the term's technical meaning. In a technical sense, feedback should be applied only to those situations in which A affects B and B affects A and there are numerous repetitions around the loop. The popular usage is not so much wrong — it is just that the popular usage is such a degenerate case that it loses its power and interest.

We can usefully distinguish two rather different behaviors for feedback loops: 1. the case in which it seems to have a purpose and/or goal and will resist disturbances that tend to displace it from its goal state 2. the case in which it tends to blow itself up. The goal seeking case is termed negative feedback and the effect on the two halves of the loop is opposite, i.e. if A causes an increase in B, B will cause a decrease in A and vice versa. Therefore, any change in either will tend to be resisted by the other. A negative feedback loop, therefore, tends to be highly stable. The 'blow itself up case' is called positive feedback and means that a change in A causes B to change in the same direction and a change in B causes a similar change in A, i.e. any disturbance is amplified by the interaction of the two. A positive feedback loop, therefore, tends to be explosively unstable.

	Pre-cybernetic causality	**Cybernetic causality**
basic mechanism	linear, **a→b→c**	circular **a→b→c→a** or **a⇄b**
results	**1.** Given initial conditions always give the same final conditions.	**1.**Given initial conditions may give different final conditions (with a positive feedback loop).
	2. Different initial conditions always give different final conditions.	**2.** Different initial conditions may give the same final result (with a negative feedback loop).

Table 2.1. A shift in understanding of causality.

The interactions between two athletic teams can illustrate both types of feedback and the subtle changes which sometimes transform a system from overall positive to overall negative. Given two teams that are roughly evenly matched, if one team plays very well and begins to pull slightly ahead, the other team is stimulated to greater effort and tends to catch up, i.e. the two function as a negative loop in minimizing the score difference between them. However, suppose one team is having a horrible night and gets completely demoralized in the first ten minutes. As the game goes on and they get more and more hopelessly behind, they will tend to play less and less well and the better team will relax and everything will go right for them. In this case, the two teams are functioning so that overall the feedback loop is positive in maximizing the score difference. This example illustrates nicely both types of feedback loops and demonstrates the point that there is nothing structural or in the 'essence' of the system, about whether the loop is positive or negative. The real point is that systems which inlude feedback loops are capable of very complex behavior and that quite subtle changes in the relationships at one point in the system can have very large scale effects in changing system behavior. The differences among the four scenarios sketched in chapter one could be explained in terms of differences in the feedback loops set up by the four different administrators.

Table 2.1 provides a pre-1940 (or pre-cybernetics) view of causality and a cybernetic view of causality:

HOLISTIC PROPERTIES

Perhaps the second fundamental insight that cybernetics had (and it shared this with other sciences, particularly general systems theory)[5] is that there are many systems which exhibit 'holistic' behavior, i.e. they have characteristics which belong to the system as a whole and don't belong to any of its parts. Your appearance is an example of such a characteristic, as is charisma, or school climate, or the 'feel' of an institution. This insight is sometimes expressed as 'the whole is more than the sum of the parts', but this statement is either false or it simply means that the characteristics of the whole are due to the *interaction* among the parts. Another way of talking about this characteristic of systems is that they have 'emergent' properties, i.e. the properties of the parts give no hint of some property that the whole possesses. Ashby[6] has shown that emergent properties are also due to interactions among the parts, and more particularly to unexpected characteristics of those interactions. If we had 'full' knowledge of the parts, there could be no surprises and the issue of emergent properties could never arise. However, since 'full' knowledge of the parts of any system is quite impossible (as I attempted to show in the first chapter), we can confidently expect the systems that interest us to continue to surprise us with 'emergent' properties. Any of our social systems provide legion examples of this characteristic. For instance, consider the examples given in table 2.2.

For each of the system levels given in Table 2.2. many other examples of 'emergent' properties could have been given. For instance, morale in a given social system is not simply the sum of the morale in the constituent units. The same is true for questions of norms and culture generally. For instance, a given university will have norms for scholarship and publication that are widely shared across campus. Within the university there are generally a few units that far exceed the general norms and the rest of the university will then treat them with a mixture of pride and derision as 'hotshots', glory boys or some similar

Example one

system levels	person	city	region	nation
Holistic properties	personality and values	city culture	regional norms	national culture

Example two

system levels	student	class	school	school dist.
Holistic properties	interest in school	class norms	school spirit	ethos about schooling

Example three

system levels	patient	pediatrics section	hospital	county health dept.
Holistic properties	illness	general mode for dealing with patients	norms for patient treatment	ethos about health care

Table 2.2. Examples of system levels and properties that characterize those system levels but are not characteristic of the lower level systems

term. Similarly there will be a few units who violate the norms in the other direction, perhaps by way of defining their mission somewhat differently (e.g. as service instead of publications). Such a unit will typically be the object of some scorn and will have a somewhat defensive attitude toward the rest of the university.

THREE BASIC LAWS

Ashby[7] wrote that, if adequate for our practical purposes, we should by all means use the classical method of reductionism (i.e. deal with the system in terms of its *parts*), and avoid the more difficult methods of the cybernetician. Ashby was, I am sure, quite serious. If we can accomplish our practical ends without recourse to the methods of cybernetics we should do so. However, if we are dealing with systems of great complexity and dynamicism, we may not be able to achieve our practical ends without cybernetics. This section will lay out several laws* of nature that, like the law of gravity or the second law of thermodynamics (entropy), apply to all systems. Just as the implications of gravity or entropy are not always clear and simple, the implications of these laws are also not always clear. However, we can be pretty sure that every system is subject to these laws, just as it is subject to gravity and entropy. The domain in which a given law is most significant is an important question. Newton's laws of mechanics are important any time one wants to understand the motion of one thing relative to another. Entropy is important in questions of organization versus chaos, in questions of heat transfer, and energy loss and so on. The laws I will discuss seem to be important when we deal with social systems and institutions. Entropy and gravity also apply to these systems, (because all natural laws apply to all systems) but they may or may not be significant in terms of my (or your) practical purposes at a given point in time.

Law 1: SELF ORGANIZING SYSTEMS LAW. Complex systems organize themselves; The characteristic structural and behavioral patterns in a complex system are primarily a result of the interactions among the system parts.

We are accustomed to saying, when we see some phenomena, 'I wonder what caused that?'. For sufficiently complex and dynamic systems, the answer turns out to be 'it caused itself'. Now that is not a terribly satisfying answer (and we will go into some of the mechanisms in a moment) but it nevertheless seems to be the case. Another way of stating this law is 'the system is the way it is because of the mutual adjustments the parts have made in the process of interacting with each other'. Your family is the unique family that it is, not because someone designed it that way, but because you, your spouse, the kids and all the relatives, have gone through an extended process of interacting, each affecting the others. Each has adjusted to those others and at every stage the system has a configuration based upon the combination of all those interactions. For another example, your brain (and mine) has a structure that is partially specified by your genes. However, the fine structure, (i.e. the details of neuron interconnections) seems to be left to chance — our brains organize themselves in terms of the details. An ecology provides an obvious example — the foxes control the number of rabbits and the supply of rabbits controls the number of foxes that are able to survive. The way your classroom works depends upon yourself *and* upon the students you get. Some methods that work well with one group may not work at all with another and vice versa. The effectiveness of a hospital or a police force depends upon the leaders — but it also depends upon the rank and file. In particular the effectiveness of a hospital or police force depends upon the proper *match* between a leader and his/her staff, and on the proper match between the leader/staff on one hand and the community served on the other hand. In all these cases we have examples of systems that are the way they are because they organized themselves to be that way. In none of these cases can we find a regulator or designer or boss who is solely or even mainly responsible for the system state observed.

Law 1A: Complex systems have basins of stability separated by thresholds of instability.

This law means that some configurations of the system are stable and some are not. For instance, consider a marble resting on a surface with ridges and hollows. The marble will be stationary only at the bottom of a hollow. If I bash the marble, it will roll around a bit and eventually come to rest again in the bottom of the hollow. If I bash the marble hard enough to knock it over one of the hills on the surface, it will then roll off into some new hollow and the system consisting of 'marble on a surface' has a new stable state. The only way I can get the marble to perch halfway up one of the hills is to sit there beside it and hold it (or build a platform under it or some such). The point is that there is no way to get the marble to stay halfway up a hill without a continuous disturbance because halfway up the hill is a region of instability for the system. Or, for another example, I might decide to eliminate the rabbits living in the mountains behind my house because they are eating up my garden. With a strenuous program of hunting and trapping, I can perhaps decrease their number by half. If I then stop my rabbit elimination program, they will simply return to their former numbers in a year or two. Now, of course, if I eliminated all of them (or enough so that they could no longer find each other to breed) and put a big rabbit-proof fence around my mountain, then I would have really changed the system state. But killing half the rabbits is, in effect, bashing the marble halfway up one of the slopes.

The last couple of decades have seen a large number of educational experiments that, collectively are termed 'alternative schools'. These social experiments have typically involved 1. participatory governance structures involving students, parents and staff; 2. wide variety and flexibility of subject matter, scheduling, and pedagogical methods and;

3. great emphasis on student responsibility and initiative. The Ford Foundation study of these schools reported a life time of about three years for most of them — i.e. within three years the experimental school was essentially indistinguishable from the parent school system. It seems that in most cases these alternative schools rolled the marble part way up a slope and it took about three years to roll down again. If one wants to create a lasting, alternative school, one needs to make sure that the marble is pushed all the way over the crest of a hill, i.e. the configuration chosen for the school must be one that is in the 'catchment basin' of a *new* region of stability.

One of the difficulties in designing new institutions or new configurations for old ones is that very little of our social science is any help at all in 1. knowing where the tops of the hills are, or 2. knowing what the alternative regions of stability are. The reason why the social sciences are so little help is that most of the research (implicitly or otherwise) assumes the system is in a region of stability and investigates that region and the system behavior within that region. Very little of the work inquires into the questions raised here. The imperative suggested by the laws of self-organizing systems is that the reformers and designers of organizations need to understand which catchment basin they are setting their systems into. This suggests that we need some quite radical new types of social science research so that we gain a better understanding of what these catchment basins are and what the thresholds (i.e. ridges) between them look like.

Law 2: FEEDBACK. The output of a complex system is dominated by the feedback and, within wide limits, the input is irrelevant.

Let's see what this law means in a practical sense. To begin with, I am talking about any situation in which it makes sense to picture it as the diagram below shows:

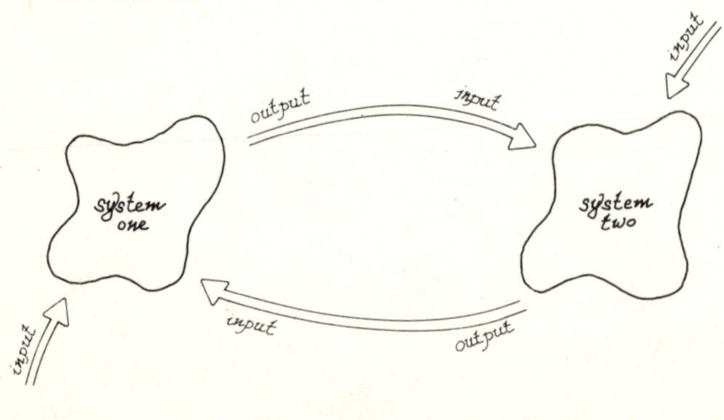

This little diagram might describe an enormous array of different situations, e.g. the two systems interacting might be a husbandand a wife, a boss and his staff, a teacher and a class, two athletic teams, two parts of an ecosystem, two parts of a corporation, a government and its citizenry, your brain and your body, etc. The law applies to all of them with one proviso: it refers to 'high gain amplifiers'. A high gain amplifier simply means that a given type of input is changed (i.e. 'amplified') a great deal. Thus the law selects out of all possible systems and system behaviors 1. those systems characterized by a process of circular interaction and 2. those inputs that are changed a large amount by at least one of the systems.

Depending upon our interests, we typically choose to call one half of the situation the system and the other half is termed the feedback. For instance, we might be interested in the school's effect on children's ability to do mathematical reasoning. In this case we would traditionally start by saying the system is, loosely speaking, the mathematics courses, the output is mathematical reasoning ability, and the feedback is rather obscure and hard to find. We can investigate the situation by looking at what happens if a given school produces very high or very low outputs of mathematical reasoning ability.

The strange finding is that nothing at all happens despite huge variations in mathematical reasoning ability on the part of the graduating students. If we really look into the situation and examine particular classes in mathematics, we will find a few teachers who are using grades, personal enthusiasm, charisma and the students' own excitement at intellectual growth as feedbacks to produce mathematical reasoning ability. Most mathematics teachers will be found to be doing almost nothing to produce this output. This suggests several conclusions: 1. mathematical reasoning skill is not an important output for the school (if it were there would be a discoverable feedback loop to regulate it). 2. mathematical reasoning skill is an important output for some mathematics teachers but not for most (again the evidence is the presence or absence of the requisite feedback loops).

We could repeat this sort of inquiry for student learning generally. The first startling finding would be that student learning makes no difference in the way the parts of the system or the school system as a whole get treated. If a school has two teachers essentially teaching the same children the same subject matter and one is superb and the other is terrible (i.e. in one class they learn a great deal and in the other they learn almost nothing) the school system treats the two teachers precisely the same. Similarly if there are two schools in the same district, one doing very well and one doing very poorly, the district treats them precisely the same. Individual teachers, parents, and students of course treat these situations quite differently (i.e. both parents and teachers will go to great lengths to get out of the bad schools and into the good ones), but the *system* has no feedback loops that in any sense affect the student learning. Thus the system is seen to be massively pathological — it cannot possibly produce the output it is ostensibly designed to produce. The successful operation of the school depends entirely upon the dedicated individual who, as teacher or principal, can somehow manage to produce student learning in spite of a system that is *systemically* indifferent.

Law 2A: All outputs that are important to the system will have associated feedback loops.

This law can also be stated as 'any desired result that has no systemic feedback loop will not be achieved *or* any system that lacks a feedback loop for a desired output is pathologically defective'. This law helps explain the intense frustrations experienced by many educators and other human service workers. The educator or social service professional chooses that field because (at least in part) he/she has a sincere desire to help people grow and develop. After a short time on the job the person discovers that the *system* doesn't care whether, for example, students grow and develop or not. The system has powerful feedback loops on system outputs such as classroom noise level, neatness of the classroom, parental complaints, student behavior in conformance with community norms, and (in many schools) the win-loss record of the athletic teams, and the grades received by students. These then are the outputs regulated by the school. The educator who wants to stimulate student growth, learning, and development is free to do so (so long as it doesn't interfere with those other 'important' outputs) but the system won't help, and in many ways the system will interfere (primarily because many of the rules, procedures, and paperwork growing out of the system's concern for these other outputs simply get in the way of or pose innumerable small problems for the teacher attempting to foster real learning). It is no wonder that many of the most sensitive teachers leave and that those who stay forget about student growth.

Lest anyone think I single out education for unduly harsh criticism, let us think briefly about several other social service institutions. One would think that the criminal justice system would be about preventing crime or perhaps even making us (the citizenry) secure. However, such evidence as does exist suggests the opposite.

The criminal justice system is in the business of exacting retribution and generally of managing criminals. It is not organized to achieve any positive effect such as reducing crime nor ensuring our personal safety or security — thus we shouldn't be surprised that we are personally unsafe and our property is insecure. The feedback loops to achieve reduction of crime or increase in safety/security are simply not there. The major output of jails seems to be more highly trained criminals.

For another example, hospitals seem to be in the business of running x-ray units, kidney dialysis units, cancer research, heart transplants, and so on. Somewhere in all those departments and research units, real patients move around and various things happen to them. Ostensibly the hospital is in the business of 'curing' people or perhaps even ensuring their 'healthiness'. But again there is a problem — where are the feedback loops for 'cures' or 'healthiness'. The best measure of the quality of care in a hospital seems to be the rate of turnover among nurses. The reason for this strange phenomenon seems to be as follows: In the whole apparatus of the hospital, the nurse is the element that deals with the patient as a human being (the rest of the hospital deals with the patient as an x-ray film, as a kidney, as a certain type of cancer, etc. etc.). If the hospital is well run, the nurse is able to put it all together and the patient is treated reasonably well and the nurse is able to feel good about his/her job. If the hospital is not well run, the nurse sees that the patient is not being well treated (oh yes, the patient's kidneys and cancer *may* be treated well, but the patient as a human being is violated). When nurses see patients are not being well treated and are powerless to give the patient the care they know should be provided, the nurses leave that hospital in hope of finding a better-run hospital. The system is defective in that we have not designed-in the feedback loops that would keep the hospital aimed at either cures or healthiness.

Feedback loops are one of the major elements that make self-organizing systems work the way they do. If one starts tracing out the chains of causality in some complex system such as an ecology or a social institution, the feedback loops quickly become very complex and interlocking. For instance (and the experts among the readers, please forgive the over-simplifications) figures 2.1 through 2.4 give some idea of the sets of interlocking loops one typically finds.

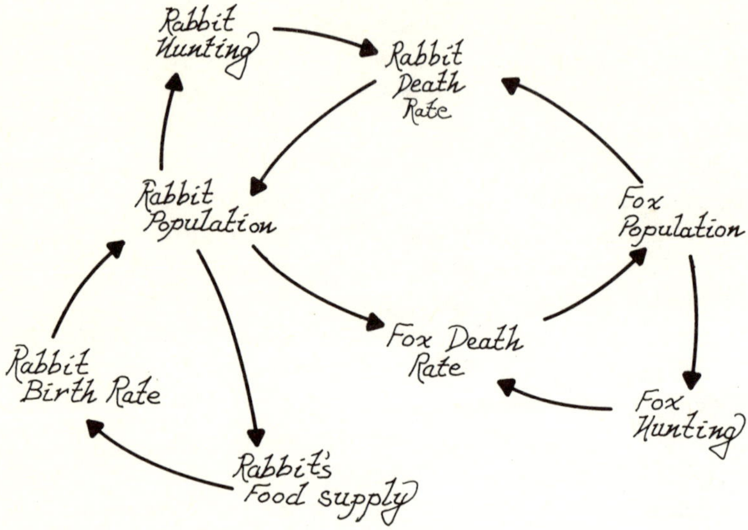

Figure 2.1. An illustration of the feedback loops regulating a fox and rabbit population system. There are four major feedback loops in the diagram.

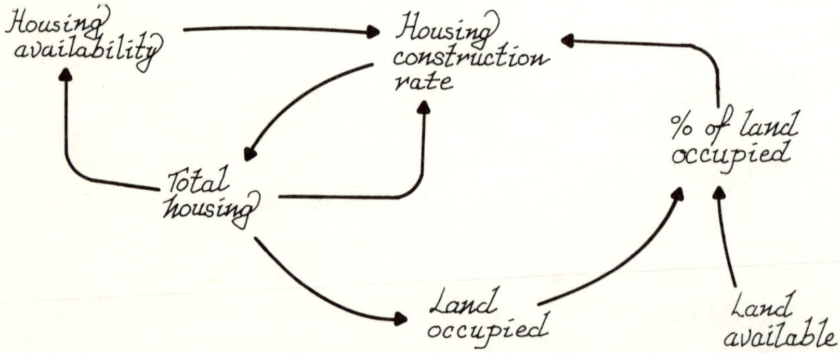

Figure 2.2. A partial representation of the feedback loops influencing house construction (adapted from Goodman[8]).

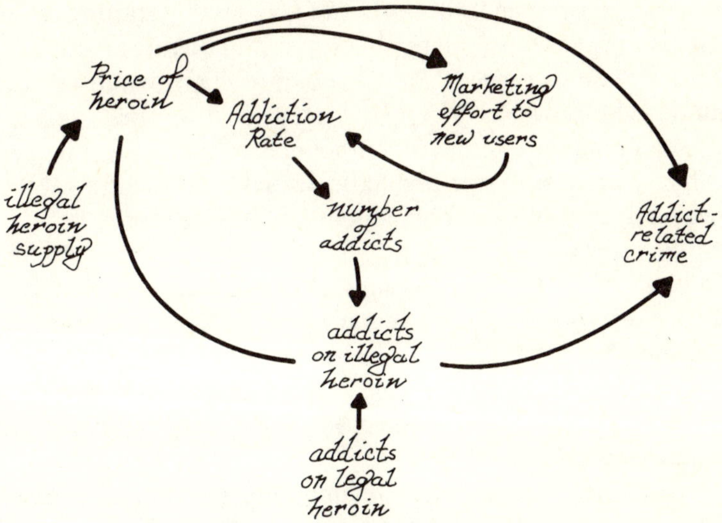

Figure 2.3. A model of policy implications on heroin addiction (from Levin, Hirsch and Roberts[9]).

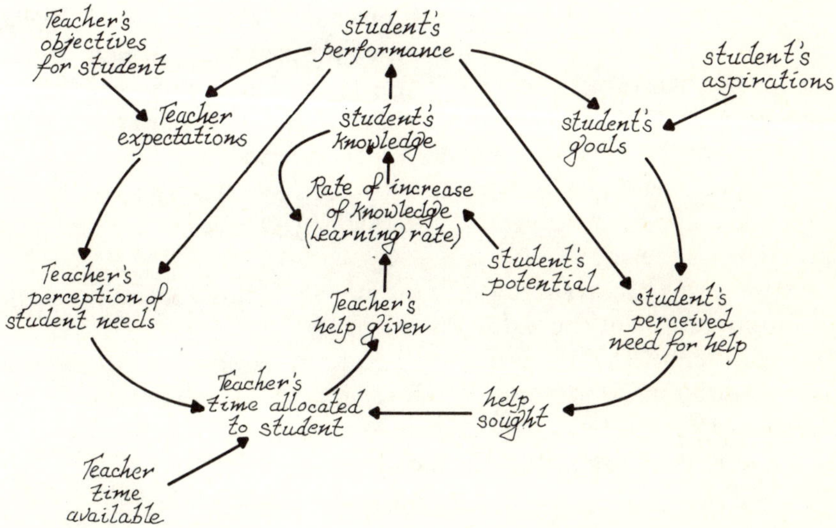

Figure 2.4. A model of student-teacher interaction (from Roberts[10]).

In figure 2.1, one can trace out one of the loops by starting arbitrarily, e.g. an increase in the rabbit population stimulates more rabbit hunting which causes an increased rabbit death rate which decreases the rabbit population. Another loop can be traced out from the same starting point, i.e. an increase in the rabbit population decreases the fox death rate which increases the fox population which increases the rabbit death rate which decreases the rabbit population. Notice that in the above two examples, after tracing the effect all the way around the loop, the loop acts to counteract the initial change. In such a case the loop tends to stabilize the whole system. Technically this is a negative (or goal seeking) feedback loop.

In other cases the original change can be reinforced and increased by the loop. Technically such a loop is a positive (or deviation amplifying) feedback loop.

As mentioned above, these feedback loops can be conveniently divided into two classes depending upon their effect upon system behavior: 1. negative or error correcting or goal seeking, and 2. positive or vicious circle or deviation amplifying. The first (negative) acts as if it has some particular goal in mind and seeks to pursue that goal. Engine governors and furnace thermostats are good examples, as are the processes providing regulation of body chemistry and temperature. The second (positive) acts as if growth or change is the purpose. These positive feedback loops tend toward explosive change which, unless limited by some other loop, will destroy the system. Feuds, arms races, mutual infatuation, and the growth of a bacterial culture are all good examples of the explosive growth of positive feedback processes.

The peculiar behavior of self-organizing systems can be largely explained by invoking sets of interlocking feedback loops. These peculiarities include:

1. - the same final state despite differences in initial conditions and differences in the pathways taken.
2. - different final states despite initial conditions that differed only in some random (and seemingly innocous) element.
3. - active resistance to attempts to change the system.
4. - spontaneous change in the system.

One and two seem to contradict each other, as do three and four. The seeming contradictions can be explained simply in terms of two characteristics of these systems:

1. The difference between a positive and a negative loop is one of degree — a negative loop can be transformed into a positive loop and vice versa by making very subtle changes in the system (I gave several practical examples earlier). Passing over the threshold from positive to negative in one key feedback loop can change system behavior from one of growth or change to one of resistance to change. Changing a key loop from negative to positive can similarly change system behavior from one of maintaining stability (i.e. resistance to change) to one of explosive loss of control (i.e. either change or 'growth', depending upon your perspective).
2. The corollary to the self-organizing system law stated that self-organizing systems have regions of stability and regions of instability. The example given involved a marble on a hilly surface. What this amounts to saying is that:
    a. a system configuration that falls within a given catchment basin will end up at the lowest point in that basin, regardless of where it started.
    b. a system configuration that begins on the very crest of a ridge or hill can go either way depending upon essentially random (and *tiny*) influences while it is perched on the ridge. The point is that whatever initial slight nudge the system gets to move it ever so slightly in any direction gets it started toward the bottom of one catchment basin rather than the other. Thus two systems that began in essentially the same configuration may well end up at radically different points (i.e. in the bottom of two radically different catchment basins).

The challenge these thoughts pose to the manager is that organizations can no more be maintained in positions of instability than marbles can be perched on the side of a hill. Managers (and students) of organizations must learn to design organizations to be stable and, when change is desired, we must learn to find a new stable configuration that involves the desired change. There are numerous examples of attempted change that involves trying to perch a marble halfway up the side of a hill — one such is the huge number of 'alternative' schools appearing over the last decade or so in the U.S.

Law 3: THE LAW OF REQUISITE VARIETY. Given a system and some regulator of that system, the amount of regulation attainable is absolutely limited by the variety of the regulator.

What this law really means is that the relative complexity of the regulator and the system to be regulated is crucially important. In all cases, what the regulator in effect does is to deal with aspects of the system which, taken collectively, match the complexity of the regulator itself. I say 'in all cases' very confidently because this is the *best* that any regulator can ever do. It is of course possible (and common) to do much worse than this.

Let's see if we can get a sort of common sense grasp of the way this works. Regulation implies a more or less continuous interaction between some 'system' and some 'regulator'. The simplest possible regulator is one that uses its own internal state to tell the system 'more/less' or 'yes/no'. Such a regulator doesn't 'know' anything about the system controlled except that the system has some effect on the regulator itself, and based on the system's effect, the regulator instructs the system to do more or less, to start or stop, etc. Your thermostat is the most familiar example of such a regulator and it controls your house very nicely most of the time. Since I live in Maine and have a woodstove in the room where my thermostat is located, the thermostat is almost always nice and warm and thereby totally ineffective in regulating the temperature of the house. In fact, the thermostat is so ineffective under these conditions that while it sat there happily warm, the pipes in the small bathroom in the back of the house actually froze one cold day last December.

The regulator for my house is actually me — and I am more complex in this regard than the thermostat. When I function as the regulator of my house temperature, I consider: 1. my own comfort; 2. the comfort of other members of the family if they voice their concerns to me (this replaces the thermostat's internal state with our internal state); 3. the state of the storm doors (especially the one that tends to be left ajar by the kids); 4. the state of the guest room door because that room is both a drafty heat sink and usually empty, and 5. the state of the upstairs bedroom doors (closing them during the day keeps the downstairs much warmer). All in all, 'me-as-house-regulator' is a much more complex regulator than is the thermostat. And to the extent that the 'me-regulator' is more complex than the thermostat, the me-regulator is able to achieve better regulation — where better is defined in terms of dollars spent.

If I were to hook up a micro-computer to open and close thermal shades based on the heat loss or gain through my windows at various times during the day, I would then have a more complex regulator and would be able to save even more money.

Variety is a technical way of talking about the complexity of a system. The variety of a system is defined as the number of possible different states of that system (see also chapter 8). The more complex the system, the more possible states it has, and the higher its variety is. The common thermostat has an effective complexity of two (i.e. hot enough, not hot enough). The 'me-regulator' has an effective complexity something like this:

1. my comfort: too hot, just right, too cold, i.e. 3
2. others' comfort: too hot, just right, too cold, i.e. 3
3. state of storm doors: open or closed, i.e. 2
4. state of guest room door: open or closed, i.e. 2
5. state of upstairs bedroom doors: open or closed for three doors, i.e. 8

The total variety for the 'me-regulator' is the number of different permutations of these five factors, i.e. 3 times 3 times 2 times 2 times 8 - 288. The microcomputer as regulator (if I wanted to work at it a little) could easily become a regulator with a variety measure in the millions by simply making finer distinctions and using more dimensions such as the heat flow in or out of windows.

The furnace thermostat has no way of dealing with storm doors and bedroom doors. The 'me-regulator' has no way of dealing with heat flow in or out of windows. As the regulator becomes more complex, it is able to deal with more of the system (i.e. it is able to regulate more of the system's aspects). The law of requisite variety says that the degree to which a system can be regulated is always and absolutely limited by the variety of the regulator. And, just as we saw with the house temperature example, there are always aspects of the system that are potentially relevant that the regulator can't deal with because it lacks the requisite complexity.

In practical terms, quite frequently the regulator is incapable of even perceiving the relevant system aspects. For instance, the thermostat can't 'perceive' doors. You and I may not be able to comprehend an attitude of someone else or may not be able to recognize some other important aspect of our organization. The different perceptions of superiors and subordinates in the same work situation provide a good example of this point.

The other practical point is that even when the regulator is able to comprehend the relevant system aspects he/she may not be able to deal with all of them. The problem of scheduling patients with various problems through various departments of a large hospital or clinic is so complicated that it is usually dealt with by the simple (and terrible) method of simply pretending that the patients' waiting time doesn't matter. In other words, the patient becomes the regulator by absorbing (in his/her waiting) all the variety that the hospital refuses to deal with. The problem of trying to individualize education is similar — the teacher is well able to recognize all sorts of individual differences, but he/she is not usually able to do much about those differences — there is no time to do anything except give everyone pretty much the same assignment. This explains why teachers typically ignore standardized test scores and the other data in the students' central file — the teacher already knows more about the individual student than the teacher can use. The teacher lacks the variety to deal with the total variety presented by the *group* of students. Much of the teaching of colleges of education and much of the research on teaching methods is irrelevant to the needs of teachers precisely because it ignores this point — in fact it assumes that the teacher can somehow increase his/her own variety as a regulator of a class. The real question that should be addressed by research into teaching methods is something like this: 'how can the variety of a class-sized group be reduced and the variety of the teacher be amplified so that they at least roughly match — in such a way that, rather than destroying the conditions for growth, real learning is stimulated?'

In all management situations, the management is always faced with the task of regulating a complex people-plus-things that is always more complex than the management team. Thus the management is always faced with less than total regulation. The question becomes, given that you can't regulate everything, how should these limited regulatory capabilities be deployed? This is a crucial question because, if regulatory efforts are inappropriate to the situation, it is entirely possible for the regulatory attempts to be counter-productive, i.e. the system will be more out of control than it would have been in the absence of any regulation by the 'bosses'. We will examine some practical examples of this phenomenon in a moment. First, it is helpful to look at a corollary to the law of requisite variety.

Law 3A: Most of the regulation of very complex systems is achieved through the interaction of the parts (i.e. one part acts to regulate some other part).

The 'regulation' achieved by the ostensible 'bosses' is merely imposed on top of the system's own regulation of itself. In a real sense this is a restatement of the law of self-organizing systems, but it should take on new depth and meaning now that feedback and requisite variety have been introduced.

EXAMPLES

The three laws and their three corollaries are mutually supportive and it is therefore instructive to consider how they effect each other. Let us begin by restating all of them.

Law One: Self organizing systems law. Complex systems organize themselves; the characteristic structural and behavioral patterns in a complex system are primarily a result of the interactions among the system parts.

Law One A: Complex systems have basins of stability separated by thresholds of instability.

Law Two: Feedback Law: The output of a complex system is dominated by the feedback, and within wide variations the input is irrelevant.

Law Two A: All outputs that are important to the system will have associated feedback loops.

Law Three: Law of Requisite Variety: Given a system and some regulator of that system, the amount of regulation attainable is absolutely limited by the variety of the regulator.

Law Three A: Most of the regulation of very complex systems is achieved through the interaction of the parts (i.e. one part acts to regulate some other part).

The mechanism through which complex systems organize themselves is, to a large extent, through sets of interlocking feedback loops. Part A affects part B and part B affects part A and they tend to continue to interact until each is in some region of stability under the conditions provided by the other. The law of requisite variety makes explicit the amount of control one given part can have upon some other part. In particular, the law of requisite variety shows that we can forget the notion of some powerful, unitary part of a system as the major regulator of that system. For instance, a dictator with life and death control over all of his/her subordinates is still limited by the law of requisite variety. Typically, such a dictator regulates a few aspects of the system very rigidly (e.g. the way others treat him/her, the expression of political attitudes, and so on). Even achievement of this much regulation requires that the dictator manage to amplify his/her own regulatory capabilities with a large secret police force, etc. In the process of achieving regulation over these aspects of the system, the dictator typically (and increasingly over time) loses control over system aspects such as the loyalty of the citizens, legitimacy of his/her rule, and ability of the system to innovate, grow or change in a positive fashion. And as loyalty, legitimacy, and ability to innovate decreases, the need for repression grows. In this way the dictator's attempt to impose regulation upon the system sows the seeds of his/her own destruction.

Given a management situation where feedback is used to achieve some desired output, the law of requisite variety shows the limits of what can be achieved with a given feedback loop. Let's consider some practical examples. Table 2.3 shows some of the goals that our rhetoric nominates for various human service agencies. The second column in the table shows the goals that we might infer from looking at what these same agencies actually do. Many commentators have noticed the enormous gap between the stated goals and the actual behavior of large organizations. This phenomenon has been commonly understood to exist at least since 1957 when March and Simon[11] discussed the phenomenon of goal displacement. However, the common explanations of the gap between rhetoric and reality in the realm of human service institutions tend to include all of the following:

> the administrators are incompetent and/or dishonest. If we could get some good administrators, this mess would improve.
>
> the staff is lazy and/or incompetent. If we could improve the quality and motivation of the staff, this mess would improve.

Agency	Mission rhetoric	Mission inferred from action
university	to increase knowledge, to develop wisdom, to provide practical assistance in social and technological policy-making.	to develop specialities, to fragment knowledge, to treat social and technological policy issues as isolatable problems requiring technical 'fixes'.
	to teach.	publication is what counts, teaching is a necessary duty to be disposed of as quickly as possible.
	to provide a service to the public.	to secure extra income (i.e. consulting) or to secure research assistance (i.e. grantsmanship).
schools	to maximize the development of each individual, to provide basic skills to all, to prepare students for useful citizenship.	to minimize parental complaints, to keep school and classes quiet and orderly, to maximize the winning record of the athletic teams.
hospitals	to cure the sick, to ease the suffering of the ill.	to treat weak hearts, diseased kidneys, etc. (i.e. to manipulate the defective parts of the body).
	to train doctors.	to provide practice patients for beginning doctors.
	to increase our understanding of health and illness.	to get the latest and most expensive technological gadgetry.
welfare agencies	to provide assistance for those unable to help themselves.	to make people dependent on government programs.
criminal justice system	to deter crime, to exact retribution, to rehabilitate the criminal.	to train criminals; to destroy the citizen's respect for and willingness to cooperate with the criminal justice system; to keep the jails full.

Table 2.3: The gap between the intended mission and what our social institutions actually seem to do

- there is no communication among the various parts of the organization. If we could get everyone to communicate openly, honestly, and effectively this mess would improve.
- the organization is financially starved, we don't have half the resources we need to do the job. As soon as the public and legislators realize how important this agency is and give us the requisite resources, this situation will improve.

For any given situation, some or all of these factors may be true. And clearly these things cause serious difficulties. However, I want to assert that with the framework developed in this chapter, we can now see that all of the common explanations are results or symptons of more basic underlying problems, *not* the fundamental problems.

If we look carefully at the human service agencies listed in table 2.3, we see that in no case are there even reasonably well-developed feedback loops on the intended missions. This is most easily seen by asking the following question, 'if the university (or school, hospital, etc.) does a great job in achieving its intended mission, who within the institution is thereby rewarded? And if they do a terrible job, who within the institution is punished?' The answer for all these institutions is (with very rare exceptions) no one at all. Now ask the same question about the goals in the second column, those inferred from the institutions's behavior: 'If the university (or school, hospital, etc.) does a great job in developing narrow specialists, fragments knowledge, and dispenses technological 'fixes', who benefits? And if they fail to train narrow specialists, if they refuse to fragment knowledge, and resist dispensing the quick technological 'fix', who suffers?' The answer of course, is that the institution begins to lose prestige, the people are replaced, etc. The university behaves very rationally, achieves those goals that it is rewarded for, avoids those things that it is not rewarded for and the gap between what we want it to do and what it actually does grows apace. In the meantime, the individual professor who entered the university because of a love of teaching, service or wisdom becomes either more and more frustrated or more and more cynical. The same is true of schools, hospitals, and other human service agencies.

The first part of our critique of our institutions then, is to notice that there are massive structural deficiencies in the feedback loops: the goals we intend have no effective loops and another set that we do not want, do have effective loops.

Efforts to reform these institutions typically change the inputs, i.e.

they increase the training requirements for the staff or change some of the procedures the staff is to use. The reform efforts seldom, if ever, really look at the outputs in a serious way. There are two obvious difficulties with these measures: the feedback law tells us that the inputs are irrelevant over a wide range, so it is unlikely that changing them is going to change the outputs. The self-organizing system corollary tells us that there are some configurations that are stable and others that are not. And I might add that there are a lot more unstable configurations than there are stable ones so that considerable caution is called for in designing new arrangements. Every manager already knows that, however, so I needn't belabor the point for them. Those of us who attempt to reform organizations are, however, a different story — we behave as if we had never heard of the point that some configurations are unstable and therefore unworkable.

The third and final part of the critique based on our three laws uses the law of requisite variety. Compare the complexity of the intended goals with that of the goals inferred from the actual institutional behavior. The intended goals are, in every case more complex than the inferred goals. Thus it is much easier to evolve/design feedback loops for the inferred goals than the intended goals. This is a serious and real difficulty. I raise the issue here because it is real, the perceptive reader will notice it, and I need to acknowledge it. However, I have not yet developed the cybernetic framework sufficiently to demonstrate the solution. I will return to this issue in chapters 4, 5 and (especially) 6 after developing the cybernetic theory more fully.

CONCLUSION

This chapter has attempted to introduce the worldview or paradigm of management cybernetics. It has necessarily painted with broad brush strokes and has made no attempt to deal with the details. The major points of the paradigm are:

1. The nature of the observer (or more generally the observing system) is crucially important in determining the nature of reality because:
    a. The activity the observing system engages in to investigate reality changes that reality.
    b. different observing systems apprehend different aspects of reality.

Thus the observing system and reality are seen to be engaged in an essentially circular process.

2. Cybernetics and general systems theory are concerned with systems in which organized complexity is important, as compared to organized simplicity (i.e. the domain of traditional physics and astronomy) and disorganized complexity (i.e. the domain of the statistical sciences). Second order cybernetics is concerned with what might be termed relativistic organized complexity or the cybernetics of observing systems.

3. Cybernetics is concerned with systems in which circular causality is important in contrast to linear chains of causality.

4. Cybernetics is concerned with systems which exhibit a 'holistic' property in that they have characteristics that do not belong to any of their parts.

5. Three laws were selected (from a much larger set) as being representative of cybernetics and particularly interesting for management. These laws and their associated corollaries are:
   a. self organizing system: complex systems organize themselves; the characteristic structural and behavioral patterns in a complex system are primarily a result of the interactions among the system parts. Sub point: Every self-organizing system has regions of stability separated by thresholds of instability.
   b. feedback: the output of a complex system is dominated by the feedback and, within wide limits, the input is irrelevant. Sub point: All outputs that are important to the system will have associated feedback loops.
   c. The law of requisite variety; given a system and some regulator of that system, the amount of regulation attainable is absolutely limited by the variety of the regulator. Sub point: Most of the regulation of very complex systems is achieved through the interaction of the parts (i.e. one part acts to regulate some other part).

It should be clear by now that this paradigm conflicts somewhat with our traditional images of science and ways of thinking about complex phenomena such as organizations. The cybernetic paradigm developed herein builds upon and broadens our image of what constitutes science and thereby provides powerful new ways of dealing with extreme complexity.

Note

*Strictly speaking, one might argue that not all of the principles given in this chapter are laws. They are well established principles, and I have chosen to use the term 'law' somewhat loosely in this chapter.

In Chapter 8 which presents the laws and concepts of cybernetics in a more precise and comprehensive way I have been more conservative in using the term 'law'.

CHAPTER TWO REFERENCES

1. Norbert Weiner, *Cybernetics: Or Control and Communication in the Animal and the Machine*, (Wiley, New York, 1948)
2. Stafford Beer, *The Heart of Enterprise; The Managerial Cybernetics of Organization*, (Wiley, Chichester, England, 1979).
3. Stafford Beer, 'Towards the Cybernetic Factory' in Heinz von Foerster and George Zopf (eds) *Principles of Self-organization*, (Pergamon Press, Elmsford, New York, 1962).
4. The first three categories are from Gerald M. Weinberg, *An Introduction to General Systems Thinking*, (Wiley-Interscience, New York, 1975) chapter one.
5. See particularly Ludwig von Bertalanffy, *General System Theory: Foundations, Development, Application*, (George Braziller, New York, 1968) and *General Systems: Yearbook of the Society for General Systems Research*, vols. **I** through **XXIV** and continuing.
6. W. Ross Ashby, *An Introduction to Cybernetics*, (Chapman and Hall, London, and University Paperbacks, 1956), chapter six.
7. W. Ross Ashby, 'Analysis of the System to be Modeled', *The Process of Model Building in the Behavioral Sciences*, R.M. Stogdill (ed.) (Ohio State University Press, Columbus, Ohio, 1970).
8. Michael R. Goodman, *Study Notes in System Dynamics*, (Wright-Allen Press, Cambridge, Mass. 1974) p 319.
9. Gilbert Levin, Gary B. Hirsch and Edward B. Roberts 'Narcotics and the Community: A System Simulation', Edward B. Roberts (ed) *Managerial Applications of System Dynamics*, (The MIT Press, Cambridge, Mass, 1978) p 580,

10. Nancy H. Roberts, 'System Simulation of Student Performance in the Elementary Classroom', Edward B. Roberts (ed) *Managerial Applications of System Dynamics,* (The MIT Press, Cambridge, Mass, 1978) p 599.

11. James G. March and Herbert Simon, *Organizations,* (Wiley, New York, 1958) chapter five.

Chapter 3

THE CYBERNETICIANS' QUESTIONS

The cybernetician, like any other practical person, comes armed with a set of tools. This chapter explores the nature of one of the cyberneticians' basic tools: the sorts of questions he/she brings to a new situation. The questions in a person's head are one of the dominant factors that shape the sort of observer that person is. Thus, the questions that get asked are strong determinants of the reality perceived. And clearly, one's perceptions of the reality of a situation largely determines one's reactions to that situation. This chapter discusses some of the cyberneticians' favorite questions and illustrates their use by applying them to a university department, a hospital and a school.

INTRODUCTION

Herbert Simon[1] argues that finding the right question to ask is the hardest part of problem solving. Russell Ackoff[2] says that it is more helpful to get a wrong answer to the right question than to get a right answer to the wrong question. Ackoff's point is that asking the right sort of question is informative but if you are stuck on the wrong questions, you may have great difficulty learning about the situation. While there is no formula that tells you what the right questions are, there are a number of questions that arise from the paradigm of cybernetics and that have proven to be generally useful.

This chapter explores the methods of the cybernetician when faced with a messy, problematical organizational situation in which the managerial team is asking themselves 'what do we do now?' or 'how do we handle this?' Many of our institutions, including schools, universities, hospitals, jails, and governments at all levels, are not working well compared to the needs of their clients. Further, they are not working well compared to the level of service the staff and managers think they ought to be providing. I have had students from an enormous variety of different governmental and service agencies at all levels of those agencies except the very highest (e.g. I have not had a state governor or a federal cabinet level official in class). The vast majority of these people, when they talk candidly, express considerable frustration about the way their agency works, and the extent to which they have to fight the 'system' in order to do the job that they feel they ought to do.

This section is aimed at the manager who wants to make some sizeable long term changes in the way his/her unit operates. It is not so important how high up in the organization the manager is (e.g. he/she may be a teacher, a nursing administrator, the director of a clinic or residential facility, a warden, a dean or any other manager of some unit). What is important (if this section is to be of any use to you) is that you are interested in making fundamental improvements in the effectiveness of your unit and that you are interested in entertaining some fundamental questions about the unit. If those two conditions are met, read on. Otherwise, you should consider looking at the more technical methods in chapters 4, 5, and 6.

THE BEGINNING POINT

For ease of exposition let us assume that you (the manager) have called in the cybernetician as a consultant. The primary question in the cybernetician's head will be to what extent you are operating out of an essentially cybernetic paradigm or out of an essentially reductionist paradigm. Now, this question doesn't have anything to do with whether you have ever heard of cybernetics and feedback and all that stuff. The question is really whether your intuitive understanding of social systems is narrowly mechanistic or whether you have some essential grasp of the interactions and the holistic, circular sorts of phenomena that interest the cybernetician. If you are operating out of the mechanistic conception, the cybernetician will try to raise questions that help you see the holistic, circular, interactive nature of the system. If that fails (and sometimes it does) there is little choice but to politely bid you adieu and go elsewhere.

The particular words and concepts used are not so terribly important (although they are tremendously useful). For instance, a nurse who has studied the homeostasis of the body and who has long experience in dealing with human patients, generally experiences the concepts of cybernetics as being very helpful names for what she already knew about in a more limited context. An elementary teacher who has been tuned in to her kids, or a manager who is good at developing people, generally experience the concepts in this way also.

On the other hand, it is entirely possible to be a teacher or nurse or manager who has dealt with their respective systems as some mechanism whose parts can be separated and understood in isolation. Someone who has operated in this fashion for a considerable period of time will also have schooled his/her intuition in ways that simply are incompatible with the framework of cybernetics. To put it baldly, the mechanistic intuition and the cybernetic intuition look at the same social system and see radically different things. It is as if one was using a telescope and the other a microscope, or as if one had an opinion survey and the other were using a bathroom scale to weigh the people — the resulting 'facts' simply are not comparable in any meaningful sense.

Two people operating out of two very disparate frameworks are typically unable to communicate at all. If one of the two parties understands both frameworks, the two then have the option of communicating in the framework they both share. If both parties understand both frameworks, they then have to agree which one to use. The problem is somewhat akin to trying to communicate in, say, French and the language of the polar Eskimo. If one party knows only French and the other party knows both French and Eskimo, then they can talk in French. Notice that there are things that cannot be discussed because the one party doesn't know the one language (e.g. the Eskimo has thirty one different words for different kinds of snow that the Frenchman has neither words nor concepts for. Similarly the Frenchman has available in his language nuances of love and human interaction that the Eskimo has no way of talking about nor understanding).

The point that is being made is that the cybernetician's first question (but one that he cannot simply ask about), is what sort of paradigm you, the manager, are carrying around buried in your intuition. If you neither have, nor can be helped to see, an interactive (i.e. cybernetic) paradigm, most of what the cybernetician thinks is important about your system cannot be discussed with you because you don't have the requisite concepts. Fortunately for both cyberneticians and managers, most managers have an essentially cybernetic intuition about their social systems. As a side comment, it has been my personal experience that university professors are much more likely to have a mechanistic intuition than are the practicing teachers, nurses, and managers who, after all, must deal with these social systems every day. To be fair to the professors, part of their trouble may be that some of them spend much greater amounts of time studying sciences with largely mechanistic underlying paradigms. Thus some professors have more to unlearn in this respect than the practitioner. The recent revolution in the philosophy of science (Kuhn[3], Toulmin[4], and some new work in physics Prigogine[5]) is also moving strongly in this direction. At any rate, the sort of framework that you the manager operates out of is the basic question that the cybernetician is interested in at the beginning. And the answer to that question determines to a large degree whether or not it is worthwhile to work together.

BASIC QUESTIONS

I will assume that you have the essentially cybernetic intuition (otherwise you will have stopped reading before getting this far and there is no point in my continuing to write). So you say to the cybernetician:

> "here's my situation, this is the job we're trying to do, we are facing this problem, that opportunity, and we're puzzled about *this*. There are certain respects in which we are very pleased but there are some frustrations and a strong feeling that we could be doing better. So, how can you help us improve the situation?'

The cybernetician will usually want to talk some more about your intentions and history. 'How long a history does your current modis operandi have? How long has it been since the organization has really considered its basic assumptions about itself?' This question gives some clue about the extent to which it is feasible to raise fundamental questions (i.e. if the organization has just gone through a massive reorganization it is probably not politically feasible to question the basic structure).

'How many efforts have been made to improve the existing organization and how well did those efforts succeed?' If, as is typically the case, there have been many efforts to make improvements that haven't seemed to make much difference, then there is a good experiential base for raising very fundamental questions.

'How strong and widespread in the organization is the feeling that you should and could do better than you are doing currently?' If the feeling of dissatisfaction is deep and widespread, then there is good reason for asking basic questions, and otherwise not. Quite typically the experience of other similar organizations is very important in these respects. For instance, most public school educators are well aware of numerous attempts to improve schools that haven't seemed to make much difference. These attempts may not have been in the schools where these people worked, but since they are so widely known in the profession, the attempts still provide a backdrop which facilitates the raising of very basic questions. Similarly, nurses are aware of many attempts to improve hospitals and are therefore frequently ready to entertain basic questions.

Let's assume that you and your organization are ready to entertain some basic questions — what might those questions be? There are a whole lot of very basic questions that cybernetic thinking raises.* Perhaps the way to get into this is to simply list some of them.

1. What is the system? What are the relevant boundaries? What is the relevant environment?
2. What is the real purpose of the system? What purposes of the system might we infer if we looked at what the system is actually *doing* rather than thinking about the rhetoric on purposes? What purpose would we like the system to have?
3. What are the constraints on the system? Which of the recognised constraints are truly constraints and which are avoidable? Which of the currently recognized constraints could be avoided by redefining the system or redefining the environment or redefining the purpose?
4. What is the language used for thinking about the system? What built-in constraints, assumptions, and beliefs does this language contain? Does this language create unsolvable problems for us? Can we invent a meta-language that removes or dissolves the problem?
5. How does the system work? What causes what else? How can we get a grasp on a set of system parts that affect each other and *how* do they affect each other? What are the major dynamics that make the system work the way it does? What is the actual system that produces the observed results (not the public relations statement of purpose and its associated system, but the *actual* results and the actual system that produces those results)?
6. What are the outputs that the rest of the system requires of your system? If you think of your system as a black box (and after all most of what you do is in fact invisible to others), what are the outputs that you *must* produce and what are the aspects of your system that you are free to change as you like?
7. What self-organizing tendencies does this system have? In

particular, what sort of personal goals, values, and aspirations do the people of the organization hold as individuals? And, equally important, what sorts of cultural norms and values are important for the people of the organization as a group? What sort of technical imperatives are inherent in the business the organization is in? What are the important environmental feedbacks that reward/punish the organization for particular sorts of results or behavior?

Many other questions, based on any of the cybernetic laws and concepts enunciated in chapter eight could be raised, but this list is already long enough and these questions have proven to be very useful ones.

The first thing to notice about the questions is that they are massively inter-related. Let us group the questions for convenience and label them (in order of presentation above) as: 1) system definition, 2) purpose, 3) constraints, 4) meta -language 5) dynamics, 6) required outputs, and 7) self-organizing. If you think about your own organization, you will quickly see that to make a change in any one of these dimensions is usually to make a change in at least several of them. For instance, if we change our notion of the purpose of a jail, we will typically need a different sort of staff (at least in part), thereby changing the elements of the system, and we might well change the boundaries by (for instance) changing the relationship to the surrounding community. And unless we manage to change the dynamics of the way the jail works, we will fail in our attempt to change its purpose. A little reflection should convince you of the extraordinary degree to which these seven questions are inter-related.

The second important point about these questions is that every organization has already answered them and, more or less, everybody in the organization understands the answers. These answers constitute a large part of the organization's culture and understanding of itself and therefore its identity. Without this common understanding of the answers to these questions, the organization would be simply a conglomeration of people that would be unable to get anything done.

The third important point about these questions is that the answers shared by the organization members, typically have more the quality of myth or fairytale than objective reality. This is not to say they are unimportant for, as I said in the paragraph above, without them the organization couldn't function, and very often in social systems even fairy tales with no basis in reality are preferable to no common understanding. However, the fact that the answers shared by the organization members may not be rooted in reality means that there is an opportunity to invent better answers if the organization so desires. Digging into the beliefs about any one of these dimensions will typically pay big dividends *if* the culture of the organization is supportive of doing so — otherwise digging into these matters is likely to get you run out of town or at least fired.

The potential for getting oneself in very big trouble by digging into these questions is perhaps the fourth noteworthy point about them. The answers to these questions, after all, define the organization's identity, its understanding of what it is. Thus, if one digs into them uninvited or is perceived as doing so in a threatening way, the organization is likely to react as if you threatened its very existence — as in fact you are doing in the psychological sense that you are threatening the sense of identity.

The fifth point is that rethinking these questions, in those cases where the organization supports so doing, is generally very rewarding. Because the answers currently held are often either radically wrong or else only one of several possibilities, the opportunity for improvement is often very great indeed.

Chapter one included an extended discussion of alternative definitions of a system by a manager dealing with a problem of low productivity. That discussion comprised an example of the power of considering the question of just what the system is.

A UNIVERSITY EXAMPLE

This section briefly discusses the impact of asking fundamental questions about a university program for training administrators at the graduate level. The actual order in which the questions were raised and answered is now lost and may never have had much meaning. This is so because the people involved (including myself and a few others, 1. did not have an explicit list of questions (partly because the group included people with several different orientations), and 2. dealt with the questions iteratively (i.e. we would think about one and then another and then return to an earlier question and so on). Insights about what we wanted to do and how to do it gradually emerged and gradually congealed into a coherent program. All that can be reported is the difference in our answers now and what they are typically for graduate training programs for administrators. You should understand that the order of discussion of the questions is now chosen primarily for ease of reporting on a more or less finished product, and says little if anything about the process of getting there.

1. Purpose

The purpose of graduate training programs for administrators is typically couched in terms of change in administrators or would be administrators, or in terms of competencies/skills/experiences the administrators should get during the training. Our new purpose is to improve the institutions in which the administrators work. The usual objection to this purpose is that it is enormously difficult to assess. However, the distinction between change in the student and change in the institution is crucial. If our purpose is to change the student, we can set up assessment procedures, feedback loops, etc., that are entirely internal to ourselves as a training program.

If our purpose is to change the institution, we must of necessity look outside of ourselves. In the first case (assuming we are serious) we set up a learning process that is essentially narcissistic and blind (i.e. it focuses inward) and has essentially no connection to reality except that which we assume exists between a set of administrator characteristics and that reality. To say that there is little objective evidence for the assumed connection between student characteristics and the reality of organizations is to grossly understate the case.

In the second case (again assuming we are serious), we set up a learning process that focuses squarely on our relation to the reality we are supposed to ultimately effect. And if (as is the usual objection to this tack) the proposed purpose is impossible to assess, then perhaps the system needs redefining to make the intended purpose possible to assess.

2. System dynamics

The system supposedly works by having administrators take courses on the theory and practice of management and leadership. Probably no one connected with the enterprise of training administrators really believes this anyway so it is easy to challenge. The problem is to replace it with something other than the typical course. Our solution is to put students to work on practical problems.

If (as we believe) the practical administrator is frequently faced with messy problems, then it makes sense to focus the student's training on trying to assist real administrators in solving or at least managing some of their messy problems. This suggests that the program of training, rather than focusing on a set of courses to be taken, should focus on applied research teams whose task it is to assist managers with their real problems.

One of the major advantages of putting students to work on real problems is that it gets both the faculty and students out into the institutions so that it might make sense to talk about assessing the program's impact on the institution. At the same time, other horrendous problems rear up — graduate programs are expected to generate a certain amount of tuition income (and this is customarily done in courses), dissertation research must be done to exacting standards of scholarship which don't match the needs of the practitioner at all, and so on.

3. Meta-language

The language for thinking about the situation is basically our academic language of science, research, and organization theory. The clues to where we need to examine this language are that there are certain difficulties that occur over and over again and, despite numerous serious attempts, somehow the difficulties never get resolved. In our particular situation of wanting to train administrators, several persistent difficulties came to mind.

The first persistent difficulty is the theory-practice gap. Most administrators seem unable or unwilling to make much use of the theory and research that we scholarly types generate. Our usual assumption is that this is the practitioners fault or that we haven't put the practitioner through enough courses. If we contemplate the possibility that we scholars may be at fault, it then makes sense to examine the situation afresh. If we then redefine research from that which we have typically done in dissertations to that which the early operations researcher did, we get a mode of research that has demonstrated utility for practitioners. The major elements of the re-definition are shown in table 3.1.

Given an articulation of the type of research needed, there is no great difficulty in doing that sort of research — if one decides to do so. However, it does seem clear that the academic mode of research is much less useful to practitioners than is the operations research mode.

A second meta-language difficulty is that the professional students of organizations tend to be fairly specialized in their expertise. This is particularly troublesome for a cybernetician whose training emphasizes

'respectable' academic research	'scruffy' operations research
-exhaustive literature search	-literature search to get a starting point
-seeks generalizable truth	-seeks local truth
-certainty of results are critical	-rapidity of learning is critical
-practical import unimportant	-practical import is primary
-depth of research critical	-breadth of research critical
-seeks description of system in an assumed equilibrium situation	-seeks explanation of causal dynamics in assumed non-equilibrium situation

Table 3.1. Schematic comparison of academic research and operations research.

the holistic nature of organizations. However, the imperative for professional scholarship is clear and demands that we 'keep up with our field'. With the volume of writing being done today, there is only one way to even come close to 'keeping up with the field'. One has no choice but to specialize and specialize rather narrowly. University departments expect specialization, journals are built on specialization, fame and fortune are most easily achieved by specialization, and tenure (i.e. survival) comes to those who are recognized specialists.

Those who manage a broad view are *only* those who first manage to get recognized as expert in something and then go after a broad view. The logic and the institutional arrangements are clear and inexorable: *keep up with your field* and that means narrow specialization. After years of struggling with this (and conspicuously failing!) I have reformulated the language to describe what I now realize I have been doing for quite some time: 'choose reading to maximize your own change'.

Keeping up with your field results in rapid learning only if the field itself is changing rapidly. On the other hand, for any applied scientist, there are always huge gaps in your knowledge of the phenomena of interest. Reading to maximize your own change is always a prescription for rapid learning, whereas keeping up with your field may be a prescription for stagnation.

A third area of seemingly unresolvable difficulty is that of poor teaching. Professional tenure, promotion, and status depend almost entirely upon publications. And the research that leads to publication is typically quite separate from the teaching. Therefore, the rational response is to minimize the time put into teaching and devote time to research. The result, of course, is that most university 'teaching' is scandalously bad and the faculty strenuously (and successfully) ignores all attempts to improve it. My meta-linguistic reformulation of the situation is clearly not appropriate to all departments, but applies well to applied social science areas. My reformulation says 'make the research process into the major learning experience'.

In some fields (e.g. physics) one must learn calculus and an enormous body of fact about physics before the relevant question can even be understood. In social systems, however, this is clearly not the case — the issues are generally understandable by a ten year old. And when the students are graduates (typically with many years experience in the field) they have, in important respects, a *better* understanding of the situation than we professors. In other respects (e.g. in gaining an overview or in being able to examine the situation from various theoretical perspectives) we professors 'understand' the situation better than our students. Our typical procedure ignores (and thereby implicitly devalues) the administrator's own knowledge of his/her system and fairly explicitly proclaims that our perspective is the more valid one. This is both silly and self defeating. At any rate, there is clearly no necessity to subject the graduate student to large numbers of courses before they are permitted to do any research.

The practical proposal is this: put the students, from the beginning of their graduate programs, into research teams of about 3 to 8 members. Have each team work with a faculty member and tackle a major problem area with the expectation that the team will continue for several years or perhaps many years (with the professor providing continuity for successive generations of students). If such teams truly focused on the situation faced by practitioners, we might find that we could simultaneously do important research, improve institutions, and train both researchers and administrators.

4. Required outputs?

This is really a question about what sorts of change are entirely within the compass of the black box itself, and what sort of changes involve the rest of the system. The point is that the rest of the system doesn't know nor care what your particular box does except in terms of its output. Therefore, the box can make whatever internal changes it might wish, so long as its output is adequate. The output that a department of administration must produce seems to comprise the following:-

- professional publications.
- income to the university (from tuition or grants) at least exceeding some minimum level per full time faculty equivalent.
- graduates with various certificates (e.g. principals, supervisors, superintendents).
- a perception on the part of the rest of the university faculty that we are playing the game more or less according to the rules of the academic culture.

According to my reckoning, any department that fulfills these constraints may do whatever it wishes in whatever manner it wishes.

The discussion of the training program for administrators has so far touched on the questions of purpose, system dynamics, meta-language, and required outputs. Questions of system definition, constraints, and self-organizing tendencies have not been addressed directly. However, the degree of inter-relatedness among the questions is such that all the questions have been at least touched upon in what has been said so far. Thus it is possible to simply skip ahead and sketch out what the finished program looks like based upon the thinking presented so far. The next few paragraphs will, therefore, sketch out the training program as currently conceived, based upon the ideas presented above.

The heart of the program is the research team that tackles a major administrative problem such as the management of decline or the management of a change in purpose. The research team consists of 3 to 8 students and a faculty member. The team operates in the context of attempting to assist actual managers who are currently grappling with the team's chosen problem. Some of the team members should be managers facing the problem themselves. The style of research is that of the early operations research teams, i.e. the team has the dual task of 1. assisting the managers to solve their particular problem or improve their situation, and 2. learning how that *sort* of problem can be effectively dealt with. This style of research requires that a working relationship exist between the university team and the administrator in the field. In order for the relationship to work the administrator must get some concrete benefits (otherwise he/she stops co-operating) and the university must earn some publishable results (otherwise they can't survive).

The faculty member of such a team needs a rather broad background in several respects. Real problems always involve many disparate aspects and the faculty member guiding the research must be able to at least understand many of them (not necessarily all, but many). Quite typically, such a research project involves a wide variety of research techniques including field observations, interviewing, surveys, statistical reduction of various sorts of data (including especially time series), invention of new measurement devices, and quasi-experiments. There are probably none of us who are truly competent in all these methods, but the team as a whole either needs many of these competencies or needs to be able to draw upon experts in the various methods.

The breadth required of the faculty team leader emphasizes the importance of the meta-language reformulation of reading 'to maximize the change in yourself'. Typically, our graduate training programs encourage students to master an area of scholarship. The imperatives of the operations research style of research suggest that the student should not master an area of scholarship, but should dig into a given area to the extent that it is helpful in dealing with the practical problem at hand. Thus the student should be guided by the same principle we articulated for the faculty 'read to maximize the change in yourself'. The activities of the research team then become the driving force that largely determines the rest of the students' program. In particular, the research team activity should largely determine the students' research method studies, other courses taken, and the outside reading done. The faculties' judgement about the student's competence should then be largely in terms of the student's contribution to the team's efforts to solve the problem. This largely eliminates the need for the sort of artificial testing that most university programs rely upon and allows students to be judged in terms of essentially real life performance.

These research teams should result in very high quality outputs (from the standpoint of the rest of the university). Since the faculty teaching and research and service time to the field are essentially combined, the faculty member has a much greater proportion of his/her time devoted to 'research'. In addition, he/she now has this entire team of assistants in the research effort. Thus, the research team should constitute a very nice engine for producing high quality publications. Further, the teams should generate a considerable quantity of funded research, thereby buying them considerable independence and power within the university structure. The only program [10] that I am aware of that operates somewhat along the lines proposed herein does indeed generate a large volume of high quality publications and enough funded research to be essentially self supporting.

Perhaps this is enough discussion of administrative training programs, because the purpose is simply to illustrate the power of asking these basic questions.

A HEALTH CARE EXAMPLE

It may be helpful to illustrate the power of the basic questions by examining another area, in this case health care.

The avowed purpose of a health care system is something to do with health maintenance or curing illness or some such. The purpose of health care systems in the western world seems to have undergone the following transformations: initially the purpose was to fix up problems as they arose. This meant that illnesses and accidents were treated as people fell ill or suffered accidents, with the purpose of restoring the person to a state of good health. Eventually it was realized that many diseases (e.g. tuberculosis) were 'caused' by preventable environmental conditions and that many others could be prevented with simple precautions such as vaccinations. Furthermore, by eliminating dangerous practices from the workplace, from toy manufacture, etc., many accidents could be prevented. Therefore, while keeping the old purpose of curing problems, the new emphasis became to prevent the problems (i.e. preventive medicine, but also agencies such as OSHA). Today there is an increasing awareness that good health is not simply a matter of curing problems and preventing problems, but that good health is a function of lifestyle, genetics, and medical intervention when necessary.

When we look at the various pieces of the 'health system' and inquire into what their purposes seem to be, based on these observed activities, we get a rather interesting picture. Western medical doctors are trained as specialists: brain surgeons; internal medicine, eye-ear-nose-throat; cancer; pediatrics; geriatrics; plastic surgery; etc. The hospitals are similarly fragmented: x-ray, cancer, obstetrics, heart, surgery, etc. A patient entering a major hospital is treated as a collection of special parts. The nursing staff is left the job of dealing with the human being. Thus, the purpose of doctors and hospitals (which the doctors largely control) seems to be to deal with separable parts of the human being. The purpose of nurses seems generally to be dealing with the person. This is not meant to imply anything about anyone's motivation or sensitivities, but is simply an inference based on observations of what doctors and nurses do in hospitals.

Hospitals are notorious for the pervasiveness of the conflict between doctors and nurses. And this analysis suggests that it could hardly be otherwise, given the current arrangements, because the two groups clearly have different operational purposes: the doctor is out to deal with some discrete problem and the nurse tends to be out to deal with the person's health — and as we saw above the two are not the same and they lead one to suggest different remedies to the patient.

The training of the doctor involves heavy doses of natural sciences, particularly chemistry, physiology, anatomy, and pharmocology. All of these sciences are rooted in the reductionist mode and in that limited sense are antithetical to a systemic or cybernetic paradigm. Further, the doctor's training emphasizes huge amounts of memorization (i.e. there is a compelling necessity to have down pat 1. sets of symptoms, 2. diseases and defects, and 3. curative procedures, beneficial drugs, etc.

The doctor's training, then, is primarily aimed at learning symptoms, diseases/defects, and curative procedures and the proper matchups between these three sorts of things. Given the vast store of knowledge we have about these things, it takes an extreme effort to become truly knowledgeable in even one speciality and it is not humanly possible to be knowledgeable about the whole field of medicine. Since the doctor's intuition is trained in the reductionist mode, he/she will not normally notice that there is any problem with this. The patient who has to try half a dozen different specialists before finding an answer, or who gets different answers from each specialist experiences quite a problem, but the system is not set up to take notice of that. The nurse charged with caring for the person also notices that the team of doctors are looking at discrete parts of the patient and that none of them is dealing with the person, but the nurse is the low person on the status hierarchy and his/her perception has less status than does the doctors.

The difficult constraint here, seems to be the huge quantity of data that the doctor needs to have at his/her fingertips. It does not seem possible to train a human being to be a medical generalist *and* to be an in depth expert on the matchups between symptoms, diseases, and cures. Given the electronic revolution, we could redefine the system to include diagnostic computers. After all, computers are good at 'remembering' masses of data (far better than humans!) and computers are also quite good at comparing two different profiles to see if they match or not. Thus, it is well within the state of the art to have a computer take a patient's profile of symptoms and compare that profile with profiles for various diseases/defects. In fact, it has been shown that such computer diagnosis can be more accurate than the physician's diagnosis. Thus, we see that the central rationale for the dominant mode of training physicians is no longer sensible — the specialized diagnostic work can be largely left to the computer. The human doctor could be trained to think about the *person* and his/her total needs.

Suppose that medical training was truly changed so that the doctors' preparation program involved less memorization, more problem solving, more attention to the holistic and systemic aspects of human beings, and the computer took on some of the routine (but massive memorization) of diagnosis. It is impossible to really say just how this would change the practice of medicine, but I feel fairly sure that there would be less shuffling of the patient from one department to another, more consideration of the patient's feelings and dignity, less technology/drugs used in medicine, and more emphasis on the patients' choice of lifestyle and the implications of that lifestyle for healthiness. One of the clear benefits of this sort of change is that nurses and doctors would have more commonality in their approach to patient care, and the entire health care establishment would probably have a much lower level of conflict as a result.

A SCHOOL EXAMPLE

As a final example of the power of asking basic questions, let's look at schools.

There is a huge literature on the purposes of schools: schools ought to produce good citizens, or socialize people, or prepare people for the job market, or make people literate, or give people the basics, or give people survival skills, and so on. There is almost as big a literature on what schools are actually doing (and by implication therefore what their actual purposes are): schools stifle curiosity, produce conformity, prepare people for the exigencies of an assembly line sort of job, provide babysitting services, keep young people out of the job market, etc.

There are any number of ways of getting into an analysis of the schools, but the self-organizing tendencies are striking (and somehow largely ignored). The first thing that strikes me about the school system, is the essential sameness of schools in the United States. Despite huge variations in the wealth of different school districts and a strong emphasis on local control, most schools are rather alike in the role of the teacher, role of the student, curriculum covered, pedagogical methods used, and the observable results. There must, therefore, be powerful forces at work to produce this striking uniformity despite a near infinite variety of innovations, philosophies, and techniques.

Well, what sort of self-organizing tendencies are internal to the system? What about the values, goals, etc., of the individuals and the groups that make up the schools? Perhaps the most striking values are these: the students dislike school, don't see the value in it, and are basically hostile to the enterprise. Teachers, on the other hand, have typically entered the profession out of desire to help people and are convinced that the way to do that is to provide them with the content specified in the curriculum.

Given that the students don't seem to realize the value of the school's efforts, increasing amounts of coercion are applied to get the students to absorb the content that the curriculum calls for. In many cases the school ends up feeling more like a jail than a school. This result seems inevitable in all those cases where the student is seen as wrong in resisting the schools well intentioned attempts to teach the curriculum. It is clear that there is a trap here, i.e. we know full well that little if anything useful can be taught to someone who doesn't want to learn it, but there seems to be no alternative to coercing the students into doing the school work. We need to keep this trap in mind while we go on to examine other self organizing tendencies of the system.

Schools are peculiarly susceptible to environmental pressures and it is rewarding to examine the effect of those pressures. In particular, what sorts of results are rewarded or punished by environmental feedbacks? We can get into this question by asking what sort of things earn an educator rewards or punishments? Perhaps the most common 'punishment' from the environment for teachers and principals is parental complaints.

For whatever reason, parental complaints about a teacher or a school, or about some aspect of either, are treated in a way that makes them very harmful to the person complained about. In particular, the parental complaint is treated as if the school's primary goal is to *pacify* the parent. Thus, if the complaint has any sort of specific content to it, the teacher (or principal) finds out about the complaint via his/her superior's request (or order) that the aspect complained about be changed. My own experience has been that the complaints are seldom dealt with in terms of the educational program of the school, but almost always in terms of what can be done to make the complaining parent calm down in the short run. This method of coping with parental complaints has two important effects: 1. the parents can change *anything* in the way of small details of the school's operation simply by complaining about them, 2. on the other hand, the parents are completely impotent about the important aspects of the school such as the climate for learning, or teacher morale, or teacher competence.

There are, however, neither rewards nor penalties associated with the quality of teaching that goes on in a given classroom or a given school. A teacher or principal will get into trouble (perhaps even get fired) if they are unable to maintain a smooth, quiet operation. But it is rare indeed for a teacher or principal to receive either rewards or penalties on the quality (or lack thereof) of their educational program or the amount that children are actually learning. The seemingly inexorable result of these two factors is that classrooms become dead places which allow the teacher to survive (i.e. no complaints from parents) and in which students don't learn.

This twin dynamic would not be so bad except that there actually seems to be a positive correlation between real learning and parental complaints. I suspect the relationship has to do with the fact that real learning is exciting, tends to include change and therefore some degree of chaos, and frequently generates some questioning of the status quo. Thus the teacher who is doing a truly outstanding job is likely to get into trouble over some of the side effects of that outstanding job. The end result is that people stop doing those things which generate excitement in their classrooms or they leave teaching altogether. At any rate, the system tends to settle into a mode of quiescence in the classroom.

The language of the schools includes 'teaching, individualized educational program, diagnosis, learning styles, meeting the needs of the individual, behavioral objectives, competencies, and survival skills'. This language clearly makes the teacher responsible for doing those things to or for the student that will result in the student's development. The language conspicuously does not include ways to talk about the student's role in guiding his/her own development. Despite our talk about individualization, the fact is, schools are closer to treating everyone the same than they are to individualization.

The law of requisite variety suggests that individualization is impossible to achieve through the medium of the teacher as the sole or even primary regulator of the students' development. You will recall from chapter two that the law of requisite variety says that the degree of regulation attainable by a given control system is absolutely limited by the variety of that controller relative to the system to be regulated . In this case, the teacher is the control system and roughly 30 students are the system to be controlled. A teacher is quite capable of controlling the physical movements, the progress through workbooks, and so on of thirty students. The teacher is quite *incapable* of guiding the development of thirty different people *individually* through the method of detailed diagnosis of each, detailed prescription of goals, detailed prescription of methods, and supervision of the process as the student implements it. The teacher is simply not equipped with adequate channel capacity (e.g. she/he can only talk to one at a time, or watch perhaps three at a time, or listen to perhaps two at a time), not equipped with adequate time (e.g. there isn't enough time in the day to prepare all the lessons, to correct all the work, etc.) and probably doesn't have adequate intellect to understand the needs of all the students or know all the subject matter that 'meeting the needs of each' would imply. This is definitely not a criticism of the teacher. The law of requisite variety simply points out that one human being can't match the variety of thirty human beings.

There is a way to achieve requisite variety in the classroom's control system — the regulatory capabilities of the students themselves could be added to those of the teacher. As soon as we elicit the student's responsibilities in guiding his or her own development, we are increasing the regulatory capability of the classroom's control system. This is what a good Montessori classroom does and it is clearly what the English open schools have done. Most American attempts at 'open spaces' or 'open' classrooms have conspicuously *not* managed to elicit the students' responsibility in guiding their own development.

Thus we are left with a contradiction. Our purpose is, properly it seems to me, to meet the needs of individuals. Our ways of thinking and talking about schools puts the teacher solely in charge. And the law of requisite variety demonstrates that there is no possibility of individualization of education for thirty students in a room under these operational assumptions of teacher as sole regulator. Unless we find a language that includes student responsibility along with individual development we can't do it. The Montessori method and the English schools provide two such languages. Part of the key to both these systems is that they include considerable emphasis on internal discipline as a concomitant of responsibility.

One of the dismal aspects of education is that so many attempts have been made to improve it without much success. On the other hand there have been a number of success stories[11]. The present analysis reveals that many of the attempts to change education have fallen into one or more of the following fatal traps:

- they contained internal contradictions, e.g. good teaching tends to earn penalties, poor teaching carries no punishments.

- attempts to violate natural law, e.g. the attempt to individualize in a manner that the law of requisite variety clearly shows can't work.

- they work against the self-organizing tendencies of the system, e.g. the feedback loops from the environment tend to force the system to emphasize smooth, quiet operation and there are no other powerful systemic forces to counterbalance the environmental force so the system is stable only when it is quiet and smooth in its operation.

This analysis is in no way complete. However, the point is perhaps made that the basic questions posed by cybernetics provide a powerful entry to thinking about complex systems and a powerful guide to action in those complex systems.

CONCLUSION

The first question of the cybernetician, when confronted with an organizational situation, has to do with the paradigm held by the people in that situation, If the dominant paradigm is a mechanistic, reductionistic paradigm that implies the organization can be dealt with by taking it apart and dealing with the pieces, the cybernetician will find that the aspects of the situation that he/she thinks are most important are not real or observable to others. If, on the other hand, the people in the organization have an essentially organismic or holistic paradigm, the cybernetician is able to deal with the most critical aspects of the situation whether or not the participants know anything about the specifics of cynernetics.

There is a set of inter-related questions the cybernetician is typically interested in asking about any social system. One formulation of these question is:

1. What is the system? What are the relevant boundaries? What is the relevant environment?
2. What is the real purpose of the system? What purposes of the system might we infer if we looked at what the system is actually *doing* rather than thinking about the rhetoric on what the system is *supposed* to be for? What purpose would we like the system to have?
3. What are the constraints on the system? Which of the recognized constraints are truly constraints and which are avoidable? Which of the currently recognized constraints could be avoided by redefining the system or redefining the environment or redefining the purpose?
4. What is the language used for thinking about the system? What built in constraints, assumptions, and beliefs does this language contain?

Does this language create unsolvable problems for us? Can we invent a meta-language that removes or dissolves the problems?

5. How does the system work? What causes what else? How can we get a grasp on a set of system parts that affect each other and *how* do they affect each other? What are the major dynamics that make the system work the way it does? What is the actual system that produces the observed results (not the public relations statement of purpose and its associated system, but the *actual* results and the actual system that produces those results)?
6. What are the outputs that the rest of the system requires of the system? If the system is thought of as a black box (and after all most of what it does is in fact invisible to others), what are the outputs that it must produce and what are the aspects of the system that can be changed as desired?
7. What self-organizing tendencies does this system have? In particular, what sort of personal goals, values, and aspirations do the people of the organization hold as individuals? And, equally important, what sort of cultural norms and values are important for the people of the organization as a group? What sort of technical imperatives are inherent in the business the organization is in? What are the important environmental feedbacks that reward/punish the organization for particular sorts of results or behavior?

The questions provide a powerful beginning for analysis of complex social systems and a helpful guide to action in reforming these situations.

Notes

*This section uses some of the technical language of cybernetics, but does not provide definitions. Chapter 2 discussed some of these terms in their technical sense and chapter 8 'Technical Notes' provides difinitions and discussion of all of them. A difficult editorial choice was made to try to provide the general framework before going into much detail on the particulars. Those readers who prefer to get the detailed pieces before the big picture might do well to consult chapter 8 at this point.

It is necessary to make a distinction between two major types of operations research (O.R.). Many professors and practitioners of O.R. are using a set of well developed techniques that collectively might be termed optimization techniques. On the other hand, there is a brand of O.R. typified by people such as Beer[6], Ackoff[7], Waddington[8] and Blackett[9] that do *research* into *operations*. The latter sort of O.R. is the one referred to here.

CHAPTER THREE REFERENCES

1. Herbert A. Simon, *Administrative Behavior: A Study of Decision-making Processes in Administrative Organizations* third edition (Free Press, New York, 1976).
2. Russell L. Ackoff, *The Art of Problem Solving: Accompanied by Ackoff's Fables* (Wiley-Interscience, New York, 1978).
3. Thomas Kuhn, *The Structure of Scientific Revolutions* (University of Chicago Press, Chicago, 1962).
4. Stephen Toulmin, *Foresight and Understanding: An Inquiry Into the Aims of Science* (Harper and Row, New York, 1961).
5. P. Glansdorff and Ilya Prigogine, *Thermodynamics: Theory of Structure, Stability and Fluctuations* (Wiley-Interscience, New York, 1978).
6. Stafford Beer, *Decision and Control: The Meaning of Operational Research and Management Cybernetics* (Wiley, London, 1966).
7. Russell L. Ackoff, *A Concept of Corporate Planning* (Wiley-Interscience, New York, 1970) and 'The Future of Operations Research is Past', *General Systems* **XXIV**, 241-252 (1979).
8. Conrad Waddington, *Tools for Thought* (Basic Books, New York, 1977).
9. During the second world war, Blackett, a physicist by training, headed a group of scientists working on operational problems for the British armed forces. Blackett's group worked on a number of important problems, had a number of successes and became known as 'Blackett's Circus'.
10. The Social System Sciences program at the University of Pennsylvania directed by Russell L. Ackoff.
11. See for instance, Arthur Blumberg and William Greenfield, *The Effective Principal: Perspectives on School Leadership* (Allyn and Bacon, Boston, 1980), and Willard R. Duckett et al, *Why Do Some Urban Schools Succeed: The Phi Delta Kappa Study of Exceptional Urban Elementary Schools* (Indiana, Phi Delta Kappa, Bloomington, 1980).

Chapter 4

TAMING COMPLEXITY: MODELS AND OPERATIONS RESEARCH

The Manager or human services professional is always responsible for dealing with complexity — and the major part of that complexity consists of people with their needs, idiosyncracies, neuroses, hopes, talents, and abilities. The successful manager needs good intuition, and in fact, much of this book is attempting to influence your intuitive response to complex dynamic systems. Chapter three dwelt at some length on the difference between a mechanistic or reductionistic intuition and a holistic or systemic intuition.

In addition to intuition, the manager or human services professional also needs all the rational, technical, scientific help he/she can get. This chapter outlines a method for putting science to work for the manager. Many people seem to think the essence of science is the *data* it can pile up. This chapter takes the approach that the essence of science is a process for rapid learning — and rapid learning seems central to the professional concerned with people situations. This chapter, then, presents a method or process based upon science and designed to assist managers and human service professionals in rapid learning about their situations.

INTRODUCTION

Every manager is confronted with a situation of fearsome complexity. Even if the total number of people supervized is one, the manager confronts a situation more complex than him/herself. This is so because the manager is part of the situation, so that any addition to the situation beyond the manager's own person immediately makes the situation more complex than the manager. Therefore, by the law of requisite variety, the manager is always faced with a situation in which it is not even theoretically possible to achieve complete regulation. And, as all engineers know, practical results always fall short of what is theoretically possible. Thus, the manager must begin with the certain knowledge that his/her regulation over the situation will at best be partial and incomplete.

The law of requisite variety lets us easily demonstrate the theoretical impossibility of achieving complete regulation. It may be necessary, however, to explore the practical implications of this point a bit further. The manager's job is always to ensure that an organization achieves one set of outcomes (i.e. its 'goals') rather than any other of the near infinite sets of outcomes that the organization could conceivably achieve. This, in cybernetic terms, is regulation, i.e. regulation means to *select* certain results out of those that are possible (see chapter 8 for further discussion of this point).

Practically, what does it mean to say that the manager can, at best, achieve partial regulation of his/her organization? It is obvious that a manager's regulation cannot include the thought processes of subordinates nor, in most cases, the conversations among subordinates. In most cases the manager probably doesn't care about the subordinates' thought processes nor their conversation anyway. However, the subordinate's performance is clearly dependent upon his/her thought processes. And the grape vine (i.e. informal conversation) is a crucial determinant of the way employees feel, think, and *act*.

Unions and bureaucracies have long ago discovered one of the practical implications of the law of requisite variety: 'working to the rules' slows everything down to a glacial pace. 'Working to the rules' involves carefully following, to the *letter*, all the regulations. In large organizations, the *formal* rule book is generally huge. The informal rule book, the 'culture' of the organization, is also complex. The people in the organization make it work (to the extent that it does work) by constantly interpreting the formal and informal rules. Much of the informal rule book has to do with when and under what conditions the formal rules may be bent, ignored, or broken — or when the formal rules must be followed to the letter. Probably all of us have experienced frustration and rage over some seemingly trivial piece of paperwork (e.g. getting a license, registering for a course, or filing a minor insurance claim) that became a time consuming, expensive project because of the technicalities in the rules. If a union decides to give the management a bad time, it can ensure that very little actual work will get done by the simple expedient of following all the rules to the letter. For government workers, such as the police or firemen, this tactic has the advantage that it is, of course, perfectly correct and legal — no one can readily fault you for following the formal rules.

The 'work to the rule' tactic is also a favorite of managers attempting to resist change imposed from above. A manager gets things done primarily through getting *other* people to do things. If those other people are either openly or secretly resisting what the manager wants to achieve, everything is either impossible or takes forever. In this way career bureaucrats routinely defeat the 'reform' efforts of the political appointee heading their agencies.

We might summarize the cybernetics of the 'work to the rule' strategy by pointing out that the formal rule book can never be as high variety as is the real world. In other words, the rule book always attempts to define a set of standard situations and a set of responses to those situations — and the real world insists on coming to us in various shades of gray, with many 'in between' situations, with lots of complicating and messy factors that the rule book can't acknowledge. The people in the organization must interpret and apply the rules. If the staff interprets the rules narrowly and mechanistically, those of us unfortunate enough to do business with the organization characterize it as 'bureaucratic' and dehumanizing. If the staff interprets the rules liberally and flexibly, we tend to have much happier experiences with the organization and typically call it a 'human' sort of place.

Notice that the staff interpreting the rules liberally and flexibly are acting as a variety amplifier — they increase the variety of the rules to more nearly match the variety of the world. On the other hand, the staff interpreting the rules narrowly and mechanistically are doing little to amplify the variety of the formal rule book — the rule book's standard categories get imposed upon the world whether it makes sense to do so or not.

The last few paragraphs have discussed one aspect of an organization (i.e. the general attitude of a staff to interpreting and applying the formal rules) that is not fully under the manager's control. There are, of course, a great many other aspects of the organization that the manager cannot hope to directly or personally regulate. In short, it seems clear that the theoretical limit posed by the law of requisite variety represents a practical barrier of tremendous significance to the manager, i.e. the manager's regulation of the organization will always fall short of the desired amount.

The second respect in which the manager's task is difficult is that the dynamics of the situation are typically both complex and poorly understood — it is rare indeed for a manager to have a feeling of certainty that the outcome of some action will be the one that was intended. This is particularly true of those situations that involve primarily humans. The administrator of a hospital, jail, university, school, city, or other large formal organization is typically operating on the basis of 'feel', 'seat of the pants', 'intuition', and prayers. In such situations of complexity and uncertainty, even very simple knowledge of the causal dynamics can be quite useful. This chapter discusses one important method for learning about the causal dynamics of the situations that managers in large formal organizations confront daily.

SYSTEMS & METHODS

You will recall that systems are our own creations, chosen primarily in terms of their practical usefulness. The discussion that follows categorizes systems in terms of the methods of analysis they are amenable to. It happens that the available methods of analysis rather neatly categorize systems in terms of the sorts of properties that they exhibit. The whole scheme parallels the sketch of the history of science that appeared in chapter 2 during the discussion of the nature of cybernetics. Remember that any real thing or situation has innumerable characteristics and that by focusing on different sets of characteristics a large number of different systems (with very different characteristics) can be abstracted from the same reality. Note that these categories are alternative ways of looking and are not necessarily inherent in the systems studied.

Reducible systems are studied in terms of their parts. The system is assumed to be known when the characteristics of the parts are known. These are the systems referred to under the category of 'organized simplicity' in chapter 2. Typically, the relationships studied are deterministic although they may involve a random element. The laboratory experiment and the languages of algebra and calculus epitomize these methods.

Statistical systems are those that can be studied in terms of averages, where one relies upon the law of large numbers. These systems, discussed under the category of 'disorganized complexity' in chapter 2, consist of large numbers of discrete elements, each of which is a member of a few types, and all members of a given type are assumed to have identical characteristics (with regard to some criterion). Probability theory and statistics are the primary mathematical tools for studying these systems. The associated scientific methods include experimental and quasi-experimental methods in the laboratory and in the field, and a huge array of descriptive instruments such as the social scientist's survey questionnaire and the geneticist's protocols for assessing, e.g., fruit fly mutations.

Holistic systems are those whose important characteristics are not ascertainable from the properties of the system components. These are the systems (referred to as 'organized complexity' in chapter 2) made up of components which interact to generate the systemic or holistic

important to note that even a very simple situation plus a strongly coupled observer, takes on the characteristics of a relativistic system because the system then becomes the original system plus the observer. The characteristics of the original system then, by definition, become a property of the original system plus the observer. This line of thought opens up a very complex bag of worms in which you have 1. a simple system, 2. a simple system influenced by the observer, 3. an observer (you?) comtemplating a simple system influenced by an observer, 4. and on and on it goes until our patience runs out.

An opinion survey is generally assumed to deal with a statistical system, but can be transformed into a relativistic system by the simple expedient of duplicating the survey with slightly different wordings. The methods for relativistic systems thus include all the others, plus any methods that help in understanding the interaction between the observer and the system. It is an understatement to say that these methods are not very well developed. Such methods as do exist in this arena tend to be specific to particular fields. Perhaps the major guideline that can be offered is that one should specifically think about the implications of changing the nature of the observing system in some way to ascertain the change in the system observed. In this way one can begin to get some feel for the effect of the observer upon the system.

EXAMPLES

It may be helpful to provide examples of each of the four types of systems as they can be abstracted from the same reality. Consider the question of the miles per gallon for an automobile, say the Volkswagon 'bug' as compared to the Volkswagon bus. This question can be dealt with in any of the following ways:

1. Reducible system. Gas mileage depends upon mass, engine efficiency, body shape, speed, etc. in well understood and separatable ways. Therefore, we can write an equation such as the following, that shows precisely how each of these factors effect gas mileage for both of the cars:

   mileage = f(mass, efficiency, shape, speed, etc...).

   It is then possible to determine the effect of a given change in one (or more) of these variables upon the gas mileage.

2. Statistical system. Gas mileage depends upon factors such as the state of repair of the car, inflation of the tires, need for tune-ups, etc. These factors have some statistical distributions which, in combination, give a statistical distribution for the gas mileage of the two cars. The distributions look like this:

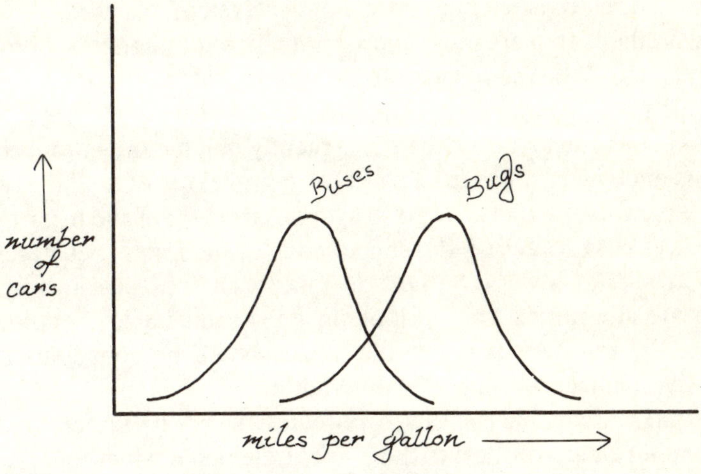

We can then predict the average gas mileage for people who drive bugs and buses, respectively.

3. Holistic system. The gas mileage achieved by a particular car depends strongly upon the type of car *and* upon the particular driver's relationship to the car (e.g. 'hot rodding' vs sedate driving, state of repair/tune-up, etc.). Thus the gas mileage is a characteristic of the particular car-driver *system*.

4. Relativistic system. Studies of the effect of driving habits and car maintenance habits upon gas mileage have themselves an effect upon those same habits. Thus, studying the situation, changes the situation to some extent.

Even though we talked about gas mileage in these four examples, it turned out that we meant different things by those words in each case and the four systems were quite different. It is important to realize that all four systems are 'correct' in that each of the four can give useful answers to important questions. It is not appropriate to ask which system is better than another, which system is right, or which system is wrong except in the context of some particular purpose — and then the question is best phrased in terms of whether or not the system meets our particular needs.

Gas mileage of volkswagons was considered under the rubric of four different system types (or ways of looking): reducible, statistical, holistic, and relativistic. The aspects of the 'system' one is apt to notice and the methods that are most appropriate for studying the 'system' are quite different, even though all four are abstracted from more or less the same thing.

Thinking about social systems is typically much more complex than thinking about gas mileage. The great complexity of social systems makes it easy to abstract all sorts of systems from them and in particular it is always easy to define systems of each of the four types described above. It should always be kept in mind that these various system aspects are alternative ways of looking at the same basic phenomenon, and that the manager and scientist alike should be conscious of the alternative choices available in this matter.

In social systems the issues are frequently so poorly understood that it is not at all clear how best to think about them. Consider for instance, the area of crime:

1. Reducible system. Criminal action is a result of a number of factors such as poverty, permissiveness, moral degeneracy (put in whatever factors you like). The point is that the reducible system approach assumes that there are parts of the system that can be treated in isolation. A corollary assumption is that changing one of the 'causative' factors will make a corresponding change in criminal behavior

2. Statistical system. The average criminal has this set of characteristics ....., while the average victim has this other set of characteristics .... The critical assumption is that these *average* characteristics are important and meaningful in understanding the system.

3. Holistic system. The social system has, as some of its characteristics, a certain level of property, unemployment, illness, crime, wealth, artistic endeavor, etc. The critical assumption is that these are total system characteristics that cannot be much changed without changing the nature of the social system.

4. Relativistic system. This way of looking at crime might build on any of the other three, with the addition that the very process of examining the situation will change it to some extent. For instance, it has been argued that treating crime as caused by poverty (or unemployment or whatever), provides a moral justification for crime among those who are poor (or unemployed, etc.) and thereby increases the incidence of crime. The critical assumption is that the process of studying the situation changes that situation.

The statements about crime were selected to demonstrate that current dialogue on these matters implicitly includes all four types of systems. Further, it is anything but clear as to whether or not *any* of these ways of thinking about crime has any scientific validity. As a start toward improving the level of dialogue on these and similar matters, we should at least find out whether or not the various participants in a dialogue are talking about the same systems or radically different systems.

Crime, considered as different system types, requires different methods of study. Reducible systems are amenable to experiments or quasi-experiments on the relationships among their parts, e.g. the relationship between poverty and crime or between unemployment and crime. Statistical systems are often the object of large scale descriptive studies. Holistic systems can be described with ethnographic field studies or simulated with games or computer models. Relativistic systems are typically studied with two or more methods at once. This note on methods is illustrative only and should not be taken as an exhaustive list.

THE ROLE OF MODELS

The manager is always faced with some 'thing' which he/she is trying to 'manage' into behaving in one sort of way rather than some other sort of way. This rather abstract description of the manager applies equally well to a cowboy herding steers, a teenager nursing along a jalopy, a teacher coaxing a class into learning, a doctor running a hospital, or the president of the United States trying to manage foreign and domestic policy. In all cases, the 'manager' acts on the basis of some framework that includes at least four elements:

1. Some image of a preferred state, perhaps a goal or perhaps merely a way of behaving by the system (e.g. a low rate of crime is desired).

2. Some image of the current state of the system (e.g. society suffers from a high rate of crime).

3. Some image of the 'way the system works'. (e.g. the reducible system view of crime noted above).

4. A belief, based on the previous three images, that the situation might be improved by a given sort of 'managing'. (e.g. Increase the penalties for criminal behavior and criminals will be deterred).

Given that the situation to be managed is always more complex than the manager, the problem of choosing reasonable actions is quite difficult. To be precise, it is quite common for gross errors to occur in all four of the elements noted above. This means:

1. The image of the preferred state may be in error;

   - it is quite common that once achieved, the desired state turns out not to be less valuable than was expected. In particular the desired state may have unanticipated negative consequences that outweigh the beneficial results.

   - typically, desired states are seen as means to some other end and the assumed relationship to the higher end may be wrong so that achievement of the desired state does not in fact assist in reaching the higher goal.

2. The image of the current state of the system is often seriously in error.

   The most common way in which this happens in large systems is that the manager is simply unable to remain informed about the relevant system aspects. Another common problem is that the manager may seriously misjudge critical aspects of the system. For instance, managers are frequently grossly wrong in their beliefs about subordinates' values, attitudes and desires.

3. Our image of 'the way the system works' is almost always inadequate and is frequently wrong for social systems.

   Errors in the image of 'the way the system works' frequently lead us to undertake actions which end up having an effect opposite to that which is desired.

4. Our beliefs about the relationship between action and outcome constitute a model of 'the way the system works'.

   Very often this 'model' is merely implicit and frequently amounts to no more than a gut level or intuitive 'feel' for the system.

The question of how the system works is clearly a central one. Most of the rest of this chapter will be devoted to a powerful method for attempting to improve our understanding of 'how the system works'.

There are several different ways of thinking about the connection between what we know (or think we know) and how we act to try to achieve a given result. Be that as it may, I will simply focus on the role of a model in this connection. Now a model is simply some representation of reality. It may be no more than a dim set of images in our head or a set of intuitions. Whatever the model consists of (and more of this later), for the moment I will simply use the term 'model' to mean that which we use to make the connections between our actions and the expected results (you may want to consult the discussion of models in chapter 8).

The question that I now want to address is this: given that a model plays a central role in our actions (i.e. the bridge between action and expected outcome), how can we put science to work to improve the models that we have available to us in managing organizations? This question comes very close to defining the province of the operations researcher and the methods of the operations researcher in fact provide the guidance we need in this area.

Before we go any further however, I need to clear away some terminological confusion. If you go to a university and enroll in a course or a degree program under the label of operations research (typically in a school of business administration, applied mathematics, or industrial engineering), you will not generally get the methods I am talking about. What these programs typically do is to give you a set of applied mathematical techniques for solving specific kinds of problems.

The problem types that these techniques address are inventory, allocation, queing, sequencing, routing, replacement, competition, and search[5]. These techniques are important and powerful methods that are appropriate whenever a problem area can be isolated from the rest of the system and dealt with in terms of a single criterion of success. The usual criterion of success is some variation of dollars (e.g. maximizing profit or minimizing costs) or some variation on the use of a limiting resource (e.g. minimizing distance or time, or maximizing the productivity of a bottleneck process).

The limitations on the applicability of the OR techniques are 1. that they are not able to deal with an entire organization at once, but only some limited aspect of it, and 2. they are able to deal with only one criterion of success at a time.

Despite these limitations, the techniques are enormously important because they permit finding the best possible solution in a wide range of very complex and costly situations. However, the subject of this chapter is not these techniques, but the approach of the operations research scientist at a prior stage, before the situation is understood well enough to make these techniques really useful.

AN ILLUSTRATIVE CASE

Let us imagine for the moment that you, as say a hospital administrator, have hired an operations research (OR) team to assist you. If you are wise, you will charge them to look around and make some suggestions. The team will want to know what your purpose is, and you will undoubtedly talk about the needs of your clients and meeting those needs and perhaps talk about the enabling legislation and the societal purpose embodied in that legislation. At any rate, the purpose (as most purposes are) will probably be a little vague, but will touch upon a number of society's values. In addition, the team spends an hour and a half getting your perception of some of the problems and opportunities the organization faces — including those aspects that are persistently troublesome or frustrating. The team will want to sort of poke around and talk to people, wander around and observe the organization in action and so forth. This will probably go on for some time.

You, as the manager who is putting out the money for all this, may begin to wonder about the impact of these folks' activities upon your unit and may begin to get a little nervous because it doesn't look like they really have much in the way of answers. Furthrmore, you begin to wonder what a bunch of egghead scientists (including, e.g., a physicist, ecologist, and anthropologist), none of whom have any experience with your sort of operation, could possibly say that would be helpful. By the approach of your lunchtime meeting with them on the second day, you are wondering how you ever fell for your buddy's line that this group could really help you. Unfortunately you did give them a contract and there seems to be no way out except to proceed and make the best of it.

The lunch time meeting is billed as a general discussion of 'ways of looking', whatever that means. After lunch is cleared away, the team leader says that their purpose today is to briefly sketch out several alternative ways of looking at or thinking about the organization and they need your guidance about which seem useful to pursue. The question, they emphasize, is not which is most true or accurate, but which is most useful. With that introduction, they plunge into the first 'way of looking').

The physicist on the team begins by describing the (to you) all too familiar difficulty of accomodating patients without large waiting times. Two years ago you had commissioned a queing theory study of the flow of patients that figured out the best possible solution, taking into account both the patients' waiting time and the cost of more facilities. On average, the patients' waiting time was small. The problem was that during a normal week, there would be several one to three hour blocks when any given facility would have almost nothing to do and then a little later would be overwhelmed so that waiting times would soar to more than an hour and a half.

The physicist suggests that there seem to be two (or possibly three) general patterns for patients to move through the various stations in the hospital (e.g. emergency room to x-ray to lab to a bed *or*, emergency room to lab to x-ray to discharge). These various pathways probably each have some more or less regular periodic surges and valleys in the patients moving through them. If two or more pathways come together at some point such as the lab, then the small peaks and valleys in the separate paths will either reinforce each other or cancel each other out (thereby causing alternating periods of empty facilities and backlogs).

The physicist then goes on to suggest that the science of acoustics provides models for handling situations characterized by waves that reinforce or destroy each other, and that if it seems warranted they could develop a method for regulating patient flow that might almost entirely eliminate waiting time. As you contemplate the work study figures from the earlier queing theory study, you realize that the facilities were in fact adequate to handle all patients with almost no waiting time if there was just some way to smooth out the flow of patients through the facilities.

The physicist then wants to know if there would be any difficulty in altering the sequence of stops that a given patient makes on his/her way through the hospital. Your reply is that the sequence is pretty flexible, but that there are some constraints — some operations must happen before others. The physicist suggests that there is a good chance that the patient flow could be smoothed out quite a lot if there was some way of monitoring the waiting time in each facility and using that to adjust the sequence of stops that the patient made. This leads into a general discussion of the feasibility of a small 'scheduling' micro-computer in each department within the hospital. If each patient was given a machine-readable, 'scheduling' card that was presented to the microcomputer upon arriving at, or departing from, any department, the computers could automatically adjust the sequence of stops to minimize waiting times.

At this point the team leader comments that the group has probably spent enough time on the acoustics model to illustrate one possible approach to decreasing patient waiting times.

The anthropologist is the next presenter, and she begins by commenting on the difficulty of maintaining adequate records on the patients. The hospital has its own record keeping system, but since most people use the hospitals for emergencies and serious illnesses only, these tend to be the only parts of the person's history that the hospital captures. Routine visits to the doctor, life style, and all that sort of thing, is missing from the patients's file.

The anthropologist begins to discuss the extent to which the information available influences the staff's treatment of the patient and the extent to which treatment would be different if other information was available. Given that both the kinds of information and the sequence in which it is considered are important determinants of the decision reached (March and Simon[6], the issue is an important one for the hospital. Because of the nature of the information available i.e. that on emergencies and serious illnesses) the treatment of the patient inevitably takes on a crisis management aspect. There is typically little consideration given to the relationship between the treatment and the patient's long term life style. Furthermore, given the information-culture of the hospital, there seems to be no way of changing this.

The anthropologist suggests that there seems to be considerable concern about the adequacy of the information base among the staff. Your own reaction at this point is to stifle a groan — you could recall only too well the good intentions of both you and the staff on precisely this point, stretching back at least five years. Unfortunately, good intentions were all you had on this score — essentially no progress had been made despite what seemed to you to be strenuous attempts.

Your attention is recaptured as the anthropologist goes on to say that the way to change the situation is to change the information-culture, i.e. the type and flows of information within the hospital. Changing the information-culture seems to mean two things: 1. combining the hospital's records with those of the doctors who used the hospital so that they could more nearly approximate a complete medical record on individuals, and 2. development of a computer filtering capability that could more adequately deal with the mass of data on individuals that would accrue. It is no good, she argues, to get a massive computer file on individuals and then expect busy doctors to be able to routinely read these files. Furthermore, she adds, the computer could find patterns in such data far better than could humans and that therefore, the computer could detect all sorts of diseases or pathologies long before the humans could.

When you ask about the details and costs, the reply startles you because the answer is that the required system couldn't really be designed in detail, but has to be 'grown in place'. As nearly as you can tell there are two reasons for this. The anthropologist maintains that you are discussing a nervous system for the hospital, and that while the characteristics of the human nervous system are known adequately for this purpose, the *body* to be served is not too clear yet (i.e. the relationships of the hospital to the doctor's private practices, to the state's medical records, etc., are not at all clear). So the nervous system has to evolve as the body grows.

Furthermore, the anthropologist points out that the nervous system for the hospital includes a large component of people talking to people, and people — doctors, nurses, and patients — talking with machines, and therefore, the cultural aspects of the organization are critical. The culture can be shaped, but certainly cannot be designed in detail in advance. So, this line of thinking requires that a nervous-system-with-the-body-and-associated-culture be 'grown in vivo'. Despite the experts' assurances and your own fascination, you are torn between the desirability of the results and considerable apprehension about possible difficulties.

At this point the team leader suggests it is time to see if either of these ideas (the acoustics model or the nervous system model) is worth pursuing. The team leader asserts that they could provide you with an 'acoustics' model to decrease patient waiting times or a 'nervous system' model to improve the hospital's decision making about patients. The key question, however, is what you as the administrator want to tackle.

THE 'WHAT' OF MODEL BUILDING

It is time to turn to explicit consideration of the model building methods of the operations research team. In the hospital example of the last few pages, we saw scientists developing interesting 'ways of looking' at the hospital that seemed to be based upon analogy. We need to examine the actual process in some detail. The process I will discuss is laid out fully in Beer's chapter six of *Decision and Control** and is discussed in *Management Science*, particularly chapter four.

By now the assertions that the observer at least partly determines the reality, should be at least somewhat familiar, if not fully accepted. The methodology presented in this chapter takes advantage of the fact that the observer's cognitive structure is a critical component of the observing system. In fact, you and I can be a succession of different observers by the simple expedient of looking at one situation through the filters (or cognitive structures) of a succession of different models. For example, in the hospital case of the last few pages we looked at the hospital, first through the filter of acoustics and waves, and later through the filter of 'culture' and a nervous system. In so doing, we noticed very different aspects of the hospital.

Let me make the boldest and most outrageous claim right at the beginning: *any* situation can be examined (or more outrageously still, modelled) through the application of *any* branch of science. Furthermore, given proper rigor in the process, the model so developed from *any* branch of science will provide a 'correct' model of the situation. The model may or may not be useful for anyone's practical purposes, but given the proper process, the model will be correct and accurate.

Let me be explicit about what is being claimed in this section. Newtonian mechanics, acoustics, fluid dynamics, genetics or whatever branch of science you please, can be applied to a managerial situation and will, given proper methodological rigor, provide a valid model of that situation. Having developed such a model, using say acoustics, the results known to the expert in acoustics can then be translated into the managerial situation. It is as if the model allowed us to import knowledge from one field into another. This then is the extreme claim that I wish to make for the method. Some readers are almost certainly outraged, but I hope to convince you in a moment that the claim is reasonable. Before doing so, however, I want to advance a more modest claim for the method.

The extreme claim, advanced above, requires a methodology based upon sophisticated expertise in the use of formal languages. I want to make clear the method's power and utility for those people who lack sophistication in mathematics and formal logic. So here is the less extreme claim: The method provides useful guides for action, including new approaches and new possibilities that were not previously available. In particular, the method provides assistance in rapidly developing useful hypotheses about the dynamics of complex systems.

The reader has probably already figured out the broad outlines of the methodology. It begins with a metaphorical link between the situation of interest and some scientific model. The method then, in essence, consists of making an analogy between the two situations (scientific and managerial), abstracting a model from each, and making the two models (managerial and scientific) formally identical. Having established a formal identity between the two models, then one has, in effect, an engine for reasoning about the managerial situation. Because of the formal identity between the two models, anything that is known about the scientific model can be translated into the terms of the managerial model, or to put it practically, knowledge can be imported from the scientific situation into the managerial situation. This paragraph describes *what* can be done, but has not really said much about *how* it all gets done. That is the next step.

THE 'HOW' OF MODEL BUILDING

We are concerned with a situation in which a manager is attempting to understand a managerial process. Let's examine an actual example that occurred in one of my seminars. The director of a branch campus of a community college was faced with a situation in which the central administration was intent on maintaining control over the campus, and the faculty of the campus was quite intent on gaining independence. The director was thus caught in the middle. Worse, as the director responsible for overall administration of the campus, he saw considerable merit in both positions but had no framework for developing a rationale for an appropriate degree of independence. The first breakthrough in this problem occurred when the director worked with a nurse on another problem using fetal development: at that point the director said 'aha! the relationship between the branch campus and the main campus, in terms of development, is like the relationship between a fetus and its mother'. The director's reasoning went something like this:

'At the moment my branch campus is not large enough to provide a full range of services for itself, we really need to rely upon the main campus for certain kinds of things. To that extent we are dependent. However, our faculty is highly skilled and we are quite capable of being totally independent in curricular/instructional matters. In fact, given the large differences between our community and that of the main campus, we are in a much better position to make curricular/program decisions than is the main campus so that we should be independent in these matters. Further, we are growing and at some point should reach a size at which it would make sense to be essentially independent'.

The next step, after the metaphor that says the two are somehow alike, is to begin to abstract a model from each. The director's thinking at the end of the last paragraph provided a basis for such a conceptual model: The fetus develops from conception until birth in such a way that it gradually becomes more and more capable of an independent existence. Similarly, the branch campus develops from its inception in such a way that it should gradually become more and more capable of an independent existence. This then raises the question of just what constitutes a 'capability for independent existence?'.

There seem to be an enormous number of factors involved in determining the fetus' capability for independence. After considerable playing around and trying out various sets of variables, the director settled on a very short, simple set: length, weight, degree of maturation of organ systems, and age (from conception). Part of the process of selecting these particular variables was a process of thinking about the branch campus and making an analogy between these variables and the campus. The analogy that emerged was:

Fetus	**Campus**
Length	FTE students
Weight	Acres of the campus
Degree of maturation of organ systems	Degree of maturation of support systems
Age (from conception)	Age (from beginning of campus)

Considerable effort was then devoted to trying to develop an equation that expressed:

degree of independence f(length, weight, maturation, age)

and that would, therefore, also define degree of independence for the campus. While this was going on, the model stimulated a rather penetrating discussion of the effect of each of these variables on the overall degree of independence of the branch campus.

In my opinion, the equation never did make much sense. Further, the model immediately raised the further question of what constitutes 'degree of maturation' and what are the appropriate organ systems/support systems. Despite these rather glaring shortcomings, the model did result in a substantial shift in policy. Both the director of the branch campus and the main campus administrators had been operating on the assumption that the main factor in the branch campus' independence was the size of its enrollment. As a result, the branch's planning efforts were going into increasing enrollments and the size of the campus. The model suggested to the director (and he decided) that he should redirect his efforts into developing the support systems within the branch. Looking back a year and a half later, the director reports that the model building exercise marked a turning point in their thinking about the relationship between the two campuses and the degree of autonomy that was appropriate to the branch campus.

The branch campus director's case illustrates the power of the method as an aide in creative thinking and as a guide to action. That model building exercise never got close to a formal identity between the scientific and managerial models that would support importation of knowledge from the scientific model to the managerial situation. In fact, that sort of rigorous application was never remotely possible in this particular case: The director of the campus did all the work himself (with a little minor help from myself and a few other graduate students), it was done within the scope of a class project, and the director's background is almost totally lacking in either scientific or mathematical training. What the director did have was a keen analytical mind and the ability to follow through the implications of his analogy. Thus, even though the model never got past the stage of a rough analogy, it was a considerable improvement over no framework at all and did in fact direct action for the next year.

I have taught this model building method to about six classes of graduate level students in an administrative training program. The students were primarily educators, nurses, and civil service people from the federal government. With the exception of the nurses, many of these behavior of interest. Their peculiar resistance to the methods of reducible systems or statistical systems stems from one or more of the following causes:

- the elements of interest are too few to treat statistically but the interconnections are too complex to permit treatment by studying the properties of the parts.
- the behavior of the elements is radically *non*-homogeneous, i.e., despite the elements being identical in nature, there are important structural differences throughout the system (convection currents and standing waves provide two simple examples). In general, under conditions that are far from equilibrium, the behavior of large numbers of identical elements may show considerable structure and the averages for the system as a whole will then be quite misleading.
- there are substantial numbers of variables (e.g. more than three) which interact to cause some system behavior of interest and there is a need to know how to change that system behavior in some respect.

The first thing that needs to be said about the methods of science in dealing with holistic systems is that they are in many respects inadequate. The methods used with reducible systems and statistical systems are very much part of the armory for holistic systems, but a number of newer (and still controversial) methods are also important. The methods of operations research, particularly simulation, are important here. A number of recent developments in mathematics also seem important, including bifurcation theory and catastrophe theory (Prigogine[1] , Thom[2], and a calculus of self reference (Spencer Brown[3], Varela[4], Hofstadter[5]). These mathematics for the first time give us formal methods for handling discontinuous changes as opposed to the smooth, continuous changes that calculus handles. Spencer-Brown and Varela have given us a framework for handling questions in which an operation refers to itself (e.g., I will finish this book unless the process of finishing it kills me first). Prior to Spencer-Brown's work we had no formal way of handling such statements (see chapter 8 on recursion).

Relativistic systems are those in which the characteristics of the system are influenced in decisive ways by the observer (discussed in chapter 2 under the heading of 'relativistic organized complexity'). These systems, apart from the influence of the observer, might have the basic characteristics of any of the other three types. However, it is students were completely lacking in any sort of scientific or mathematical background. In some cases (such as the branch campus case reported on above) the student would learn about a scientific model specifically for the sake of the exercise. In other cases, students used sailboats, flying, and running as their 'scientific' models. Clearly, these students were unable to make the formal identities between their managerial and scientific models. Nevertheless, many of the exercises in fact 'solved' difficult problems that had been frustrating traditional efforts for some time. When I say that problems were 'solved', I mean that useful strategies or approaches were invented or discovered in situations where people were previously impotent to find any helpful ways of acting.

It's time to describe the method more rigorously. The following paragraphs lay out a series of steps as if the method were a nice linear process. In fact the method typically involves a number of iterations through these steps and involves frequently going back to some previous step which then changes the later steps. All in all the process is much messier than this list makes it appear. However, there is a general sort of progression that makes it helpful to list the following steps:

1. There is an initial insight or metaphor: 'this managerial situation is like .... because ....'. The metaphor links the managerial situation loosely to a scientific situation*.
2. A rough conceptual model of the managerial situation and a rough conceptual model of the scientific situation are developed next. These two models are more or less developed in parallel and an attempt is made to make an analogy between the two in some detail.
3. A formal model is developed for the managerial situation and for the scientific situation. The attempt here is to arrive at two models that are isomorphic (i.e. whose parts can be put into a precise one-to-one correspondence).
4. Given two rigorously formulated models that are isomorphic, the final step is to express them as a formal model that can be manipulated (i.e. in one of the formal languages or within a computer) so that conclusions about the managerial situation can be deduced.

These four steps provide an outline of the method. Figure 4.1 provides a graphic description of the method.

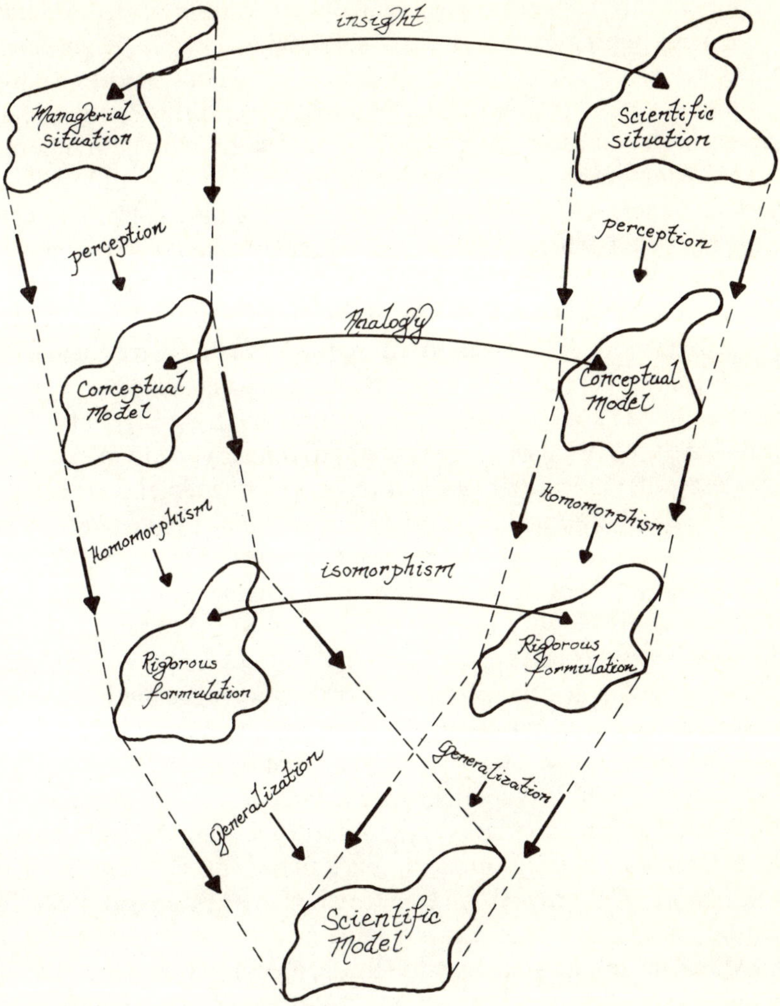

Fig.4.1. The process of building a 'Scientific' model of a managerial situation (S. Beer, *Decision and Control*, (Wiley, London, 1966)

A MORE 'FOLKSY' METHOD

When one's client is a major steel company or a very high level government official, the project is likely to involve several different varieties of scientists and both a mathematician and a logician. Such a team is well equipped to carry the process through fully. When Stafford Beer was developing the method, he frequently worked on such large scale projects. On the other hand, there are enormous numbers of teachers, human service administrators, government officials and others who face complex and intractable problems and who are never going to have the wherewithal to hire a team of scientists (perhaps not anyone at all). Thus it is vitally important that the method can be employed in a looser sort of way by these folks who don't have access to a whole battery of specialists. As a matter of fact, my own use of the method has been entirely in cases where we always lacked some of the formal expertise that we really should have had. At any rate, I will spend some time discussing the process so that anyone at all can use it regardless of technical background or access to specialists.

The following outline of the process is one that I have successfully used with large numbers of educators and human service administrators. It requires very little in the way of technical or mathematical background, although both are helpful. The method does require the ability to look at a situation from various perspectives and to think analytically about a model and the managerial situation. Furthermore, the methodological sketch given here also applies to someone attempting to use the method in the stronger, more rigorous sense mentioned earlier (the only difficulty for the rigorous application is that the last stages of the method are not spelled out in detail — the interested reader should consult Beer's *Decision and Control*[6] *, part two and perhaps Ashby's *Introduction to Cybernetics*[10] on transformations and mappings). The process is outlined in the next few pages.

1. Make an initial statement of the problem. Make sure that the problem as stated is one that you own, i.e. that you have control over. An example of a common problem that the problem formulator does *not* own is, 'my boss is incompetent' or 'my boss treats me like an irresponsible child'. While these are common problems they are not problems that one can do anything about. If one finds himself/herself with such a boss, a better problem statement would be something like this 'given that my boss is incompetent, what can be done to improve the work situation?'. A good guide to the initial problem statement is that

you should focus on those aspects of the situation that you feel strongly about — you may be massively frustrated or intensely curious or very apprehensive or all excited about some particular aspect of the work situation. Finding a good problem statement is at least as much art as science, so you might as well be guided by your intuition and your feelings in picking a starting point.

2. Analogies. Brainstorm analogies to the problem situation. The usual difficulty people run into here is that they are much too conservative, i.e. they make analogies between the work situation and other similar situations. This is sometimes helpful, but nothing very startingly new will come out of it. For instance, someone worrying about planning a conference may make an analogy to planning a course. The advantage of this particular analogy is that, for someone who is an expert in course planning, a model of the course planning process will provide a very helpful tool in making sure that most of the details in planning a conference are thought of (one of my students was an expert in course development but was feeling extremely insecure about his assignment to manage a conference and actually used this example. It worked very nicely). The disadvantage to using this sort of analogy is that you won't learn very much about the underlying dynamics of the problem area.

One of my classes was just getting underway the month after Mt. St. Helens blew its top. That particular class used volcanic eruptions as analogies to organizational change in a federal bureaucracy and developed some quite intriguing insights. In general it is a good idea to deliberately seek at least a few analogies from fields that are far distant from the situation facing you. The analogies can be written down as follows: 'my NAME OF PROBLEM is like SCIENTIFIC SITUATION because ....'.

3. Choose an analogy. After you have a number of analogies, you should pick one that seems provocative, i.e. one that seems to get at the heart of the matter or that looks like it may provide some insight into the dynamics of the situation. Again, picking a good analogy is more art than science. The sort of model that is helpful will depend on what you are trying to accomplish.

If your problem is to design and implement some sort of process, then a model of a process may be the most helpful. If however, you are faced with a recurring or chronic problem, or simply a complex and poorly understood situation, you will probably do better to pick some model that deals with causal dynamics, i.e. some model that explains how something works.

4. Develop the analogy. This step typically involves a good bit of mucking about. In essence it consists of identifying the particular variables in the scientific situation that are relevant and the corresponding variables in the managerial situation. My usual procedure is to make two lists:

scientific variables	**managerial variables**
variable 1	variable 1
variable 2	variable 2
.	.
.	.
.	.
variable n	variable n

I usually try for lists of about three to seven variables. Fewer than three is too simple to help and more than seven is too complicated to manage.

The intention at this stage should be to get variables in the two lists that correspond, i.e. that seem to play the same sort of role in terms of the dynamics of the situation. I almost never get this right on the first try. The possible errors are many, including:

- a list of variables on the scientific side that are inappropriate, i.e. they direct your attention into unhelpful avenues.
- by definition, the dynamics of the managerial situation are largely unknown (otherwise there is no point to the exercise), so there is every likelihood that even when you have an appropriate list of variables on the managerial side that you will have them somewhat shuffled relative to the scientific variables.

At any rate, you discover that you have errors when you begin the next stage.

5. Implications. This is a matter of working out the logical implications of your scientific model. As you begin doing this, you periodically check to see if the same implications make any sense for the managerial model. Typically, you will find that there are some nonsensical results because you have made some incorrect correspondences. At this stage you have to go back and rework the lists of variables. This may involve rearranging the correspondences or it may involve the more fundamental step of changing the managerial variables.

6. Model utility. After a number of iterations through steps four and five, you should have results from the scientific model that make sense when translated into the managerial model. The next step is to ask whether these results are helpful or not. It is entirely possible to have a

model that is valid in a strong, rigorous scientific sense and that is also totally useless in that it doesn't help the manager at all. More commonly, the model may be valid but not really address the manager's most crucial concerns or it may raise new questions that have to be answered before the problem can be dealt with. If the model is totally useless, one must go back at least to the stage of picking an analogy (or a new slant on the old analogy) and perhaps all the way back to the beginning to find some radically different analogy.

The first two times I attempted to teach this method to graduate students, I began by explaining it much as the text above does. As preparation for my explanation, students were assigned the relevant sections of *Decision and Control* and *Management Science*. At the end of my explanation, I would ask if there were any questions. There always were — in fact the questions kept coming and coming and eventually took up all of several classes. We never did get to the end of those questions.

These classes were made up of very sharp graduate students trained in the social and behavioral sciences, but somehow the process just didn't make any sense to them. Finally in despair, I said, 'look here! We are going to try an experiment. Just humor me for about two hours and we are going to simply walk through the entire process'. In both cases, the class was willing to suspend their disbelief for two hours and we walked through the process. In both cases the exercise was a great success and the class learned to use the method.

In subsequent classes I never tried to explain the method nor did I ask anyone to read about it in advance — we simply did it, under my direction as group facilitator. These exercises always began by getting the class to list problems they were concerned with and then the class selected one to work on. In several cases, I accepted their choice with great trepidation because it seemed to me that there was no way to do anything about the situation. Nevertheless, we worked on the problem they chose. Then we brainstormed analogies and I kept urging them to think of outrageous ones because they tended to choose situations very much like the problem situation. After getting a long list of analogies, I would ask them to choose an outrageous but interesting one. I would then guide them through the remaining steps in the method.

In every case, where I simply walked a group through the exercise, the following results accrued:

- in about two hours they more or less understood the method and were interested in learning how to do it on their own.

- by the end of the two hours, the group had gotten excited about what they had learned about the initial problem. In some cases they simply learned that the problem couldn't be dealt with as stated and in other cases they got some interesting insights into the dynamics of the situation. The key point to me was that the students learned and knew they had learned and knew that the learning was due to the method.

The real point of the last few paragraphs is that you, the reader, are very unlikely to learn this method except through doing it. None of my classes ever learned the method until I simply walked them through it. When I finally caught on, stopped trying to explain, and walked people through, almost all of my classes developed reasonable facility with the method. So, reader, I am suggesting that if you want to learn this method there is no alternative to sitting down and just going through it. And further, you will probably have to start through the process *before* you understand it.

I realize that what I am asking of you is contrary to most of your training (i.e. university courses insist on rational clarity before trying something), but if you pretend you are learning a new dance or a new sport it may be easier. After all, if you are going to learn to waltz, you eventually have to stop talking about it, turn on the music, and try to move your feet. Similarly, if you are to learn the model building skills of operations research, you must stop reading, get your pencil, and start model building.

I have not run into any university people who admit to using this method in spite of the fact that *Decision and Control*, the book that spells out the method, has long been considered a classic among management theorists. I do know that some natural scientists use the method, without ever having heard of Stafford Beer or *Decision and Control*, but I know of no management theorist within a university that will admit to using the method. On the other hand, I know of practitioners who use the method. This is all by way of repeating that you can't understand the method without using it. I suspect the academics have attempted to gain rational clarity before using it and they failed — therefore, they never got to use it or understand it. The practitioner, on the other hand, is more likely to try it and therefore is likely to learn it. So, go ye and use the method — and don't wait for total clarity before beginning. Just pretend you're learning to waltz and off you go.

FURTHER READING

After you have attempted to use the method a few times you will undoubtedly run into some difficulties. The following books may be of some help to you if you want to follow up on developing your skill.

Stafford Beer, *Management Science* (Doubleday, New York, 1968) gives many examples and is very easy reading. Unfortunately this book is only available through libraries because it is out of print.

Stafford Beer, *Decision and Control* (Wiley, London, 1966) is the definitive reference. It describes the method in its full scientific rigor and shows the relationship of this method to the standard techniques that operations research has developed.

Charles Lave and James G. March, *An Introduction to Models in the Social Sciences* (Harper & Row, London, 1975) gives a very nice introduction to the art of model building and to the sort of reasoning that is required to derive implications from the models.

W. Ross Ashby, *An Introduction to Cybernetics*, (Chapman & Hall and University Paperbacks, London, 1964) gives a formal but easily understood explanation of the process of mapping one model on to another, of the process of mapping some situation via a model, and of the relationships among various models.

The manager who gains facility with the methods described in this chapter may well want to learn how to take advantage of the more formal and mathematically sophisticated methods of operations research. There are numerous difficult and costly problem areas that simply can't be handled without recourse to methods that require sophisticated mathematics. This chapter has been concerned to introduce methods that permit rough modelling and, hopefully, rapid learning about the managerial situation. In order to get that job done, the more technical methods have necessarily been ignored. This does not mean the technical methods are unimportant, but it does reflect my conviction that managers need to start with the (relatively) crude methods that help in discovering the rough dynamics of a situation. Having done that, the manager can begin worrying about the details, including use of the mathematical tools of operations research. Lest the manager fear that I am recommending a graduate course in mathematics, it is important to add that the manager can understand the uses and limitations, the times to use and the times not to use the mathematical tools of operations research without delving into all the mathematical detail. Stafford Beer's *Decision and Control* (Wiley, London, 1966) and Russell L. Ackoff and Patrick Rivett's *A Manager's Guide to Operations Research* (Wiley, London, 1963) provide excellent starting places.

CONCLUSION

Managers are always responsible for regulation of a situation more complex than they themselves are and they therefore can be only partially successful. The manager's beliefs about the way his/her situation works constitutes a model of that situation. Quite typically these models are implicit and unexamined and therefore not very amenable to learning from experience. This chapter presents a model building method designed to assist the manager learn about his/her situation. The method works through a process of explicitly making analogies from some scientific model to the managerial situation. The model building process culminates in a scientific model and a managerial model that have a precise one-to-one correspondence between their respective elements. This one-to-one correspondence allows use of the scientific model as a framework for reasoning about the managerial situation. It is as if one could import knowledge from the scientific model into the managerial situation. Even when the model building process is not ultimately successful (in the sense just described) the method frequently stimulates a good bit of creativity in thinking about the managerial situation.

Notes

*See under Further Reading.

**'Scientific situation' means the phenomena dealt with or described by a particular science.

CHAPTER FOUR REFERENCES

1. Perhaps the most important and certainly the broadest work (in the sense of touching the most disciplines) to extensively use these new mathematics is that of Prigogine and his co-workers. This framework, which earned a Nobel prize in physics, has had applications in both biological and social sciences. See for instance, Ilya Prigogine, 'Order through Fluctuation: Self-organization and Social Systems' in Erich Jantsch and Conrad Waddington (eds.) *Evolution and Consciousness* (Addison Wesley, Reading, Mass, 1976); J.L. Deneubourg, A. De Palma, and D. Kahn, 'Dynamic Models of Competition Between Transportation Modes' *Environment and Planning, A* **11**, 665-673 (1979); Peter Allen 'Self-organization in Human Systems' in *Essays in Societal System Dynamics and Transportation: Report of the Third Annual Workshop in Urban and Regional Systems Analysis*. Report No. DOT-TSC-RSPA-81-3 (U.S. Department of Transportation, Research and Special Programs Administration, Washington D.C., 1981)
2. Rene Thom, *Structural Stability and Morphogenesis: An outline of a General Theory of Models* translated from the French by D.H. Fowler (Benjamin/Cummings, Reading, Mass. 1975).
3. G. Spencer Brown, *Laws of Form*, (Julian Press, New York, 1972).
4. Francisco Varela, 'A Calculus for Self-Reference', *Inter. J. Gen. Systems* **21** 5-24 (1975).
5. These are Russell L. Ackoff's categories. See his *A Manager's Guide to Operations Research* (with Patrick Rivett) (Wiley, New York, 1963) for a good overview of the techniques. Stafford Beer's *Decision and Control* (Wiley, London, 1966) provides another way of describing these techniques and an excellent discussion of the role of the formal languages of mathematics, statistics, and logic (chapters eight through ten).
6. Beer, *Decision and Control*, p.114.

Chapter 5

THE DESIGN AND REGULATION OF ORGANIZATION: THE VIABLE SYSTEM MODEL

The first four chapters have given the general framework and some of the major principles or laws of cybernetics. Some methodological points have been dealt with (in chapter three the 'cybernetician's questions', and in chapter four on model building). However, the material so far leaves us in rather the same position as an expert in physics who decides to invent a small vehicle propelled by its passenger's leg muscles — should it have one, two, or three wheels? what size? where should the seat go? and so on. The history of the bicycle demonstrates how difficult the design question is even after the relevant physical laws are well understood.

Even after understanding the principles of cybernetics, there is a serious design question remaining: what sort of pieces should an organization have and how should they be inter-connected? This chapter addresses that question. Stafford Beer used the method of chapter four to develop a model for organizations analogous to the human nervous system. The resulting model is called the viable system model.

INTRODUCTION

Brain of the Firm and *The Heart of Enterprise* represent the culmination of over twenty years of managerial experience and research into organizations. The basic problem Beer was concerned with solving is something like this: Given the twentieth century, with its totally new degrees of:

- complexity; more people, organizations, technology, problems, opportunities, information, etc., than ever before.
- rate of change; all sorts of things are changing at an unprecedented rate.
- interdependency; our organizations, social systems and personal lives are inter-mixed and interdependent to the extent that we can hardly do anything without a complex ripple effect that influences scores of other people, things and organizations.

All this means that survival requires an increasing amount of learning and change on the part of individuals and organizations. The bottle neck is typically the rate at which we (individually and organizationally) can change ourselves to adapt to new circumstances.

Given that the computer could be effectively yoked into the information processing aspect of the problem (but so far has not been), and given the nature of the twentieth century as spelled out above, then the question for the student of organizations becomes:

- how can we create organizations that continue to meet the needs of their clients?, or
- how can organizations learn and adapt rapidly? or
- how can we create an effective nervous system for the organization that is capable of maintaining it, learning, and adapting? In short, how to create a brain for the organization that will improve its effectiveness?

This then is the nature of the problem Beer set out to solve.

Cybernetics and Management sets out the discipline (i.e., cybernetics) that provided the general framework. *Decision and Control* gives the methodology for model building that was used. *Brain of the Firm* and *The Heart of Enterprise* provide the model or theory of organization that resulted. All of the books and innumerable papers report on applications. Now this chapter will attempt to provide you, the reader, with enough insight into the model so that you can begin using it in your own situation.

A LANGUAGE OF EFFECTIVENESS

Think of some organization, preferably one you are quite familiar with, or best of all, think of the unit that you yourself are responsible for, whatever that may be. Represent that unit by an amoeba shape, thus:

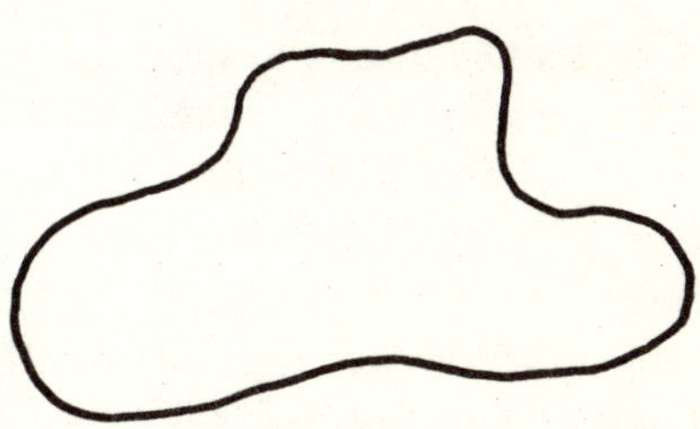

Now, this unit is not isolated, but is rather embedded in some environment with which it carries on a complicated set of interactions. So let us distinguish between the environment and the operation of the unit itself:

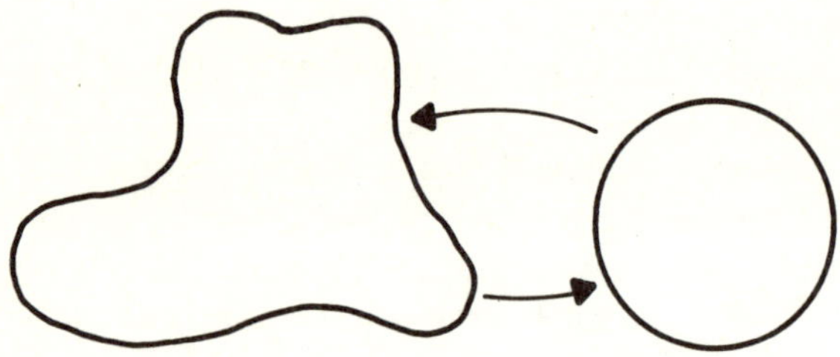

The arrows represent a flux of interactions between the two.

The operation also has some management (you, if you followed my suggestion to think about your own unit). Let us also make a distinction between the management and the operation.

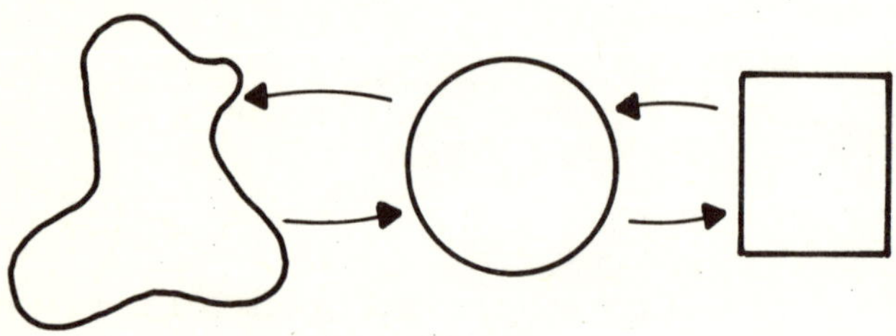

Finally, let us distinguish between the management and the models of the unit that the management holds. These models may be partially explicit (e.g. a computer simulation or the balance sheet), but they are always at least partially (and often almost entirely) implicit, buried in people's heads in the form of intuitions, biases, prejudices, guesses, etc. In whatever form these models exist, they constitute the management's view of the unit that is being managed. Let us represent the models held by management with a triangle:

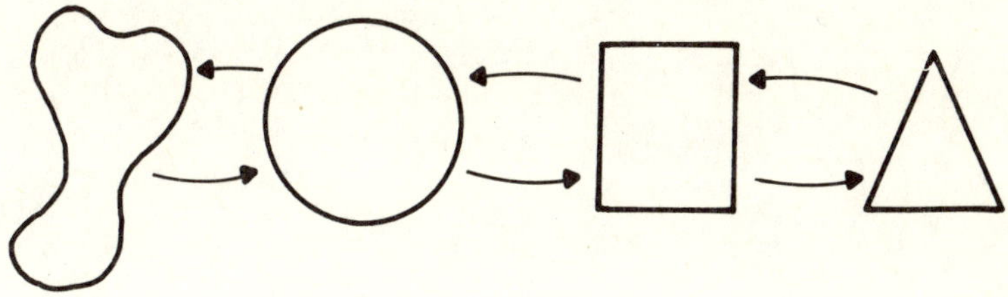

So far we have taken an organizational unit and developed four conventions for talking about different parts of that unit. As we move from left to right, each part is actually embedded inside the previous part. In actuality the unit looks like figure 5.1

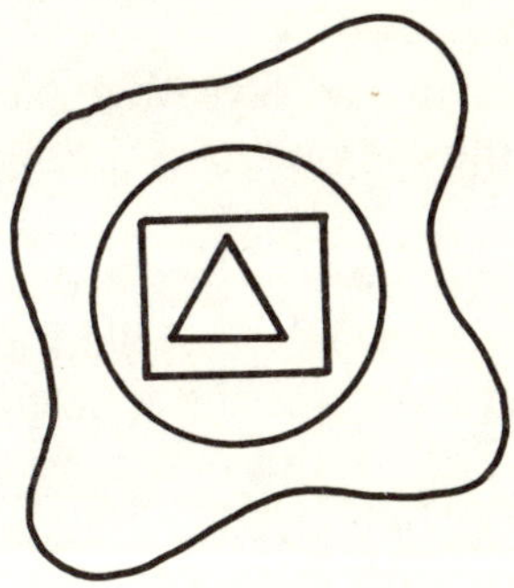

Figure 5.1. An operational unit showing the parts embedded

Figure 5.1 shows the embedding of models in managers, managers within their operation, and the operation within some environment. However, it is convenient to stretch the whole thing out so that we can examine the interconnections. It will be helpful if you keep in mind that the reality is that the parts are embedded as shown in figure 5.1

The model so far is a very simple one. Let us see what this simple model allows us to say about the practical business of management. The model includes four aspects plus arrows representing the interconnections (see figure 5.2).

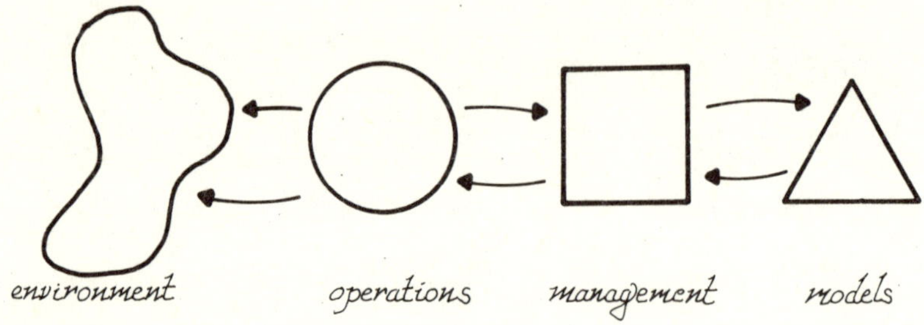

Figure 5.2 An operational unit pulled apart to show the major interactions.

Perhaps the first noteworthy observation is that the environment represented by the amoeba shape is the most complex (since it includes all the rest, plus more), the operation is the next most complex, and the models part is the least complex of all.

The law of requisite variety says that the degree of regulation achievable is limited by the complexity of the regulator compared to the complexity of the system to be regulated. This demonstrates that no aspect of our system can hope to achieve complete control over the piece just to its left in figure 5.2, i.e., the management can at best partially control the operation, and the operation can at best partially control the environment. The management must be less complex than the operation because it is embedded in (i.e., is part of) the operation.

Similarly the operation must be less complex than the environment because it is embedded in (i.e., is part of) the environment (see figure 5.1). Further, the models (which represent the management's view of how to manage) are not sufficiently complex to completely control the management. In all aspects of the system it is at best partially under control and partially out of control of the supposed controller. We might shrug our shoulders and comment about the role of the fates or random happenings at this point, but there are deeper lessons.

First, without some element of chance or error there is no possibility of learning or growth. Some degree of lack of control is necessary to avoid being totally rigid and unable to adapt. Genetic mutation provides a good example of the importance of random 'errors'. Some people have difficulty accepting the role of 'chance' and 'error' in learning and growth.Without going too deeply into the issues involved perhaps three points will suffice for present purposes. First, 'change' always means, by definition, that the system undergoing change is in some sense destroyed and then reborn. Regardless of the details of the change transformation, from the standpoint of the old system the change must be an error. Second, probably all of us are aware of the fundamental role that mistakes play in our personal development. Third, Ken Boulding has pointed out that science never proves anything. What science *does*, is to discover errors (i.e., untenable hypotheses or theories) and then move away from those errors. For all these reasons, some level of chance and error are important to an organization. What degree of control is best is a deep question, the answer to which varies enormously with the given environment and the purposes of the people involved.

The second lesson is that since the supposed controllers lack the variety to do the full job, the systems must always be in part *self*-regulating. This self-regulating ability is both necessary (for without it the systems would collapse) and troublesome (because we so typically ignore it and then run into trouble when we try to change something). It is entirely possible, and in fact fairly common, for the management to behave in ways that interfere quite seriously with the system's ability to be self-regulating. The result is that the management's efforts at regulation result in a net loss of regulation.

Third, there are several general strategies available to management (or any regulator) and some are enormously more effective and efficient than others. Managers seldom pay much attention to these alternative strategies, probably because they have never been introduced to the fact that there are alternative strategies.

Fourth, systems left to themselves may or may not evolve in directions that we humans find desirable (the dinosaurs, for instance, presumably would have preferred to stay around). It behoves us (if we wish to survive) to design the parts of our organizations in such a way that we have appropriate mixes of regulation and randomness.

Fifth, the arrows stand for some sort of flow from one part to another. The flows could in fact be anything: materials or things such as people, lumber or dollars; energy such as electricity, heat, etc.; or information such as speech, electronic codes, memos, etc. From the standpoint of learning, adaptation, and regulation (or in short, long term ability to survive) it is convenient to treat *all* of these flows in terms of the information content of the flow and ignore the differences in *medium* between say speech, paper, electrical signals, or the arrival of a person or a load of steel. The medium may be the message (as McLuhan says) in a psychological sense, but a nervous system can only work if it has some basic unit (e.g., the information content) to compute with.

I will return to elaborate on all five of these points later in the chapter. Before doing so, however, I want to give you a little more of the overall model of the effective organization.

OPERATIONAL ELEMENTS

We spent a couple of pages showing that an organizational unit could be represented as an environment, an operation, a management, and a set of models. Typically, however, such a unit has a number of brothers and sisters. Therefore, to represent the whole organization we need to draw several sets of these pictures as in figure 5.3:

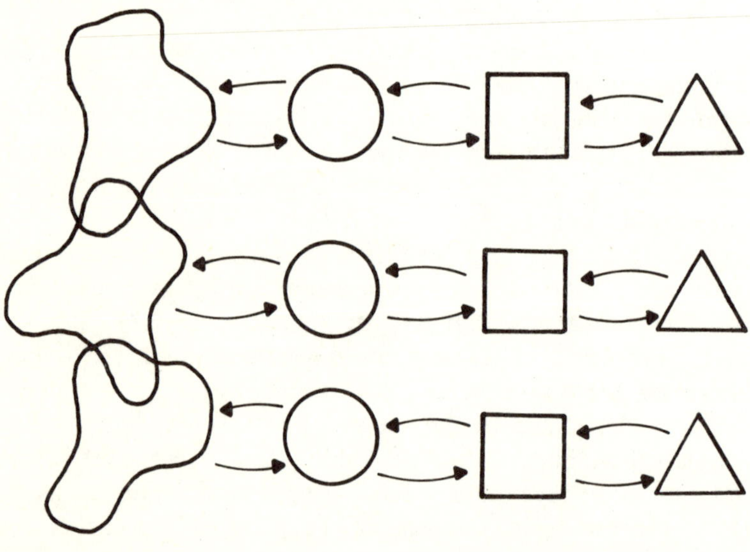

Figure 5.3. A set of related operational elements

The environments in Figure 5.3 are shown as overlapping because they almost always do so. In fact, each environment is likely to overlap with *all* the others, but the limitations of a two dimensional drawing make it difficult to show. Anyway, we now have a picture of three organizational units that, together, make up a larger organization.

Our picture in figure 5.3 is massively defective, however, because we have shown no interconnections except that the environments overlap somewhat. As drawn, this is no organization at all. The management of each unit certainly interacts with the others so that sets of arrows should be drawn to show this. Furthermore, the operations interact with each other directly. In the case of a functionally departmentalized organization such as a large hospital or a city govenmnent the operational interactions may be very strong indeed. In the case of the hospital the patient actually gets passed from one operation to the next and so on right around the hospital. In the case of a city government, the highway department's actions effect the parks department, the recreation department, the welfare department (by displacing families), and so on.

Finally, the models in figure 5.3 (i.e. the little triangles) interact also. It may seem strange to say that a set of models (ebedded in management A's brains) affects some other set of models (embedded in management B's brains), but in fact each manager's view of his/her own unit is influenced by the other unit manager's views. Thus our diagram needs to be redrawn to show these interactions. Again, due to the limitations of drawing in two dimensions, the model fails to depict each operation interacting with all the others, fails to show each management interacting with all the others and fails to show the interaction of each model with all the other models. This entire collection (except for the environments) is called system one. Each of the environment —

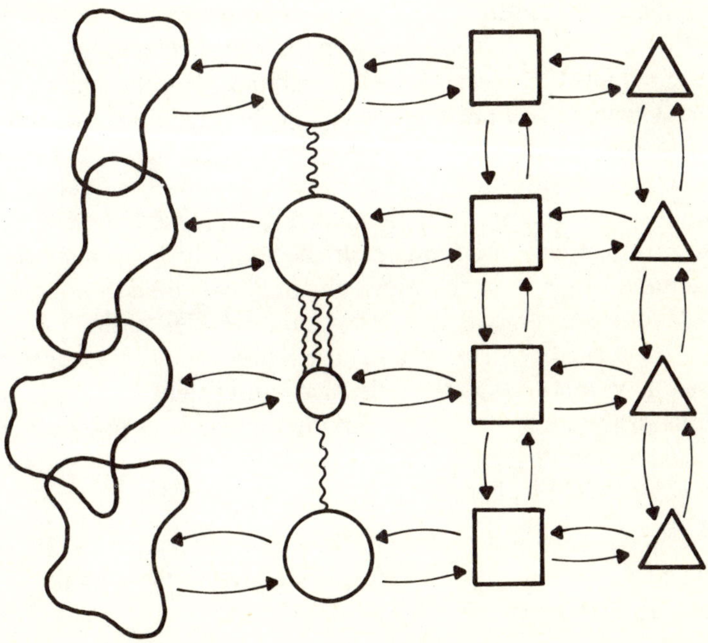

Figure 5.4. System one. A set of operational elements which collectively make up an organizational entity.

operations — management - models complexes will be referred to as an operational element. Figure 5.4 shows four operational elements which together constitute an organizational entity called system one.

THE HOLISTIC MANAGEMENT

A group of organizational units needs someone to manage it. Even if we have a perfectly running set of organizational units, something would happen that would result in one of the units making a change. Even that might not upset the apple cart right away, but sooner or later (and usually sooner) one of the units would make a change that posed a problem for one of the other units that was not resolvable by negotiations. One of the simplest and most common of such cases is when two or more units compete for limited resources from the larger organization. This line of thought raises the question of keeping the entire organization running smoothly.

In cybernetic terms we are talking about the need to maintain the homeostasis of the organization, to make sure that all the critical variables are maintained within their normal limits so that the overall organization can continue to function effectively (see chapter 8 for a discussion of homeostasis). This function has everything to do with trying to achieve a synergistic relationship among the units.

The management of each unit is charged with making that unit work well. The survival and effectiveness *of that unit* is the primary concern of that management. However, the survival and effectiveness of the larger unit may require that the unit be decreased in size or even abolished altogether. Such choices are necessarily the province of some management other than the unit's own. Thus we see the need for a higher level management. It is convenient to refer to the higher level management as the meta-system to system one (see chapter 8 for discussion of meta-system). It is also convenient to divide up the functions of the meta-system as outlined in the next few paragraphs.

Internal and Now Function

The maintenance of homeostasis within the organization as a whole is a full time job for a management team. For convenience we will label this function 'system three'.

External and Future Function

Exploration of the environment and the future of the organization is also a full time job. Label this function 'system four'. The psychology of thinking about the external and future is quite different from the psychology of thinking about the internal and now. System three (internal and now) is taken up with homeostasis, maintaining a smooth operation, conserving, using the lessons of the past. System four (external and future) is oriented toward growth and change, toward new threats and new opportunities, toward changing things around to make them more efficient or more effective. Furthermore, system three has the whole power that comes from control of the productive resources of the organization. System four, of necessity, will have command of those resources left over after the needs of the 'productive' system three are met.

Identity Function

The built in tensions between systems three and four require a 'boss' to mediate between them. Call this function 'system five'. The primary role of system five is to make sure that the interaction between three and four is at an optimal level. Practically, this means that the balance between stability and rate of change must be about right. The most important prerequisite to successfully carrying out this function is that the identity of the organization be clearly maintained. This has everything to do with defining and clarifying the organization's basic purposes.

Co-ordination Function

If we look at the managements of each of the sub units from the standpoint of the meta-system (i.e., systems three-four-five), we can consider the interaction of each management with its own unit in terms of a feedback loop. This means the management is considered as a feedback loop and the operation is a process to be controlled, i.e., the management is a feedback designed to ensure that the operation produces the desired output. However, there are feedback loops for each operation (e.g., four in figure 5.4), each of which affects the others in several ways. There is a real danger that such a system will begin oscillating, i.e., an action that intends to have one effect has the opposite effect and the correction of *that* makes the original difficulty worse. This point is explained at length in the next section, but it may be helpful to first review the model as explained so far (see figure 5.5).

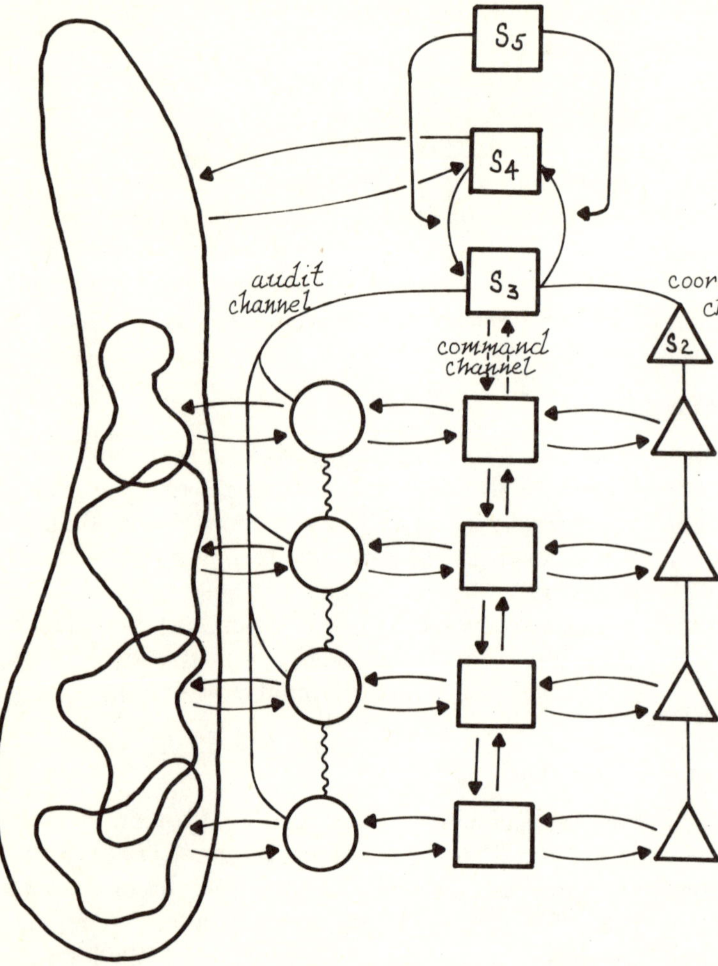

Figure 5.5. An outline of the structure of the viable system at one level of recursion. The aggregation of unlabelled triangles, boxes and circles is system one.

In figure 5.5, system one consists of the set of four operation-management-model units taken as a whole. System two consists of the anti-oscillatory mechanism that operates through the models of system one, under the direction of system three. System three is the management unit responsible for the internal and now (i.e., homeostasis) of the system one. System three uses system two, a command channel for giving orders (shown as coming straight down from three to the managements within system one), and an audit channel for those occasions in which an indepth exploration of one or more operational units is necessary (shown as coming in on the left of the circles). Remember that the two dimensions of the paper interfere with an accurate drawing of the situation — in particular, system three's command and audit channels go directly from system three to each of the units in system one, as do system two's channels.

System four is responsible for the external and future (i.e., learning and change) and therefore must have channels directly to the outside world. Furthermore, the environment explored by four includes all those dealt with by the system one units and any apsects of the larger environment that is important to the overall organization. System five monitors the interaction between systems three and four.

Notice that system four and the operational elements have direct connections to the environment but system three and system five do not. This is not to say that a person fulfilling the function of system three or system five would not have access to the environment. The point is that the system three function is *internal* and system five is concerned with the integration of the whole and neither of them interacts directly with the environment.

FEEDBACK AND OSCILLATIONS

The major difficulty that tends to cause oscillations in feedback systems is that of improper timing. For instance, suppose that it took your furnace one minute to heat your house by one degree. Suppose also that it took the thermostat ten minutes to send the signal that the room was warm enough and the furnace should stop. Under these conditions, the house would get at least ten degrees too hot before the furnace could stop. You might be very tempted to open the windows to cool off, but if it also took the thermostat ten minutes to signal to the furnace that it should start up, you would then get too cold.

Being a prudent soul, you will likely turn the thermostat down about ten degrees to prevent it getting so hot next time. However, this means that the house now gets very cold before the thermostat turns on the furnace. If you are just a bit impetuous you might suddenly realize that it is freezing, get quite irritated and go turn the thermostat up above its original setting. This of course causes the temperature to (eventually) go even higher — thus making you more over-heated than the first time. At this point your heating system is in a fine state of oscillation (and you are in a fine state of misery!). Your actual furnace-thermostat combination is carefully adjusted to minimize these oscillations.

The problem of system oscillation is also very severe at the national level in terms of regulating the economy. Suppose there is a six month delay in gathering the economic statistics and that the item to be regulated (e.g., the supply of money, the interest rate, etc.) has a natural sort of periodicity that also amounts to about six months. Thus an oversupply of money is recognizable after about six months and the government acts to decrease the supply of money. But suppose that in the meantime the actual supply of money has begun to decrease all on its own. Then the government policy designed to bring the money supply back to the level desired is going to cause a shortage of money. The recognition of the shortage will be six months in coming so that the problem might be quite severe by the time it is recognized. If in the meantime, the economy's own internal dynamics have begun to increase the supply of money, the government will be acting (six months later) to increase the supply of money just when it should be doing the opposite (see figure 5.6). In this way the supposed regulator can make the system's instability worse.

Instability or oscillation due to time lags is very common when dealing with interconnected sets of feedback loops and is quite likely to occur in the organization as depicted in figure 5.5. Therefore, we need system two whose job is co-ordinating the various units so that they do not go into oscillation. Ideally, system two should consist of an explicit set of models (those used by the unit managements) and a capability to identify and guard against those conditions that might lead to oscillation. Thus system two is a servant to the unit managements collectively. System two shouldn't have the right to tell anybody what to do, except insofar as particular activities need to be prescribed or regulated to avoid oscillations. The unit managements cannot themselves avoid oscillations because it is their own interactions that cause the problems

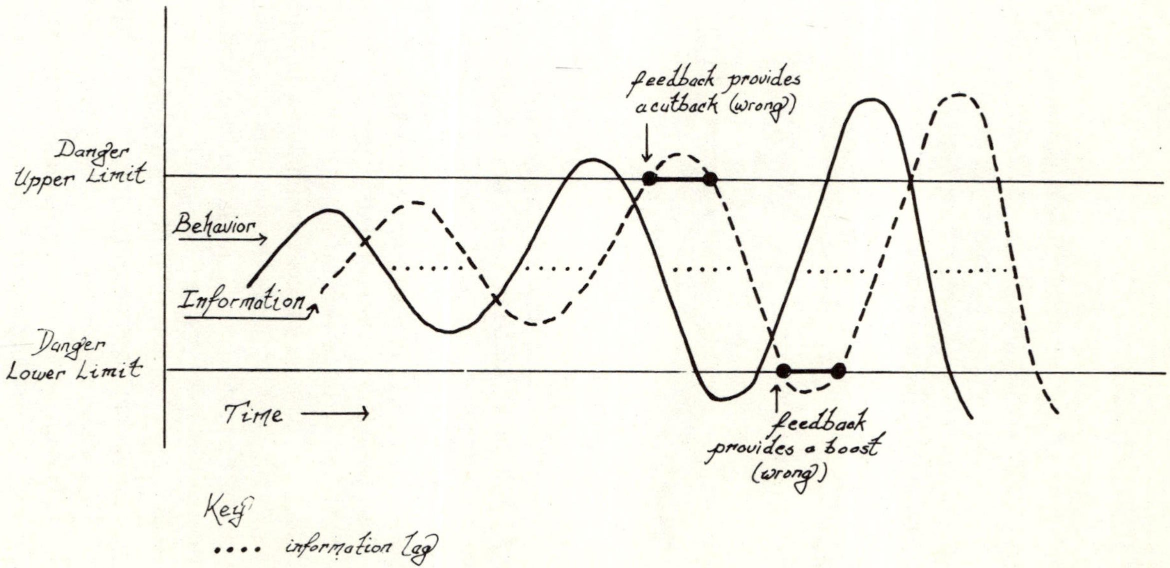

Figure 5.6. An illustration of a feedback increasing instability by being out of phase.

(adapted from Stafford Beer, *Platform for Change.* Wiley, New York, 1974 p.430)

— system two must be able to take an organization-wide view that includes all of the units.

LEVELS OF RECURSION

Consider again figure 5.5, with its operational units making up system one and the meta-system consisting of systems 2-3-4-5. If we lump all the environments together into one big amoeba, lump all the operations (with their managements) into one big circle, and lump systems two-three-four-five together as the management of this thing we get:

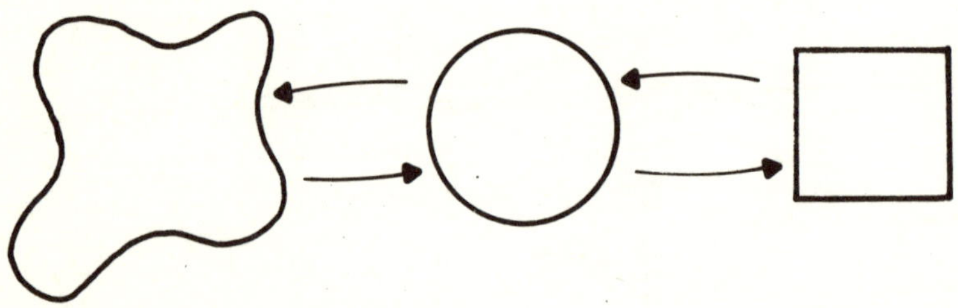

or the same model that we started out with many pages ago. However, in this case we are talking about a representation of a much larger unit than before. To be precise, at the beginning of this chapter we were talking about your own unit, the one that you yourself manage. Now we are talking about a larger organizational unit that includes your unit and several others (i.e., your unit's brothers and sisters, so to speak).

If you work for a really large organization, such as a state or the federal government, we could now repeat the analysis that we have just finished, i.e., we could lump together the brothers and sisters of this larger unit to constitute a system one at this larger level, and this system would obviously need its own systems two-three-four-five.

Alternately, if your unit has several different departments within it, we could apply the full model to your unit alone. This means we would identify the units that make up your system one, your anti-oscillation system two, your system three for maintaining homeostasis, your system four for managing learning and change, and your system five to balance the three-four tension.

In effect, these diagrammatic conventions constitute a language for discussing the requirements for effectiveness. They can be used to describe a giant organization as a whole or to describe one small department or any level in between. And when we go to the level of detail of the individual human being, the model still fits because that's where it came from to begin with. The methods of chapter four were used to model the nervous system of the organization in terms of the nervous system of the human being.

Figures 5.7 and 5.8 show multiple levels of recursion. In this way the model can be used for any organization or any part of an organization. This does not mean that some box from the existing organization chart can (necessarily) be sensibly described with the model. The viable system model describes the requirements for simultaneously maintaining internal stability and adapting. Those requirements are, in the language of cybernetics, the same for organizations of any size.

On the other hand, the boxes found on organization charts are frequently *not* coherent wholes — i.e., the organization chart boxes were not devised with the requirements for autonomous entities in mind. Therefore, the reality for many organizations is that the units recognized by the organization chart are rather artificial from the standpoint of either the intended purpose, or the way the organization is actually working. The viable system model applied to such a box from the organizational chart will, if carefully done, reveal only that the box is not a viable system because it doesn't have all of its necessary parts.

The claim that is made for the model, then, is that it describes any organization, of whatever size, that is able to maintain its internal stability and to adapt to new conditions.

Before the example of figures 5.7 and 5.8 can be explained, a short digression is needed. The proper application of the model to a real school system depends quite critically upon the purposes of the school. To be precise, if the purpose is for students to produce something, then students are the operational elements at the lowest level. If, however, students are expected to be *produced*, then something like 'lessons' or 'assignments' are the operational elements at the lowest level.

There are clearly profound questions of educational philosophy tied up in this choice. The viable system model, when applied in these two different ways, makes clear what some of the possibilities and limitations are. In particular, the viable system model specifies the necessary sphere and degree of autonomy for the operational elements. If the student is to produce something, then a certain amount of autonomy is *required* (the proper amount of autonomy depends upon what is to be produced). If the student is expected to *be* produced, there

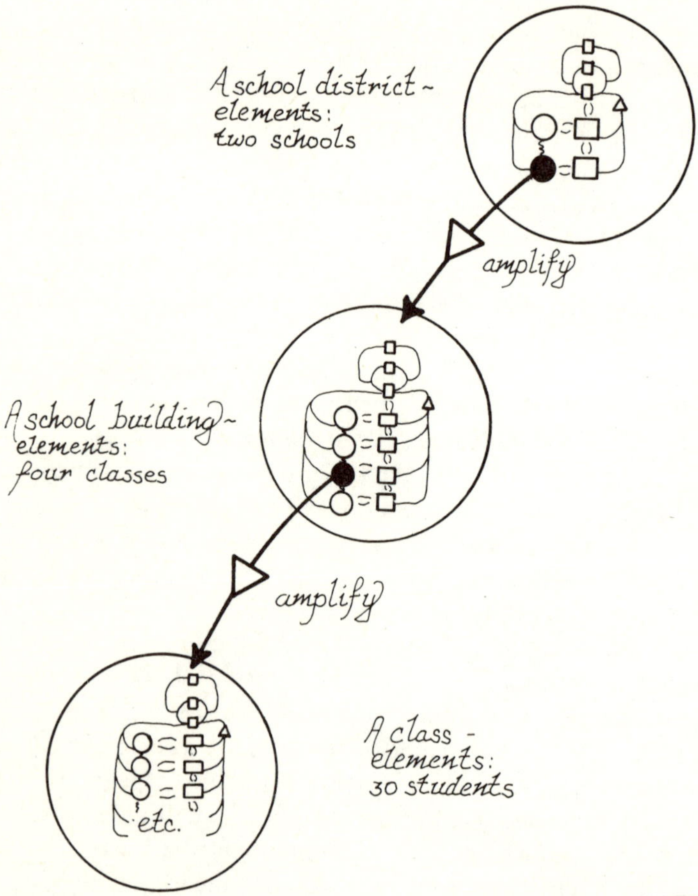

Figure 5.7. An example of the recursive application of the viable system model. Note that this is based on particular purposes for the school and other purposes require different breakdowns.

(adapted from Stafford Beer, *The Heart of Enterprise,* p.315)

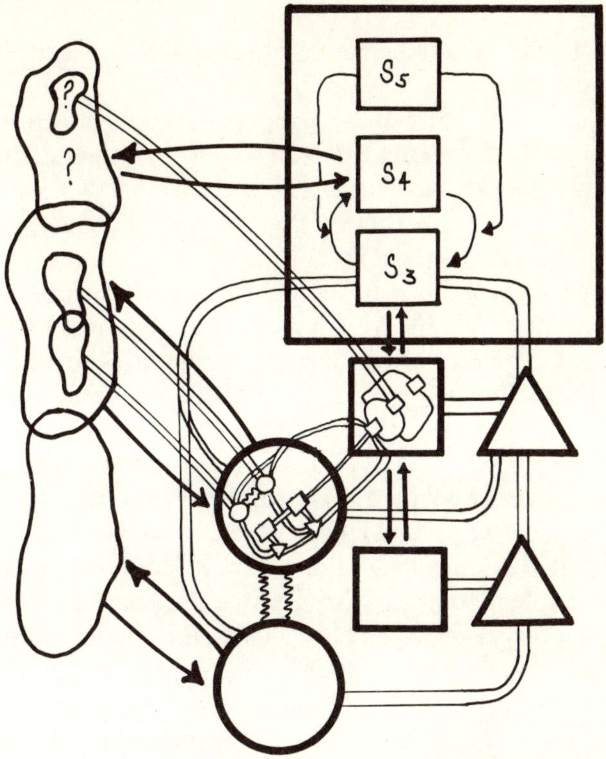

Figure 5.8. An example of two levels of recursion of the viable system model. Overall it shows an organization of two elements. One of these is shown in further detail (on the diagonal).

(adapted from Stafford Beer, *The Heart of Enterprise*, p.321)

is no necessity for student autonomy. The latter situation seems appropriate for a training situation, i.e., to produce a mechanic or typist. The former situation is required for education in the root sense, i.e., a responsible citizen or lover of music must largely produce him/herself.

In order to provide an easily understood example of recursion and to avoid the issues raised in the paragraph above, the example used in figures 5.7 and 5.8 has been absurdly simplified to deal with a school district with only two buildings, each of which has four classes and 30 students per class. The limitation to only 2 buildings and 4 classes per building is merely to permit a relatively uncluttered drawing — the principles are the same for more realistic situations. Further, each class is assumed to have students as its operational elements.

In figure 5.7 the viable system model is applied to three different levels of recursion in a small school district. In a larger district, it would be useful to define another level of recursion between the levels of building and district.

In figure 5.8, the entire drawing represents the school district with its management (i.e., systems 2-3-4-5) and its two operational elements (i.e., the two school buildings). The entire viable system model, with systems 1-2-3-4-5 and all of the inter-connecting channels is shown for the school district as a whole.

When we examine one of the operational elements (i.e., a school building) in more detail, we can see all of the viable system model applied to it. The school building management, which looked like an undifferentiated black box from the district's standpoint, is now seen to consist of a tiny system two, system three, system four, and system five. Furthermore, the school building operations, which also looked like a black box to the school district, is now seen to consist of two separate operations (i.e., classrooms), each of which has its own management.

If we wanted to use a magnifying glass we could repeat this trick and draw the next level of recursion (i.e., the students) inside the smallest circles. But the point is already made: the model is recursive. At whatever level the model is applied, it looks precisely the same (except for the number of operational elements). And whenever one looks inside a part of the model, the same parts are always there. To be precise:

- operations (i.e., a circle) include smaller operations and their associated managements.
- managements (i.e., a system one square) include the systems 2-3-4-5 for that management.

And if one looks for the big picture, whatever system 1-2-3-4-5 is being considered, it always makes up an operation with its management for the next higher level of recursion.

There are numerous ways of discussing organizations, including that most familiar one given by the organization chart. The viable system model outlined above is a way of discussing organizations designed to facilitate questions of organizational effectiveness and adaptation.

USING THE MODEL

In general, the translation between the viable system model and the organizational chart is complex. A good beginning to using the model, is to decide what parts shall constitute the operational elements of system one at whatever level the analyst is working. The major guideline for identifying the operational elements of system one is that they are the parts that do or produce whatever the organization is supposed to do or produce.

It is crucial, in this regard, to keep in mind that an organizational unit always develops goals of its own. Not only does every organizational unit develop *goals* of its own, each unit also develops reward/punishment systems, accountability systems, norms, and feedback loops to attempt to achieve those goals. In short, every organizational unit becomes an integrated system devoted to achieving its own goals.

In many organizations, the goals of the various units are at least in part in conflict with each other, or in conflict with the intended overall mission, or merely irrelevant to the intended overall mission. This point was discussed at some length in chapter two under the heading of 'examples'. That section examined the actual feedback loops in schools and universities, among other institutions. It was clear, for instance, that neither good teaching nor learning (under any of our common definitions of those terms), was an operational goal of school buildings or university departments.

The question of whether or not sub-unit goals, taken as a group, support overall goals is a thorny one. Purposes are often not easily separable into pieces. If we are building a house, we can divide it up into foundation, frame, electrical system, etc. and be relatively sure that all the parts are contributing to a 'house'. Even so, we sometimes build houses whose parts are not appropriate to each other. It is quite difficult to ascertain whether or not the goals of, say, a hospital's various departments, combine to form a reasonable purpose for that hospital.

The problem is complicated because the goals for the units are hard to determine and the units' goals, once determined, cannot be simply added together in any mechanical fashion. Unfortunately, determining what the goals *actually* are takes considerable digging into the actual modus operandi (see chapter two, Feedback and chapter three, Purpose). And determining whether or not the units' goals are supportive of the overall purpose is a major exercise in applied philosophy.

One possible solution is to divide up the organization so that all parts have essentially the same goal as the total organization. This is ostensibly what the schools do — the goal for a classroom is to 'educate' 30 students, the goal for the building is to 'educate' 300 and the goal for the district is to 'educate' 3000. The problem of making sure that the sub-units really do have the intended goal remains. Making sure the sub-units have the correct goals is operationally the task of making sure the sub-units have the appropriate internal structure, e.g. the appropriate feedback loops, or to be more precise about it, the functions and network specified by the viable system model.

In the last section, in order to illustrate the recursive nature of the viable system model, an example using schools deliberately suppressed most of the complexity of purposes by simply presenting one way of looking at a school. To return to that previous example in a slightly more realistic way, consider a school system in which the purpose is firmly defined as students developing responsible citizenship. The simplest way to structure this system is to begin with the student as the operational element at the lowest level of recursion. Since citizenship implies functioning in a society, at some level the school will have to have operational elements that look like 'societies', i.e groups. Finally, various societies must relate to each other, so this suggests a third sort of operational element.

The three notions at the end of the last paragraph (students, society, and inter-society relations) are adequate to structure the entire system. If we think about a large school system, it looks like:

R1 - the school system; made up of several coalitions.
R2 - a coalition, made up of several societies.
R3 - a society, made up of a group of 5-10 neighborhoods.
R4 - a neighborhood, made up of a group of 10-30 students.
R5 - a student.

Each of these levels of recursion has an important goal that is fairly clearly tied to the overall goal of responsible citizenship:

- the student is expected to demonstrate increasingly responsible citizenship as he/she matures.
- the neighborhood level is responsible for those very local concerns of care, and nurture of the individuals in the group. This provides the first arena for the student to demonstrate his/her citizenship.
- the society (corresponding perhaps to a small school building), must have a government in the same sense that a town or small city needs one. This provides a second, larger arena for the student to demonstrate his/her developing citizenship.
- the coalition; consisting of several societies, takes on the character of foreign relations, bargaining, and so on. This provides a very large arena for exercise of citizenship.

It is not clear exactly how many levels are desirable — and the number might even change from time to time. If we take our basic purpose (i.e., students developing responsible citizenship) seriously, we must obviously give the students a major role in making this whole structure work. And that implies a very different role for teachers and administrators. In particular, it implies putting students (largely) in charge, and making teachers and administrators into advisors, facilitators, and resources.

In order to picture the sort of school this structure implies, imagine the following combination (see also figure 5.9):

- the new structure would be initiated one year at a time beginning with grade one (i.e., after 4 years it would include 4 grades and after 12 years would include 1st-12th).
- the students would be responsible within some *broad* limits set by the adults, for the rules, procedures, schedule, curriculum, etc.
- sports, extra-curricular activities, dances, etc. should be the responsibility of the students.
- students should have control over a considerable piece of the finances (e.g., the sports budget).

The students are obviously going to make some horrible mistakes under these arrangements. But, given the purpose of students developing responsible citizenship, making mistakes and living with their consequences is an indispensable part of the students' development. The staff's role would include trying to prevent those few mistakes that would have very long-term consequences, i.e., those mistakes whose consequences would be visited primarily on someone else.

The example of the last few paragraphs was not intended to argue in favor of one kind of school over another. The example was intended to demonstrate the way in which the viable system model can be used to structure an organization, once a purpose has been firmly chosen. The example discussed only one aspect of structure, that of the operational elements at the various levels of recursion. All the other elements of the viable system model (i.e., systems one through five and the various channels, etc.) more or less fall into place if the operational elements are appropriately defined.

It might be helpful to take an example of a school structure based upon a different purpose for the school. Suppose the purpose was to produce students who would conform to community norms, i.e., the students would be 'good citizens' in a very narrow and passive sort of way, they would do what they were told to do. In the previous example

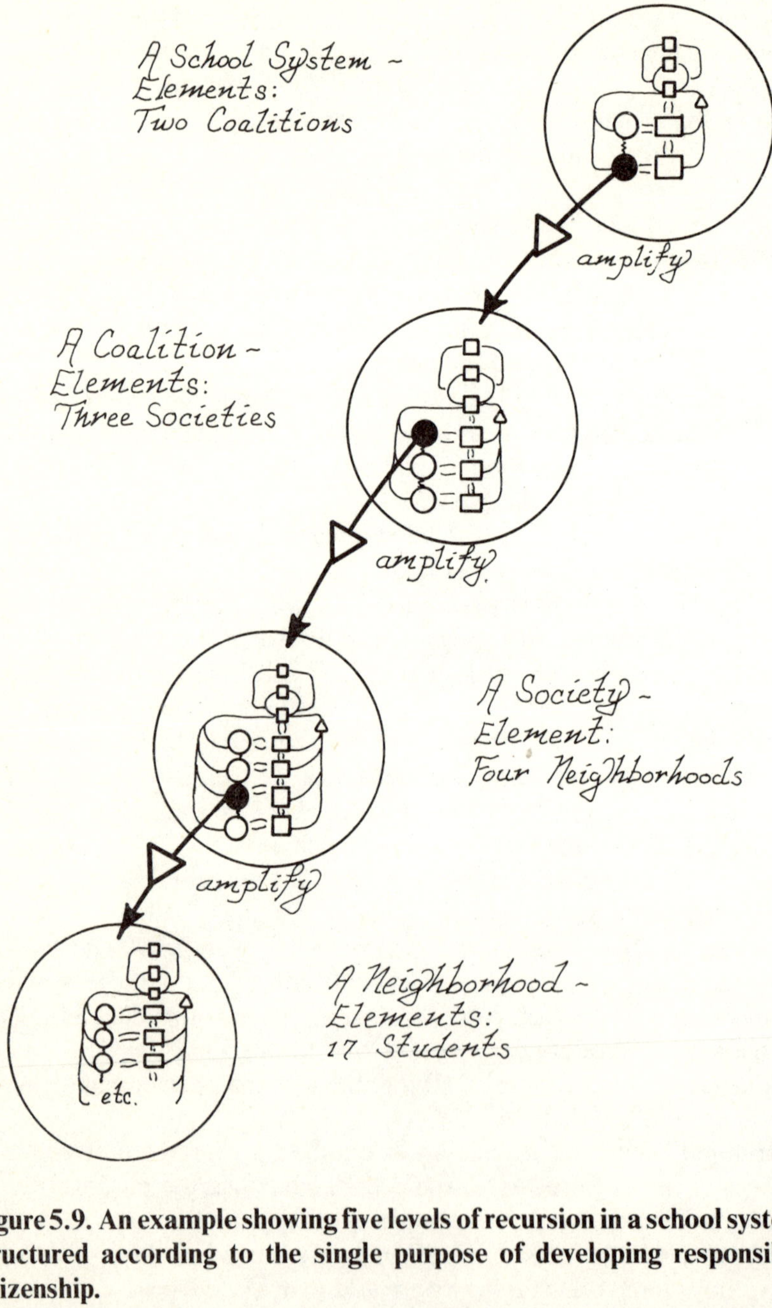

Figure 5.9. An example showing five levels of recursion in a school system structured according to the single purpose of developing responsible citizenship.

the purpose was for the *student* to produce certain sorts of characteristics in him/herself. In this case the school is going to produce certain sorts of characteristics in the student.

The previous case required the students' active assistance in directing their own development, they had to amplify the staff's efforts. Thus, the goal had to be one that the student would freely endorse and the process required a great deal of autonomy on the part of the student. In this case, the system is going to produce a student who conforms to a higher authority, i.e., community norms, and there is no reason why the student would freely choose this goal nor for that matter is there any need for the student to choose it — the system can mold the student in the desired way.

The operational elements for the system intending to produce conformists would probably be, going from the lowest level to the highest: a lesson, a set of lessons, a course, and so on up to the total curriculum. Each operational element would be judged in terms of the extent to which the students passing through it did, or did not, have the desired habits or conformity.

In the previous example, the student was judged in terms of his/her long term performance as a citizen of the 'school society'. In the second example, the teaching activity is judged in terms of whether or not it molds students in the desired way. The viable system model can be used to follow through the implications of either purpose. The model does have the advantage that it helps make the implications of a purpose clear and thereby helps assess whether a given purpose is really what we want or not.

Let us consider, as a final example, the hospital. There are obviously a number of ways that we could subdivide a hospital, e.g., there are units for surgery, convalescent wards, laboratories, cancer research, obstetrics — the list can get very long. The key requirement in defining the operational elements for the viable systems model, however, is to find a way of defining the operational elements that reflect the purposes we have for the institution. If we define the purpose of the hospital in terms of curing diseases and defects, then it makes sense to define operational elements in those terms. Perhaps the levels of recursion look like this:

R1 - Hospital, made up of centers devoted to disease types, e.g. infectious, degenerative, accident, cancer, parasites, childhood, old age, etc.

R2 - Center for Infectious Diseases, made up of centers for influenza, etc.

R3 - Center for Influenza, made up of several doctors specializing in treatment of influenza.

Alternatively, we might define the purpose of the hospital as part of a health system whose purpose it is to keep people as healthy as possible. This implies, of course, that our first level of recursion is bigger than the hospital. The levels of recursion might look like this:

R1: Health system: hospitals, county centers, etc.

R2: Hospitals: pediatrics, geriatrics, obstretics, etc.

R3: Pediatrics: Doctor Y, Doctor X ...

R4: Doctor Y: Patient 1, Patient 2 ...

In this case, where the entire structure is built upon the individual patient, units such as surgery, x-ray, cancer research, etc. are all *support* units, i.e., they become part of system three (at appropriate levels of recursion) and they are *servants* to the needs of the operational elements under the watchful eye of a system three. In this case, system three would be focusing upon questions of 1) needs of the operational elements for the *services* of surgery, x-ray, etc., 2) questions of synergy among the operational elements as that is affected by surgery, x-ray, etc. and, 3) the constraints, paperwork demands, etc. upon the operational elements arising from the surgery, x-ray, etc. The constraints and paperwork placed upon the operational elements by the support services, could then be restricted to those required for the efficient use of the services *after* the needs of the operational elements were met. This last point is important in helping to ensure that the details of the hospitals' modus operandi do not actually interfere with its purposes.

The decision about system ones and their division into operational units constitutes the basic structure for the organization. This division of the organization into system ones is crucial for several reasons. First, the system ones (at the various levels) both represent and simultaneously determine what the organization is all about.

Second, each system one must have an associated system two-three-four-five if it is to be an effective unit (this does not mean some individual must be appointed to each of these roles — you and I have all these functions being nicely carried out inside ourselves all the time). The functions of systems two-three-four-five must be taken care of, or the system ones will lose the ability to maintain internal stability or lose the ability to adapt, or both. And at the higher levels of the organization, unless there are designated individuals, a great deal of experience strongly suggests that the system two and four functions will be almost totally ignored and then system five becomes absorbed into system three.

Thirdly, we are so accustomed to thinking in terms of the standard organization chart that there is a real temptation to simply take the existing departments, divisions, etc. and plug them into the viable system model. This is almost always a mistake because the organization chart is both a historical relic (representing mainly the historical accretion of power blocs within the organization), and was designed mainly to apportion responsibility and authority, not to reflect what the organization purpose is *now*.

A great deal has been made of the enormous complexity facing every manager. One of the most important ways of cutting that complexity down to size is for the manager to define a set of operational units for his organization. This then allows the manager to focus on managing the whole (i.e., the collection of operational units that we have been calling system one). The manager's role is then defined in terms of system two-three-four-five functions for that system one. The operational elements of his/her system one should, must, be treated as black boxes.

The manager discussed in the paragraph above is in charge of an operational element in the next higher manager's system one. Thus the manager of the last paragraph is both in charge of an operational element (within his/her boss's system one) and is in charge of (i.e., is part of systems two-three-four-five) a set of operational elements at his/her own level. Since each level is made up of a set of operational units that are treated as black boxes, several advantages accrue.

The first is that the organizational structure is essentially the same at every level. This essential sameness in structure provides an enormous simplification in thinking about or discussing the organization.

Secondly, this structure of black boxes within black boxes, solves the old and intractable problem of centralization versus decentralization. The entire structure is linked and integrated by the outputs of the boxes. The entire structure is loosened up by allowing *each* box autonomy in its internal workings. The integrity of the whole is achieved by careful definition of purpose and structuring of the black boxes (i.e., the operational units) to achieve those purposes.

The management's job, at every level, is to make sure that its constituent boxes produce the intended outputs. The management, at every level, is also free to achieve its own outputs in the way that it thinks best. The flexibility, autonomy, and ability to adapt to new conditions is given by the freedom of each of the boxes to organize itself internally according to its own preferences.

This approach shows that integration of the whole, and autonomy of the parts is both possible and desirable. Probably the biggest obstacle to rethinking the organizational structure, is our familiarity with the pyramidal organization chart conventions and the existing organization structure — in other words, we are accustomed to thinking in particular ways and it is difficult to get out of those grooves.

THE LAWS OF VIABILITY

This chapter has so far posed a question and presented some diagrammatic conventions. The question posed was 'given extreme complexity and rapid change, how can we make our organizations more humanly effective?'. The diagrammatic conventions provide a language for discussing certain aspects of organization that are invariant across levels from the smallest units of an organization to the entirety of the largest organization. This section will attempt to make explicit the cybernetic laws built into the model. Or, to make the point another way, this section will attempt to explain the cybernetic laws the consideration of which this model facilitates.

As an overview, I can say that the laws and principles of cybernetics dealt with in chapters two and eight seem to be of paramount importance to the functioning of organizations, in that they provide the theoretical limits within which the organization must operate. An example may make this point clear. The laws of mechanics provide the limits within which vehicles must operate, e.g. the second law (entropy) demonstrates that an internal combustion or steam engine can never be 100% efficient. Similarly the law of requisite variety, the Conant-Ashby law, the self-organizing systems law, and the feedback laws, seem to provide crucial sorts of limits for organizations.

The second point about the model is that cybernetics has discovered a number of very general 'tricks' or mechanisms for accomplishing regulation, learning, and adaptation. Several of these are also built into the model. Again an example may be helpful. There may be innumerable ways to build engines based on the laws of thermodynamics, but the gasoline engine and the diesel are extraordinarily useful gadgets that get used over and over in all sorts of machinery that needs a power source. The point is, these engines embody thermodynamic laws in such a way that we can put them to use in a wide variety of situations. Similarly, there may be many ways of constructing motors based on the laws of electromagnetism, but we have the type with a rotating armature and routinely use it in all sorts of applications.

Cybernetics has similarly discovered that one can construct 'devices' (often by modelling them on nature's own) such as filters, amplifiers, self-vetoing homeostats, transducers, black boxes, etc., and can use these devices in a wide variety of situations. Now the model described in the previous section was developed precisely to facilitate talking about these cybernetic laws and cybernetic devices. It is intentionally quite different from the traditional model that we are all accustomed to (i.e., the organization chart) because the organization chart obscures the cybernetic points that permit a meaningful discussion of effectiveness. Again, an example may make this point clear.

Imagine that four engineers from four different planets were examining an earth-type automobile. Each of these engineers comes from a culture whose technology developed in one very narrow way and they know nothing about any other sort of technology. The first engineer, named Hydro, comes from a planet where hydraulic systems (i.e., fluids in pipes) form the entire basis for their technology. Hydro looks at the car, discovers the radiator, heater, and the associated pipes and declares the car is a simple system designed to transfer heat from the large iron mass under the hood, via a water exchanger, toward the front and, via an air exchanger, into the interior. He is a little puzzled by all the confusing accessories to this simple system — they make no sense at all.

The second engineer, Electro, is from a planet where the entire technology is based upon electromagnetic phenomena. He examines the car briefly and proclaims it is a simple signalling device, capable of about 2 to the eighth power different signals (i.e., it has about that many different combinations of lights controllable by the driver). The Electro engineer confesses massive confusion about all the extraneous and unnecessary parts under the hood and in the operator's compartment. However, he is quite certain that it is primarily designed as a signally device.

The third engineer, Chemo, is from a planet where the only technology involves chemical reactions. He is massively confused until the car is demonstrated and then gets very excited. 'Aha, it is an elaborate set of beakers for mixing air and petroleum and producing a veritable cornucopia of exotic compounds including NO, NO_2, N_2O_5, CO, CO_2, H_2O and so on'. He does wonder about a race that has so much confusing fol de rol surrounding its test tubes and beakers, but he finally assumes they are doing it for religious or aesthetic reasons. 'Oh well, don't criticize the native religion!', he says to himself.

To conclude our little parable, we need to note that each of these three engineers wrote out a fully detailed set of technical specifications for the machinery they had studied (i.e., the results were technical descriptions of the car in terms of its hydraulics, its electrical system, and its chemistry of combustion). The matter would have rested there except that their reports went to the research department of Interplanetary Vehicles Incorporated. The reports were then given to a senior engineer who was instructed to answer the following questions:

- top speed of the car
- cruising speed.
- maximum acceleration
- amount and type of raw materials needed to produce one vehicle
- aerodynamic drag at various speeds.

Six weeks later the unfortunate engineer was fired because he had been unable to answer even one of the questions. His supervisor ignored his attempt to explain that the descriptions provided by the three observers were totally useless. After all, his boss reasoned, the observers were highly qualified engineers and provided very detailed reports — he just couldn't believe they were totally useless for his purposes.

The parable of the 3 engineers reminds many people of the old story about the 3 blind men and the elephant. In that story the three blind men encounter, respectively a leg, the tail, and the side of the elephant. They then report that an elephant is like a tree trunk, a rope, and a wall, respectively. The problem with this parable is that we are accustomed to feeling superior in that we know the tree, rope, and wall are *really* an elephant. The parable of the three engineers suggests that the tree, rope, wall, and elephant are not only equally correct but that, depending upon your purposes, any one of them might be more *useful* than the others.

The viable system model has a number of uses, but two will perhaps illustrate its utility: it provides a way of structuring an organization and it provides a language for discussing viability (or in ordinary managerial language perhaps we could simply say 'long range effectiveness'). The first of these (structuring of an organization) was discussed in the last section. The language of viability needs some comment.

Cybernetics was defined (chapter three) as the science of effective organization. Chapter eight discusses 20 principles, theorems, and laws of cybernetics, all of which have to do with the way complex, dynamic systems work, i.e., with 'organization'. The viable system model is an attempt to embody many of those laws in an effective way, much the way an expensive racing bike is an effective embodiment of the laws of physics. Let's examine some of the ways the model uses the various laws of cybernetics:

1. Large organizations are treated as relatively autonomous systems nested within larger autonomous systems nested within larger systems. This characteristic reflects the following laws (these laws are discussed in chapter 8).
   - System Holism: each autonomous system is treated holistically.
   Recursive Systems: each level within the overall structure has the same internal structure of systems one-two-three-four-five.
   - Darkness: it is not possible to know a system fully. Fortunately, there is no need to examine the details of a unit's operation so long as it produces the desired outputs.
2. Attention is focused on the communication flows within the organization. The following laws are important in this respect:
   - The Law of Requisite Variety: all of the many double-arrow loops in the model are governed by the Law of Requisite Variety. This means that, in effect, the amount of *useful* information in each of the two arrows making up a loop, will become more or less equal. Thus, if managers are to have any real insight into the systems they are supposedly managing, the filters and amplifiers on these loops had better be designed carefully.
   - The feedback laws: any of these loops can be treated as a feedback situation and can, therefore, be set up to more or less run automatically if proper feedbacks are implemented.
3. Each system one is treated as a self-organizing (i.e., autonomous) system by its two-three-four-five meta- system.
4. System two is necessary primarily because feedback loops (particularly when they are multiple and inter-laced one with another) show complex oscillatory patterns based on the time lags around the various loops.
5. System three is the monitor for internal homeostasis. It also provides a meta-language (see Godels Incompleteness Theorem) for discussing synergy among system one units.

6. System four embodies the Conant-Ashby Theorem 'Every good regulator must be a model of the system regulated'. In addition, system four provides a meta-language for discussing change and adaptation.

Enough! I could go on but the point is probably made: The viable system model rests upon and embodies the Laws of cybernetics.

VARIETY ENGINEERING

Let us return to the simple model of one operational unit of system one:

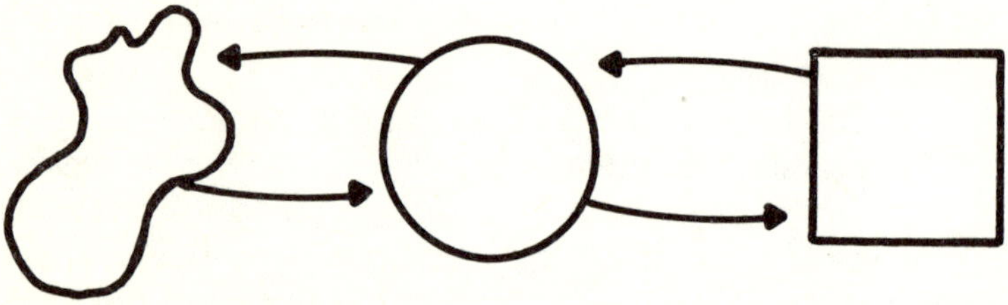

Consider the interactions between the management and the operation (i.e., the square and the circle). The first question we might ask has to do with the relative variety (or complexity) of the two. As we saw earlier the operation is always somewhat (and usually massively more) complex than the management. For instance, a teacher tries to 'manage' a class of thirty students. A case worker tries to 'manage' a caseload of forty or ninety people. A superintendent tries to manage a school system of thousands. And so on. We might draw our diagram to represent the *potential* flow of variety from one to the other like this:

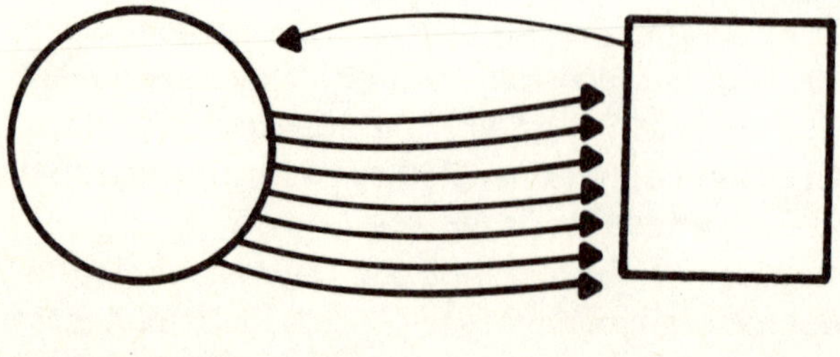

In fact, the variety flows never look like the picture above. In the absence of any better filters, the overwhelmed management just closes its eyes and ears and ignores most of the flood of data.

In a well designed information system there will be a set of explicitly designed filters to extract meaningful information from the massive variety of the operation. Similarly, the management has a relatively small capability to send information back to the operation, so that some sort of amplifier is helpful. Simple examples of amplifiers include the management saying 'This is what we want done. Please figure out how to do it and then do it.' or 'There is a new machine that just came on the market that looks promising for our operation. Check it out'. Similarly, the xerox machine and the 'company newsletter' have become important amplifiers for many of us. Thus, a well designed information system will make our model look something like this:

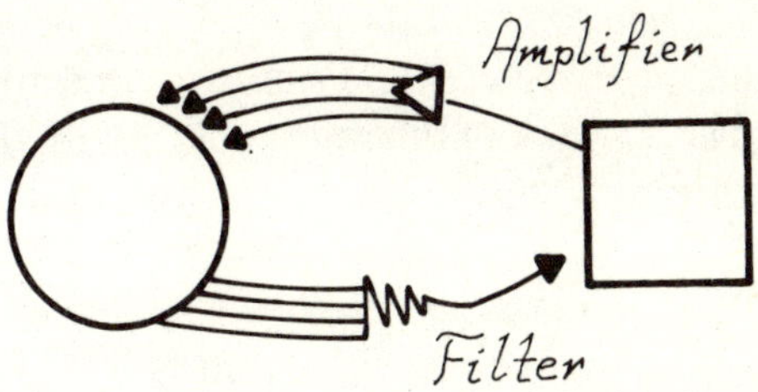

Notice that all organizations actually look something like this. It is utterly impossible to accept and digest all the information generated by even a small operation, so there is always some sort of filter between the operation and the management. And there is always some sort of amplifier on the management's activity toward the operation, although in the limiting case this may be no more than the people in the operation trying to psyche out the boss's mostly incomprehensible actions.

The design of these filters is quite critical, because if the filter is suppressing the crucial information, the operation may be on the verge of ruin and the management not even know it. This may sound very esoteric, but there are many well known examples:

- it is now well documented that teachers tend to think that gifted boys are below average in intelligence. And it is certainly an 'objective' fact that these boys don't 'achieve' very well. The teacher's filters (i.e., what they attend to about these boys in the classroom) is apparently irrelevant to the boys ability.

- the accounting system for a business firm filters out information on short term profits and losses, out of a huge welter of financial data. This filter provides very little information on the long term financial picture for the firm. As a consequence, many large firms find themselves in serious trouble or even bankrupt before they are aware of any difficulty.

- many married people faced with a divorce suit are taken quite by surprise. They keep exclaiming, 'I don't understand — everything was fine until he (or she) just walked out'.

In general, these filters are a result of historical accretion, like Topsy they 'just growed'. Filters that 'just growed' may have little or even no relationship to the most important aspects of the operation. In particular, the filters typically do not deal with some of the fast changing aspects of the operation and the relationships between the operation and its environment. The reason for these omissions, I suspect, is that these have only become important in the last few years or decades. In other words, when the world was less richly interconnected and more stable, the need to keep track of the interactions with the environment or of the fast changing internal elements was much less than it is today.

We might say that the management needs to know two basic things about its operation: is the unit healthy and is it doing what it's supposed to? These really are two separate questions, for the unit might have superb people, equipment, and materials, all working at a high level of competence and motivation at purposes that the management disapproves.

An army that stages a coup against its government provides an excellent example of an incorrect purpose. The social system among convicts typically opposes the purposes of the jail's managers. A university where the faculty are mostly doing those things that interest *them*, may be carrying out purposes very far from those of the legislature that funds them. And a hospital may be mainly in the business of helping doctors become financially comfortable.

On the other hand, the organization may be doing its absolute best to achieve the purposes its management wishes. In this case there will be a great deal of difference between the results achieved by a robustly healthy organization and one that is very ill. A good example of the difference between a healthy and a sick organization is provided by the contrast between a smoothly functioning football team accustomed to playing together, and a newly assembled team of all-stars. The teams have the same purposes, and the all-stars may be individually superior, but the winning team will usually be the one with the better teamwork (i.e., the healthier organization).

Other examples of sick organizations include those whose technology is badly obsolete or whose equipment is ill-repaired or worn out. The organization might also be ill in the sense of inappropriately structured for its intended mission, by being unable to stay well informed about its own state or the state of the relevant environment, or by being unable to reach decisions. Organizations that differ along these dimensions may be attempting the same purpose, but they are unlikely to be equally effective.

The basic difficulty with the argument that the management needs to know about the health and output of the unit is simply that both the health and the output of the unit are difficult to assess. This then, should be the first task for the system four function of our model: system four should be the focus for the organization's attempts to explicitly model and understand itself.

To begin with, system four can attack the problem of assessing the health of the organization via the methods of chapter four. Here you have your unit. It is supposed to accomplish something: how does it go about doing it? How does the unit work? What are the major dynamics within the unit? The methods of the last chapter allow a model of the unit to be prepared pretty simply.

It is not necessary that the organization's model of itself explain all the details (in fact it shouldn't and couldn't anyway). No, this model should be such that it could be drawn on one piece of paper and have about a half a dozen or so key variables that, if they were monitored, would give some insight into what was happening within the unit. The other things that are typically worth watching are some measure of output and some measure of the crucial inputs. Thus it should be possible to identify a set of variables which, taken together, provide a snapshot of the state of the unit at any one time.

What is critical for the management to know, is not so much the actual value of any of the variables from the model, but that today or this week such and such a variable changed *so much* and that this change likely means *this*. Always supposing that we have some idea of how our unit works, we can thus set up a monitoring system to let us know if anything of interest changes. This whole line of thinking suggests that time series need to be utilized.

The usual approach to measuring things is to try very hard to get accurate, objective measures. However, in this case what we need is some more or less reasonable idea of the value of our key indicators and whether or not those key indicators are changing. Thus we needn't be too picky about accuracy in any absolute sense. What we do need is some set of conventions on how each indicator is to be assessed. The problem is no different, in principle, than the problem of measuring your foot size, or in keeping track of the financial aspects of the organization: measurement *always* requires an agreed upon set of conventions, and if the variable is a new one we will have to devise the appropriate conventions. Again, this is a job for system four.

SYSTEM FOUR

Let us be clear about what is being suggested for system four. A way of monitoring the organization's health is wanted and there is no way to do it. System four will not have succeeded unless they come up with something that the organization can actually use. For instance, an elaborate computer simulation model consisting of dozens of variables and hundreds of equations is not a reasonable beginning effort for most organizations, simply because the relevant managers won't understand it and therefore won't have anything to do with it.

Thus, the task for system four is to come up with a (probably simple) model that, a) provides some insight into the workings of the unit, and b) can be used in the sense that the relevant managers will work with it, at least enough to discover its flaws. Notice that the second requirement is not very stringent, but it has the great virtue that it specifies a learning process that can proceed very rapidly.

In the process of discovering the flaws in an explicit model the managers are doing two important things:

- they are gaining insight into the workings of the organization.
- they are gaining a common framework for discussing the organization.

Every large organization has some effort devoted to various aspects of the task of system four, including typically the accounting framework, some sort of forecasting of environmental variables (e.g., demographic factors), some sort of 'market research' or needs assessments, etc.

The difficulty is that the organization's system four functions are typically divided up in terms of the functional divisions of the traditional organization chart so that no one has any notion of how the whole thing fits together. This is, for instance, the primary reason so few organizations have any notion about their overall health — no one has ever been charged with assessing it. Nor has anyone ever been charged with assessing the totality of the organization's environment (and this should be repeated for the various levels within the organization), nor for assessing the possibilities for synergistic relationships among the various pieces of the organization, nor even for assessing the various impacts one part of the organization has on another.

System four is charged with the external and the future, as contrasted with system three which deals with the internal and the now. Most organizations have no explicit models of themselves, i.e., the various managers focus on and understand different aspects of the whole — and of course these managers then *manage* these different aspects of the whole.

There are three major difficulties with the organization lacking any explicit model of itself. First, the various manager's 'models', since they are mostly implicit and unconscious, neither fit together nor include all of the organization. Second, the variety of models almost always make the various managers at least partially incomprehensible to each other (see chapter 8 on the complementarity law for an explanation of why this happens). The third major difficulty is that the organization has no way of assessing the reasonableness of proposed new actions or of assessing why some action turned out the way it did. In short, without explicit models of itself the organization has difficulty learning from its experiences.

The first job for most system fours is to create an explicit model of the organization: what does this organization do and *how* does it do it? The second and related job for system four is to model the organization's environment. Every organization has an environment that is enormously complex and that is filled with things that potentially affect it in critical ways. However, for most organizations, there are huge differences in the degree to which the various aspects of the environment actually do affect it.

System four should find out which aspects of the environment are actually critical, which aspects the organization can affect, and which aspects actually affect it. These parts of the environment might be termed the problematical environment and should be watched carefully. The rest of the environment, no matter how important it *seems* to be, should be more or less ignored. Our environment, after all, consists of those things that either affect us or that we can affect for our own purposes, and the rest of the outside world is irrelevant.

The third job for system four is to deal with the future. Given that the organization has a model of itself and a model of its problematical environment, then it has a base upon which it can begin to build its desired future. This role, again, involves the development of explicit models. It is impossible to choose a course of action to bring about some desired future without a 'model' of how things work. Our usual models are implicit and intuitive, but it is usually worth a good bit of effort to develop explicit models that link 1) the organization's current state, 2) future alternatives, and 3) current choices.

These then, are the tasks allocated to system four. We might sum them up by saying that system four is charged with 1) providing a focus for the organization's explicit self knowledge, 2) providing a focus for the organization's explicit knowledge of its problematic environment, and 3) *creating* the organization's desired future. And we need to remember that the viable system model is recursive, i.e., starting at any given level of analysis the structure repeats itself as we move to bigger or smaller levels of analysis. Thus, everything said about system four at one level of recursion applies to every level of recursion in the organization. This means that all of the autonomous operational elements must have a 'system four' appropriate to their own needs. This does not necessarily mean some elaborate, expensive operation (although at the higher levels it probably does) — it means that the *function* needs to be carried out appropriately for the given level or the unit will be reduced to simply reacting to the pressures that happen to impinge upon it.

SYSTEM THREE

While system four is off devising models, system three is charged with actually keeping things running. System three must maintain internal homeostasis and must ensure that the various operational units are in fact producing what they are supposed to be producing. System three's traditional way of doing this is to concern itself with the methods and procedures that the various operational elements utilize. The first thing that we might notice about this is that the variety of the operational elements is always huge compared to the variety of system three (or for that matter the variety of any management team). So the first question that the management cybernetician asks is 'how can we cut down on the huge variety of the operational elements without losing sight of the critical aspects of their operations?'.

The first rough answer is to treat each operational element as a black box and worry only about the outputs of those boxes. This is fairly easily done *if* we have already identified the parts of our organization that are to count as operational elements at various levels of recursion. The model is designed so that when operational elements are properly defined each is a relatively autonomous entity and therefore easy to treat as a black box. So, given that system three has identified its own operational elements, one big variety reducer is to identify the critical outputs for each operational element and to decide to ignore the internal working of those units so long as their outputs are reasonable.

System three, then, is charged with several tasks;

- system three must ensure that its organization, as an entity, produces the outputs that the larger organization requires of it.
- system three must ensure that its internal operational elements each produce the outputs that it is assigned to produce.
- system three must ensure that its internal operational elements are able to secure the resources (people, machines, raw materials, money) that they need to function.
- system three should be concerned that the workings of its internal operational elements are co-ordinated and do not generate 'vicious cycle' effects (this is a system two function, under three's direction, and will be discussed further in a moment).
- system three must be concerned about the possibility of synergistic relationships among its operational units. This function involves assistance from system four (e.g., modelling) but it pre-eminently involves maintaining a perspective that is logically superior to that of any of the operational elements, i.e., system three must be concerned with the nature of the organizational unit as an entity and with the systemic, holistic properties that it has (or could have) that none of the parts have (see Chapter 8 for a discussion of meta-language, Godel's incompleteness theorem, and system holism).

System three is the management function that traditional management teams generally fulfill the best. Even so, the viable system model articulates aspects of that function that are typically neglected or done poorly.

SYSTEM TWO

System two was described as functioning to prevent the various operational units from affecting each other adversely through inadequate co-ordination. This seems to be a fairly trivial point — we are all aware of the need for co-ordination and typically set up a multitude of special mechanisms to attempt to co-ordinate this, that and the other. These attempts, however, generally work only because the people involved end up doing the adjusting in a continuous, ad hoc fashion.

In general, if any two elements are to be co-ordinated, the co-ordinating mechanism must operate at least as often as either of the two elements makes a significant change. For instance, a sheep herder attempting to 'co-ordinate' the motion of the flock toward another pasture must have some way to intercept and turn back any sheep who strays. This is typically accomplished with dogs who have much more energy and run much faster than the sheep, so that every sheep that begins to stray very quickly has a dog chasing it back into the flock.

To take another example, the secretary trying to set up a meeting between two people must make at least one phone call every time one of the two changes his/her schedule. And if there are numerous people involved in the meeting, the secretary (in the role of co-ordinating mechanism) typically has to make *many* phone calls every time one member changes his/her schedule.

Thus we see that it is quite common that the co-ordinating mechanism may have to operate much faster or much more often than the relevant changes in the elements being co-ordinated. The co-ordinating mechanism will have to operate much faster than the changes in the co-ordinated elements anytime the co-ordination involves matching some aspect of the co-ordinated elements, such as free time for a meeting. The point is that we quite often set up co-ordinative mechanisms that couldn't possibly work by the criteria just enunciated: the co-ordinating mechanism is unable to operate as often or as rapidly as the elements to be co-ordinated change in relevant ways. These mechanisms are therefore bound to fail.

To the extent that our co-ordinating mechanisms actually do work, it is usually due to the informal efforts of the people involved, not the formal apparatus. In summary, the function of system two is to be a real-time co-ordinative mechanism for the operational elements. In this sense, system two should be a servant of the operational elements and should not be another boss. At the same time, system two is located within the meta-system (specifically within system three) so it has the power of three behind it. Beer suggests that in order to avoid problems of system two becoming another tyrant, its communications with the rest of the system be on a special color paper and that all concerned would know that these papers had to do with co-ordination only and tyranical tendencies could then be more easily resisted.

SYSTEM FIVE

The text so far has discussed system one (the collection of operational units), system two (the co-ordination function), system three (the internal and now), and system four (the external and future). At this point, the organization looks a little schizophrenic: system three is firmly focusing on maintaining the status quo, and system four is equally firmly focused on all sorts of improvements. This arrangement is bound to cause some tension and conflict. In fact, it looks like conflict is structurally built in. We might argue that the nature of reality is such that stability and change are *always* in conflict, but that argument is unlikely to persuade the practicing manager that the systems one-two-three-four structure so far described is in any sense viable.

The practicing manager is going to rightfully ask 'Given that we set up very powerful and dynamic systems three and four, what's going to hold it together? What's going to prevent the people in these two systems from killing each other or at least engaging in a war over who is to run the organization?'. In this way we get to the role of system five. System five has, as its primary function, the maintenance of a creative tension between systems three and four.

It is easier to talk about 'creative tension' than to specify what that actually means. To begin with, it is probably not possible to maintain any sort of reasonable balance between stability and change unless there is a clear sense of identity for the organization. This is so because both stability and change imply some framework, some thing, some variable(s) that are to be either changed or kept stable. In the absence of a clear sense of organizational identity, both stability and change will be dealt with out of personal interests and personal visions of organizational needs. Thus it is not even possible to have a corporate discussion (much less reach any decisions) about stability and change unless there is a shared view of organizational identity. Maintaining this shared view of identity is thus the primary responsibility of system five. Given this identity, then the proper balance between stability and change, between system three and system four, can be found and maintained. Without this identity, there is no way to decide what the balance should be, no way to recognize it if it should occur, and certainly no way to try to achieve it.

When people first start to study the viable system model, they generally want to equate system five with 'the boss' and in a way that is right, but it is also profoundly misleading. System five provides identity, as argued in the last paragraph. In terms of Godel's Incompleteness Theorem (see chapter 8), system five provides closure. In other words, systems three and four are logically superior to system one in that they have a broader view, they see the whole, and they speak a meta-language competent to resolve issues that are undecidable in the languages of the operational units (e.g., resource allocations among the units). By Godel's theorem, systems three and four must also face undecidable issues. System five provides closure by saying '*this* is the sort of outfit we are and when all else fails we decide in terms of *this* self-image'.

The system five role of providing closure (i.e., a sense of identity) is the function of the corporation's Board of Directors and the function of the School Board or the Hospital's Board of Directors. And to the extent that the Board of Directors or the School Board is the agent of the stockholders or the citizens, then it is the stockholders or citizens who provide identity. The question of who constitutes system five is thus a thorny one and the practical issue of just how the organization's identity gets defined and maintained is also difficult. A great many of our institutions today are seriously ill, partially because no one is successfully playing the system five role of defining and maintaining the organization's identity. Boards of Directors and Chief Executive Officers are *both* trying to play the system three role and in the process are:

- carrying out internecine warfare with each other
- totally neglecting the system four role of the external and the future
- causing serious problems for the organizational units trying to achieve the intended mission.

In most cases in which the organization is successful, the system five role of identity definition gets played out by someone (or a small group) acting in the capacity of chief executive officer or chairman of the board. The key dynamic here seems to be the embodiment, by this individual, of the identity that 'fits' the organization at that given point in history. When an individual is thus successful in embodying the organizational identity, he/she is then symbolically very powerful and is able to maintain appropriate relationships among the other groups in the organization. Thus, a system five which provided identity would also be able to maintain the proper balance between systems three and four.

EXAMPLE

This chapter has so far briefly introduced the viable system model. It would probably be helpful to run through an example for a large organization. Since everyone knows a bit about schools, they are useful examples (see table 5.1). The example of table 5.1 is an attempt to specify levels of recursion and system one through five for each level of recursion. Notice that this example has operational elements different from both school examples given earlier in the chapter (in the section titled 'using the model').

In the earlier examples, the intended purpose provided a starting place to figure out what the operational elements *should* be. A different procedure was used for table 5.1. Table 5.1 was constructed by examining a school district and attempting to map what they were *actually* doing onto the viable system model. Rather than having a clearly nominated purpose to work from, in this case there was an ongoing institution. The purpose and the appropriate structures both had to be inferred. This work was done in conjunction with the superintendent and was used to help the Board of Education learn to play the system five role.

Table 5.1 shows five levels of recursion (i.e. school district, school building, class, student). Each level of recursion includes (or at least ought to include) systems one-two-three-four-five.

Table 5.1 shows some of the structures and functions the viable system model highlights when applied to a school system. There are several structural deficiencies that show up in the table, including:

SYSTEM / RECUR. LEVEL	SYSTEM I	SYSTEM II	SYSTEM III	SYSTEM IV	SYSTEM V
	Monitoring the 'Autonomous' Subunits	Dealing with the exceptions	Managing what we do	Dealing with the emerging future and pressure for change	Making strategic choices
STUDENT	Monitors physiological and psychological functioning	Interruptions: illness, distractions	Learns to study, manages time, gathers material	Explores topics for project, aspires to college or career	Chooses: project topic, next piece of learning, appropriate behavior
CLASSROOM	Monitors learning of students	Interruptions: firedrill, student illness	Maintains plan book, gathers materials	Explores: course content, strategies, texts, PET IEP's	Articulates: course goals syllabus, plans for PET IEP
BUILDING	Monitors classrooms, programs and services	Interruptions: heat fails, specialist out	Manages: meetings, wk.-shops; master schedule; field trip trans.	Explores: curriculum change, staffing needs - cohort study	Sets yearly goals with teachers, recommends staff changes to Supt.
DISTRICT	Monitors schools, food services, transportation, custodial, and accounting	Interruptions: budget cuts, city water fails	Integration of system I units; manages dist.-wide programs	Assesses shifting resources, values and mores of the environment	Articulates identity and purpose of school district

Table 5.1 A school system as viewed through the viable system model

1. System five, at the class and building levels, really doesn't have an institutional embodiment. For the classroom that is working well, there is perhaps no short run problem in this regard. For the class in which the teacher is having trouble, however, there is no mechanism for defining system identity and, therefore, there are all sorts of other problems. For the building level, the principal, staff and involved parents are all important in determining the school's identity. The fact that there is no real structure or mechanism for doing this is often a serious problem.
2. System four is almost totally missing from all levels above that of classroom. This reflects what we already knew: the schools have little or no capability for planning, for exploring their environment, or for explicitly knowing themselves.
3. There are a number of system two mechanisms, but these primarily establish a static structure. Ongoing co-ordination among the units is accomplished primarily by not permitting deviation from the pre-established routines. Insisting that all classes maintain rigid adherence to the time table is administratively convenient; it is not necessarily educationally desirable. The point is that we could, given a proper structure for the system, deal with questions such as flexibility in the time table, whereas these questions are impossible to entertain under the current system.

The example of table 5.1 illustrates one of the important uses for the viable system model: it provides a ready diagnosis of system structure and highlights functional deficiencies.

CONCLUSION

Cybernetics is the science of effective organization, i.e. the science that describes the general principles of growth, learning, and adaptation in complex, dynamic systems. To the extent that these general principles are known, they provide limitations on what is possible and guidance towards what is efficient. In the same way that a racing bicycle embodies the laws of physics, the viable system model embodies the laws of cybernetics. And just as there are many possible designs for a bicycle, there are many possible designs for a viable system model of formal organizations.

The viable system model is Stafford Beer's design for effective formal organizations. This model, since it is explicitly based upon the principles of cybernetics, facilitates consideration of what is and is not possible within formal organizations and provides guidance in creating efficient structures. The viable system model uses a set of conventions:

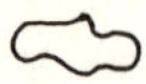	environment.
	operational element, an autonomous entity,
	management unit within an operational element,
	models held by a management unit
	information flow
	amplifier
	filter
S1	system one, the collection of operational elements
S2	system two, the co-ordinating function
S3	system three, the internal and now management function
S4	system four, the external and future management function
S5	system five, the closure and identity management function
Rn	level 'n' of recursion — one level in an hierarchy of autonomous entities, each of which has an S1, S2, S3, S4, and S5.

These conventions provide, in effect, a language for discussing effectiveness. It would be more accurate to say that the conventions of the viable system model *along with* the concepts of cybernetics provide a language for discussing effectiveness.

The viable system model specifies five broad functions that *must* be carried out in any organization that manages to both maintain internal stability *and* adapt to a changing environment. These functions were labeled system one through system five. The viable system model also specifies the information flows (i.e., the interactions) among the parts of the model. The major interactions include:

- the operational element interactions of environment with operations with management with models.
- the system one interactions among the several operational elements.
- the system two channels among the operational element models to co-ordinate efforts and avoid oscillations.
- the system three command channel.
- the system three audit channel.
- the system four interactions with the environment.
- the systems three to four interactions.
- the system five monitoring of the three-four interface.

These various channels need to be functional, balanced relative to each other, and adequately large to handle the variety present at each point in the network.

A particular organizational purpose implies some things about appropriate structures for the organization. Most fundamentally, a purpose implies that the organization needs parts that can do identifiable parts of the purpose. But, since we know from the princples of cybernetics that wholes and parts generally do not have the same characteristics, very careful analysis of the purposes and subpurposes is called for. Erroneous ways of subdividing overall purposes is perhaps one of the most common ways of making it quite impossible for an organization to achieve its intended mission.

Second, a given purpose and sub-purposes imply some specific variety. For instance, training a carpenter (or training the carpenter to hammer nails) is a task with a measurable variety. Training a kindergarten teacher, as usually conceived, also has a measurable variety but it is considerably greater than that involved in training the carpenter because we want the teacher to take into account the variety within his/her charges. Therefore, the organization training the teacher needs a variety that is measurably greater than the variety needed by the organization training carpenters. Most organizations have never thought about themselves in these terms and therefore sometimes attempt tasks that are clearly not possible with their current structure. Stafford Beer maintains that an impressionistic drawing of the viable system model showing the relative size of information flows in the various channels, is frequently adequate to find serious structural defects. It has certainly been my experience that crude estimates of the variety flows within the viable system model frequently pin point needed changes in organizational structure.

Notes.

Stafford Beer *Platform for Change* (Wiley, New York, 1974) p.430.

Chapter 6

ENVIRONMENTS OF DECISION

Chapters one and two provided an introduction to cybernetics, including the role of the observer and several of the key laws of cybernetics. In chapter three we began to apply the cybernetician's tools to management, with the questions that the cybernetician likes to ask.

The cybernetician, like everyone else, likes to understand how things work. Chapter four presented a method for quick and dirty modelling of managerial situations. Most fundamentally, the method of chapter four is important because it facilitates rapid learning.

The first four chapters presented a general orientation, some methodology, and a number of important laws. Nothing in those first four chapters, however, really addressed the question of the design of organizations: how should the beast be *structured*/. Chapter five addressed that question. The viable system model prescribes the functions and structure that an organizational 'nervous system' must have if it wishes to simultaneously maintain internal stability and be adaptive to changing environmental conditions.

Chapter six addresses the question of how the human manager is to use all this stuff: given that an organization sets out to use the tools presented, how does it actually work? What exactly do the tools look like, what will they be, and how does a manager interact with them?

INTRODUCTION

There are innumerable ways of talking about the processes of running an organization, e.g., the following terms are all commonly used to describe various aspects: planning, organizing, staffing, directing, controlling, evaluating, communicating, problem solving, decision making, policy making, motivating, co-ordinating, budgeting, etc. For our purposes it is useful to focus on the decision making — where decision making is conceived as a more or less continuous process of *selection*. The decision making process is a process of selection because there are always numerous possibilities, and the manager or leader must select one out of the many possibilities.

The decision making process is essentially continuous because each decision creates a new situation (or to say the same thing another way) each decision changes the situation somewhat. For instance, I could have worded the last sentence differently and that would have changed what was needed for this sentence. And literally everything that you as a leader do (or don't do) affects the situation you face. No matter which of the ways we choose to talk about running organizations (i.e., communication, motivation, budget, etc.) decision making runs through it. Thus, I am going to focus on decision making.

I said above that decision making is always a process of selection. The selection may be unconscious or habitual (e.g., your response when someone says 'hello, how are you?', or when a cigarette smoker lights another cigarette) or the decision may be as self-consciously rational as possible (e.g., when a cost-benefit study is used to choose between two alternative machines or dam sites, or when someone chooses a new job after carefully weighing as many factors as possible). In either case (and all the cases in between) the act of making a decision is part of an ongoing process of selection of one alternative act (or non-action) out of the set of perceived possibilities at that moment. The topic of this chapter is the question of how to facilitate that process within organizations to make the resulting selection as effective as possible.

DECISION MAKING

This whole topic is difficult to talk about because there are various kinds of decisions or levels of decision making. For instance, one way of categorizing levels of decision making is policy making versus implementation or administration. Another way is to talk about strategic planning, tactical planning, and implementation. Beer talks about normative planning, strategic planning, and tactical planning. All of these amount to different ways of discussing the long range policy choices versus the short run, detailed choices.

Another way of looking at decision making is in terms of the accepted language framework versus alternative frameworks. This raises the question of the extent to which the customary assumptions should be questioned or accepted and has everything to do with Godel's theorem (remember, every language framework has undecidable propositions) (see chapter eight).

Another, similar way of thinking about decision categories has to do with the internal milieu versus the external environment. This is an increasingly important issue as organizations get larger, for the danger is that the organization will increasingly make decisions based entirely upon its own internal needs while the imperatives flowing out of environmental and client needs get increasingly lost and ignored.

Another way of thinking about decisions attempts to categorize them in terms of their degree of value content versus fact or scientific content. And some authors have discussed the degree of uncertainty associated with decisions of various sorts. My point in running through these examples is to suggest that there is no simple, static solution to the question of how to handle decision making within the organization. Rather, what is needed is a grasp of the nature of the process and ways of effectively grappling with that process.

One of the most pernicious myths about decision making is that more 'facts' are somehow needed or would be helpful. Many millions of dollars are put into computerized 'management information systems' every year based upon this notion that more facts will improve decision making. On the contrary, the process of organizational decision making or problem solving has a number of important characteristics that imply that 'more facts' are not the critical need. For instance, organizational decision making is necessarily political.[1], Second, the most difficult aspect of problem solving often is defining the problem.[2] Third, most decision makers already suffer from an overload of data.[3] Fourth, the toughest decisions, the ones that occupy top management, are problems of values and judgments about the implications of facts, rather than problems about 'what the facts are'.[4] Finally, for top managers, much of the critical data originates from outside the organization[5].

There is considerable debate over the details, but there seems to be general agreement on the broad characteristics of the organizational decision maker. These characteristics include:

1. Satisfying Organizations generally search for solutions to problems only until a satisfactory answer appears. They seldom try to find an optimal solution[6].
2. Information overload: Most managers have far more information than they need; the problem is that most of the information is irrelevant or in a form that is not usuable.
3. Political: Managers are necessarily political animals. The goals of any complex organization are partially contradictory and are arrived at by a process that involves bargaining among competing groups. Thus, there is a large element of the non-rational in the decision making of managers.

4. Unknown Future: The manager can't tell you what he/she needs. The manager is not able to specify the problems that will need to be solved in the future, nor the decisions that will have to be made[7].
5. Tried and True: Managers use what they understand and are familiar with. A manager won't use an automated system unless he/she understands it. This means that a system built in isolation from the manager and that simply delivers information will not be relied upon[8].

In addition to an understanding of the decision making qua *individual*, an understanding of the *organization* as a decision maker is needed. There are a number of important points about the organization, including:

1. the organization is made up of *individuals*, each of whom has his/her own framework, knowledge, values, purposes, etc., so that there are *always* massive differences, conflicting purposes, confusion, misunderstandings, etc. By the complementarity law*, we can be sure that at least some of the insights and 'truths' held by the various participants will be both incompatible and mutually incomprehensible.
2. the decision making process within the organization will be largely self-organizing and in many cases the particular people involved will be unique to that particular decision situation (by the self-organization law and the redundancy of potential command law).
3. the culture of the particular organization provides a powerful orientation that, in effect, pre-judges a) what is to count as 'fact', b) what the important issues are, and c) what the possible solutions are. These three consequences follow from the insight that the observer partially determines the observation (see chapter one).
4. Godel's incompleteness theorem guarantees that in at least some cases lower levels in the organization will find the decisions of the higher levels totally incomprehensible. This phenomenon is, of course, very damaging to morale and the level of trust within the organization.
5. by the law of requisite variety, the decision making capability of the organization will be inadequate to regulate the organization as fully as the management will wish.
6. by the Conant-Ashby law, the management can regulate only

those aspects of the organization that they have, in some sense, modelled. In terms of accomplishment of overall objectives, this amounts to a requirement that the organization have some shared models of what it itself is.

Given that the individual and the organization have these sorts of characteristics as decision makers, the question is 'how can we make the decision making processes more effective?'.

Let us begin answering the question posed above by articulating a number of guidelines. Ideally, the decision making process would have these characteristics:

1. Very high variety (Law of Requisite Variety).
2. Explicit models (Conant-Ashby theorem).
3A hierarchy of models and languages (system holism principle, darkness principle, Godel's Incompleteness theorem, and the hierarchy law).
4. Redundancy of information and potential command (the redundancy principles).
5. Operating effectively in 'real time' (circular causality laws and relaxation time law).
6. Makes explicit the degree of autonomy and the degree of integration at each level in the organization (viable system law).
7. Makes explicit the processes and structures devoted to internal stability and to adaptation at each level in the organization (viable system law).
8. Makes explicit the recursive nature of the organizational control system at the various levels in the organization (recursive system law).
9. Automatically monitors homeostasis (homeostasis law).

The nine points above constitute a set of desirable characteristics for an effective organizational decision making process. The next step is to see how closely this ideal can be approached.

THE OPERATIONS ROOM

Stafford Beer's solution, designed to come as close as possible to the guidlines listed above, was to set up a special operations room. For large organizations, such as a hospital, university, or large school district, the operations room would be a rather elaborate and sophisticated facility. In all cases, the operations room is conceived as a meeting room for managers, task forces, etc., where there are relevant support systems for decision making. The 'ops room' for a university might look like the following scenario.

At first glance the University ops room looks like any large seminar room: the large square table in the center of the room has space for about 15 people comfortably spread out, and 22 people elbow to elbow. The walls, however, are strange. One wall has three screens which permit display of three different levels of recursion of the viable system model (VSM), each of which is animated to show the relative sizes of the various operations and the size and speed of the information flows among them. Figure 6.1 shows one such picture. Creation of such a model forces you to decide what you are about and then shows the relative amounts of regulatory efforts that go into each aspect. Figure 6.1, for instance, reflects the fact that most universities make no real attempt to provide much regulation of the undergraduate training program (note the small size of the management) — the faculty's real interest is on graduate training and research. The second noteworthy aspect of figure 6.1 is that S3 and S4 are badly out of balance — there is no way this organization can maintain an adequate balance between maintenance of internal stability and adaptation unless the environment is rather stable. The reason three screens are required for this section is that one would typically want to look at two or three levels of recursion at once. For example, the VSM of the total university might be on one screen, while the VSM of graduate education was on a second, and a sub section of graduate education was on the third.

The second wall of the ops room is devoted to screens that display models of the dynamic workings of the various operational elements. For instance, the operational element from figure 6.1 labeled 'undergraduate education', might be modelled to show the interaction among university reputation, tuition rates, admission standards, number of applicants and tuition income (see figure 6.2). The operational element labeled 'graduate education' might be modelled in terms of the interactions among university reputation, number of applicants, admission standards, amount of funded research, etc. These models might, at first, be relatively simple attempts to show how changes in one aspect would affect other aspects. They should be capable of being displayed on a screen as a dynamic picture (see e.g., figure 6.2).

The very survival of the university depends upon reasonable decisions being made about admission standards and fees, but the knowledge base

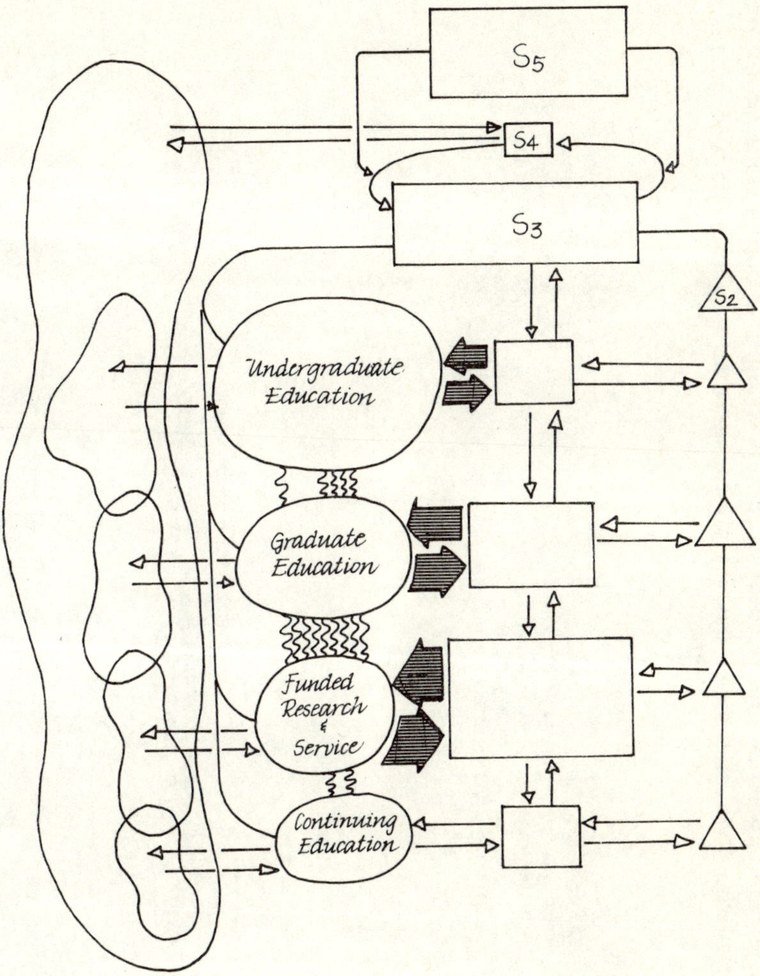

Figure 6.1. One version of a viable system model for the total University.

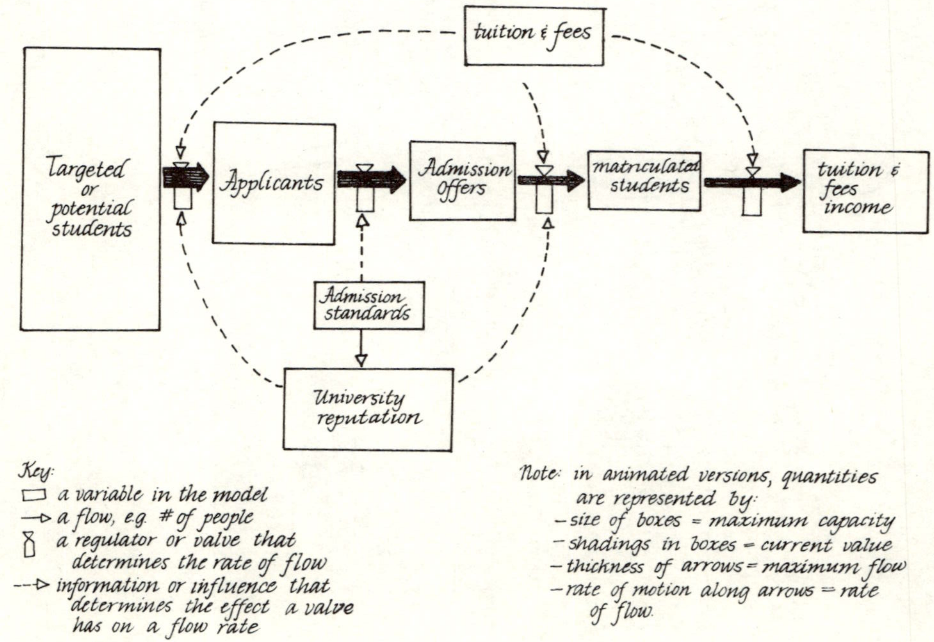

Figure 6.2. A model of the interaction between tuition/fee schedules and income generated. In animated versions, quantities are represented as follows: size of boxesmaximum capacity, level of shading in boxes-current level, thickness of arrowsmaximum flow, rate of motion along arrowsrate of flow.

for making those decisions is weak in the extreme. We know that admission standards and reputation are linked, but we have only the foggiest idea about the relevant time scales or the strength of the effect. The tuition and fees schedule clearly affects the number of students and the total income generated, but unfortunately, raising fees (to generate more money per student) tends to reduce the number of students so that universities raise tuition fees from year to year (to generate cash for the coming year), with no idea of the long range financial implications. At any rate, the point is that even very simple models of system dynamics (i.e., the way the system works), can be an enormous improvement over making decisions based upon the unaided intuition.

The third wall of our university ops room should be a data bank. The screens on this wall should be able to display the following sorts of data:

1. Pictures and maps of each campus and the geographic regions served. These should include a variety of special maps showing, for instance, population densities of various age-occupation-educational level, etc., land use, transportation networks, other colleges and universities, etc.
2. Pictures of all the buildings and facilities owned by the university, including the major scientific equipment such as linear accelerator, observatory, or other expensive equipment.
3. Up-to-date vitae on all faculty and administrators.
4. Such tables and graphs as prove useful.
5. Time series on all essential variables.

One screen somewhere in the room should be devoted to the stability monitor. This is a screen that would display, in essentially real time, time series showing the recent behavior of any of the essential variables that had undergone a statistically significant change.

STABILITY MONITOR

The stability monitor is the mechanism for drawing attention to any significant change anywhere in the system. The usual way of doing this is to monitor a huge array of different variables and to produce a report on any that seem to be changing. This requires a large and sophisticated data storage and processing capability. Furthermore, it requires a large staff to input the relevant data, and to make the changes to the software system, so that it continues to reflect the reality of the changing organization. The ops room approach is both simpler and more useful. The viable system models and the system dynamics models are *operational* definitions of what are to count as essential variables for the organization. This immediately cuts down on the number of variables that need to be monitored.

There is one further trick, however, that Beer learned from neurophysiology. The body's nervous system does all its computing with undifferentiated electrical signals — i.e., the impulses for sight, touch and taste are all the same, as are the impulses from seeing chairs, people, and mountains. We can aproximate this very efficient and flexible nervous system if we set up a monitoring system to operate on pure numbers rather than on categories such as 'pupil grade level' or 'patient stay in hospital'. The key insight is that any variable of interest can be handled as a ratio between some desired or ideal value and the actual value. This simple trick allows for the modularization of the entire system.

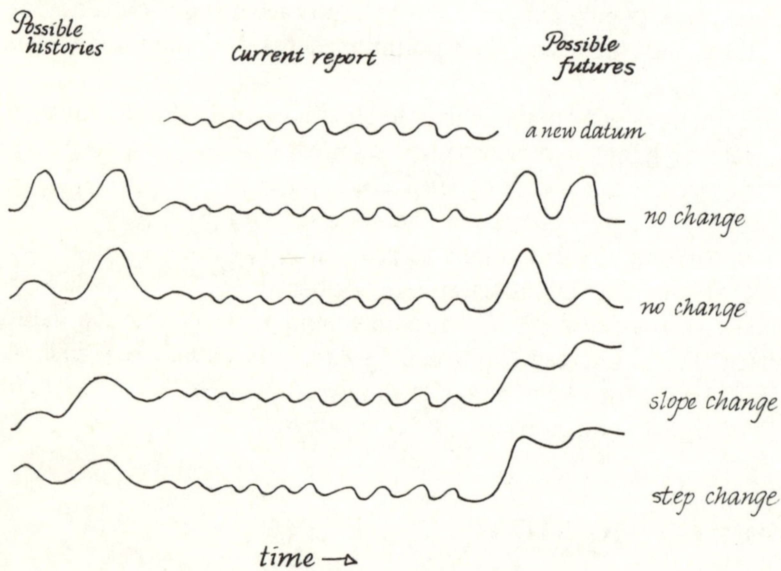

Figure 6.3. An illustration of time series data and the computer's assessment of the probability that a new, higher than average number is meaningful or not.

The models permit a set of essential variables to be defined. These variables can then be transformed into ratios of actual to ideal. These ratios can all be treated by the same software package to determine 1) the statistical characteristics of each time series, and 2) at every moment, the probability that the current value represents a significant change in the value of that variable (see figure 6.3). Considerable experience has demonstrated that a system of the sort outlined above will spot important changes long before the human being can notice that anything is going on. This 'early warning' capability is crucial because it allows managers to correct problems before they become serious and to take advantage of opportunities before they disappear. The fact that the software is processing ratios means that all sorts of changes can be made in the rest of the system with no changes whatever to the stability monitor software.

The facility described for the university ops room is intended to support decision making processes at the level of the university, i.e., by the president and the top campus administrators. Clearly those people one level down in the hierarchy (i.e., the people involved with undergraduate education, with graduate education, and so on) would also find the system useful (although to be most useful to them, the system should include models, data, etc. tailored to their needs).

At any rate, the system should be built for the overall system first. The ops room described could be appointed with a couple of powerful micro computers, about six television sets, and several slide projectors. If one wished to get fancy, all sorts of interactive graphics, including the new computer-videodisc-television combinations could be used. The point is that the technology required to set up the ops room is readily available and is not expensive unless one insists upon state of the art capabilities. For instance, an ops room with all of the capabilities described above could be set up with an outlay of between ten and twenty thousand dollars for equipment.

The ops room for the university was described as having four major components:

1. Viable system model screens — to display animated versions of the viable system model.
2. System dynamics models — screens to display models of the way the system works in some relevant respects.
3. Data bank — photographs, maps, charts, etc., of relevant data.
4. Stability monitoring system — a software package constituting a statistical filter to monitor essential variables and to sound an alarm if any of them deviate from normal limits.

These four aspects of the ops room seem very generally relevant to all levels of the system, although their particular embodiment certainly needs to be different for various levels.

ANOTHER EXAMPLE

The next few paragraphs will examine a possible ops room for a university department. The characteristics of a university department that distinguish it from other departments in the same university probably involve the following factors:

1. The relative emphasis given to teaching as compared to research.
2. The stature of the people in the department.
3. The extent to which the department is or is not responsible for the training and licensing of some professional group.
4. The extent to which they do undergraduate or graduate education.
5. The extent to which they draw their clientele from the local region or from some larger (i.e., national or global) region.

Different departments that differ on these or other dimensions will have different needs for an ops room. The example I will work through is for a small department that does almost exclusively graduate education, is responsible for the licensure of a professional group, serves the needs primarily of a rural, multistate region, and puts considerable emphasis on both teaching and research. There are a number of very real difficulties facing such a department, including:

1. The clientele are geographically dispersed and in the midst of a career (i.e., almost all are at least 25 years of age or older and have several years work experience).
2. The state imposes numerous licensing requirements.
3. Meaningful graduate education is generally very expensive and the department has, at best, very modest stature within the university because of its practitioner orientation.
4. The requirements for teaching and research tend to be interpreted in a way that makes them incompatible.
5. The orientation of the practitioners and the professors is usually such as to reinforce the theory-practice gap.

Given these and related issues, what might an ops room look like for such a department? I will proceed by considering the same four aspects that were discussed for the university as a whole.

The viable system model is important for the department because, just like any other entity, it must fulfil the criterion for effectiveness that the model reflects. In particular, the department must decide what its purposes are (i.e., its identity must be established). This is done partially through deciding what the operational elements are for the departments. Our department has tentatively said that its overall purpose is to improve the institutions our graduates administer. Our operational elements seem to be of two sorts; a. some people simply use our courses to get licensed, b. our program has also identified several fundamental problems that provide the focal point for the training of a group of students — each of these problem areas thus constitutes an operational element for the department. The second sort of issue that the viable system model raises for us is the relative allocation and effectiveness of systems one-two-three-four-five. A diagram reflecting these ideas is given in figure 6.4.

Figure 6.4 makes explicit a number of crucial issues, including:

1. Who are the people in charge of each of the operational elements? This must be a faculty member in each case.
2. Who is to play the role of system three? The total faculty? What about system four? and system five? Clearly the total faculty trying to play all three roles puts us back into saying the faculty meeting governs and therefore doesn't say anything at all beyond what is traditionally said.
3. What about system two? In what ways might these operational elements need co-ordination, in what ways might they go into uncontrolled oscillation or interference with each other? Certainly this is an issue in scheduling meetings, classes, seminars, etc.
4. What are the relevant environments and how do they differ?

All of these questions are thorny and should be held in mind while the other aspects of the ops room are examined.

The second aspect of the ops room is that of system dynamics. This aspect attempts to explicitly represent the major workings of the system: how does the department work? What are the major connections to the environment? There are four sorts of models that come immediately to mind.

1. How do you prepare a professional practitioner? How would you know if you succeeded (or failed)?
2. How do you meet the needs of a large geographic region with a small staff? How do you schedule your faculty's efforts/activities across time and geography most effectively?
3. How do the institutions administered by your graduates work?

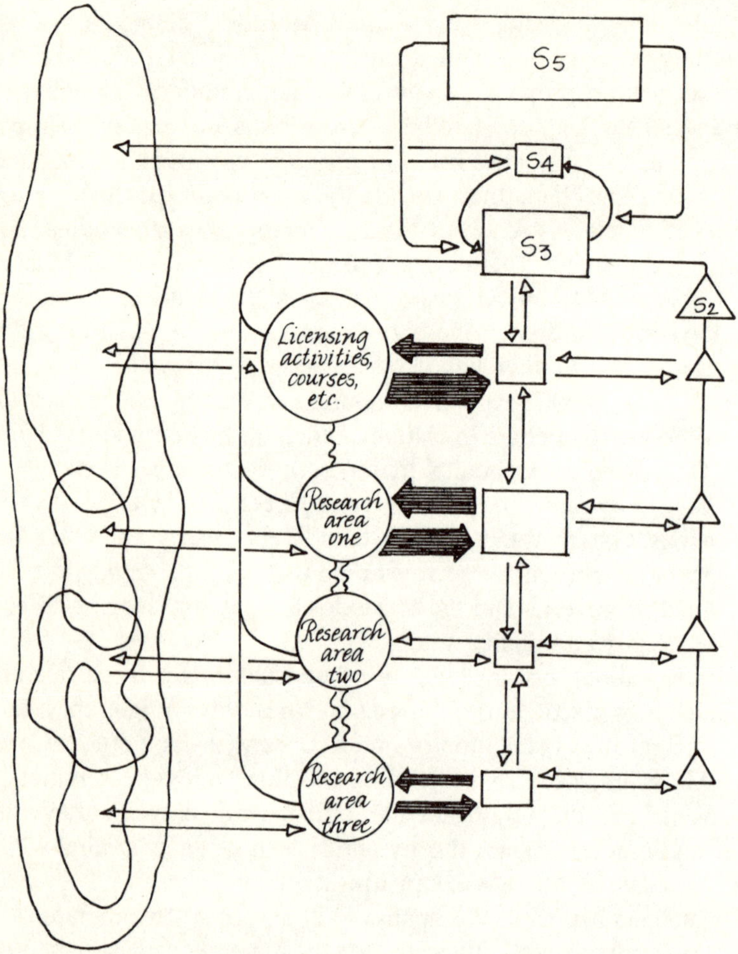

Figure 6.4. One version of a viable system model for a university department that trains professional practitioners.

What would constitute improvements in those institutions? How would you know if you improved them (or failed to improve them)?

4. What is the relationship between your operational elements and your overall purpose?

Question three (institutional improvement) seems a good starting place. Since the institutions in question are public, locally controlled ones, it seems that some measure of local public satisfaction is the key to institutional effectiveness. As a rough start, we might use the model of figure 6.5

Figure 6.5 does little more than say 'we really ought to assess this thing called citizen eudemony'. The real point is, however, that something like citizen eudemony *must* be measured if we are to assess the effectiveness of our public institutions. And it is no good saying that we will assess the 'objective' goodness or quality of, say, a hospital or school, because the extent to which a given institution meets the needs of a given community depends upon the characteristics of the institution in some sense *matching* the particular needs of that particular community. Thus the imperative is for the applied social scientist to get busy and figure out how to measure citizen eudemony and the contribution thereto from the various institutions in the community.

A few paragraphs ago, I posed the question of meeting the needs of a large geographic region with only a small department. This question suggests some sort of model that takes into account the abilities and interests of the staff, the needs of the clientele, the geography of the region (including aspects such as transportation networks and population densities), and modern electronic communication devices (e.g., computer-teleconferencing, interactive TV networks, etc.). There are many students in our department that drive one to three hours *one way* to attend classes and seminars. These people would probably pay a great deal for communication devices that would permit participation in seminars without actually traveling.

As usual, it is not precisely clear what sort of model would be most useful in figuring out how best to use our limited resources in meeting the needs of the region. However, there are several sorts of models that clearly seem useful in learning about the situation. To begin with, we need maps showing things like 1) overall population density, 2) distribution of our students, 3) road networks (perhaps this ought to include a capability to distort the actual distance to reflect the time it takes to drive along the various roads so that the resulting map would

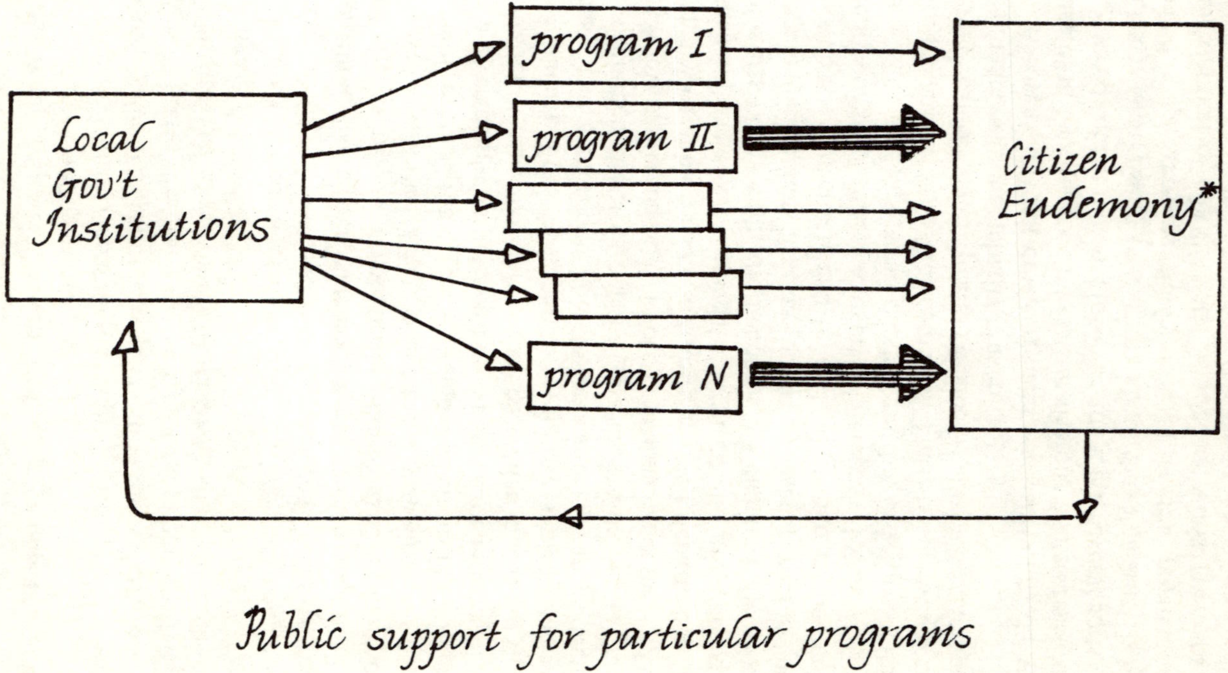

*Eudemony — a general sense of well being. See Stafford Beer 'Questions of Metric' in *Platform for Change* pp.162-191.

Figure 6.5. Initial Model of Public Institutional Effectiveness.

shorten the interstates and elongate the directions served only by small mountainous roads), 4) distribution of other professional resources we can call upon within the state.

The second sort of model that we clearly need is an explicit model of what we intend to provide our clients. This is a tricky point, because the obvious way to approach this is through a behavioral framework that specifies the skills, competencies, or objectives to be met. The trouble with this 'obvious' solution is (as has been argued throughout the book), that the cure is almost worse than the disease. To rehearse those objections in brief, they are, 1) we don't knowwhatthe relevant content is, 2) the world is a very redundant place so that the logically necessary competencies are in fact not necessary (and the logically necessary competencies are always too long a list to cover), 3) focusing upon the competencies directs attention inward, evaluation becomes narcissistic and the connection between real world performance and practitioner training gets lost. Therefore, the model of what we intend to do to or for our students must include what they do within their institutions on the job. Figure 6.6 begins to sort this out.

USEFUL MODELS

We could go on for some time in discussing the models that would be useful for a university department in governing itself. However, it is already clear that the issues raised by the models suggested are complex and not easily unravelled — in short, the models already sketched out would require a major research project before one would begin to have any confidence that they adequately represented what was actually going on.

The point from the last paragraph also applies to the models sketched out for the ops room for the university as a whole. In fact, a great deal of experience suggests that for any organization at all, as soon as one attempts to be explicit about the thorny issues facing the institution, an enormous research effort is required. And, in fact, an enormous research effort would generally be very helpful. The problem is that the resources are never available — in particular, the money required isn't in the budget, the skilled people are not locatable, and the time to carry out the research isn't there because a decision has to be reached by 'next Tuesday' at the latest. However, this line of thought paints too gloomy a picture.

In chapter four a distinction was drawn between academic research and operations research. In academic research, one is typically trying to be as sure as possible about the conclusions. There are, in consequence, a whole series of methodological and stylistic conventions that must be observed and that, in toto, make the entire process both time consuming and typically rather narrowly focused. In operations research, in contrast, the goal is to provide some knowledge or insight that will be practically useful. This almost always puts severe time limits upon the research (i.e., the knowledge or insight is worthless if it is unavailable when a decision must be rendered).

Furthermore, the criterion for judging the administrative utility of a research result is not the absolute certainty of the result, but whether or not it represents an improvement over the degree of certainty that was previously available. And since many (perhaps most) administrative situations involve massive uncertainties and a style of operating that could be characterized as 'seat of the pants flying' it is not at all hard to reduce the uncertainties and provide useful results — if (and this is a big *if*) we scientists can get past our academic training and deploy our skills in a mode to facilitate the administrator's rapid learning.

VIABLE SYSTEM MODEL REPRISE

The most important function of the viable system model is to facilitate maintenance of the continuous balance between autonomy of the parts and integration of the whole. System three has the job of maintaining a synergistic pattern of relationships among the various operational elements of system one. Without constant attention to this synergy of the whole, operational elements of system one (which after all are by definition viable systems themselves) will follow their own tendencies toward autonomy until it pulls the organization apart. Similarly, system four provides the self-conscious and explicit models of what the organization is and how it relates to its larger environment. We might characterize system three as the 'organization in being' and system four as the 'organization in becoming'. Both systems three and four must deal in terms of the totality of the organization. Now, this requirement to deal with the totality of the organization seems utterly obvious — unfortunately there are numerous reasons why it is not so easily done.

First, the major portion of any one individual's career is always with some part of the organization. Typically, the administrator has been

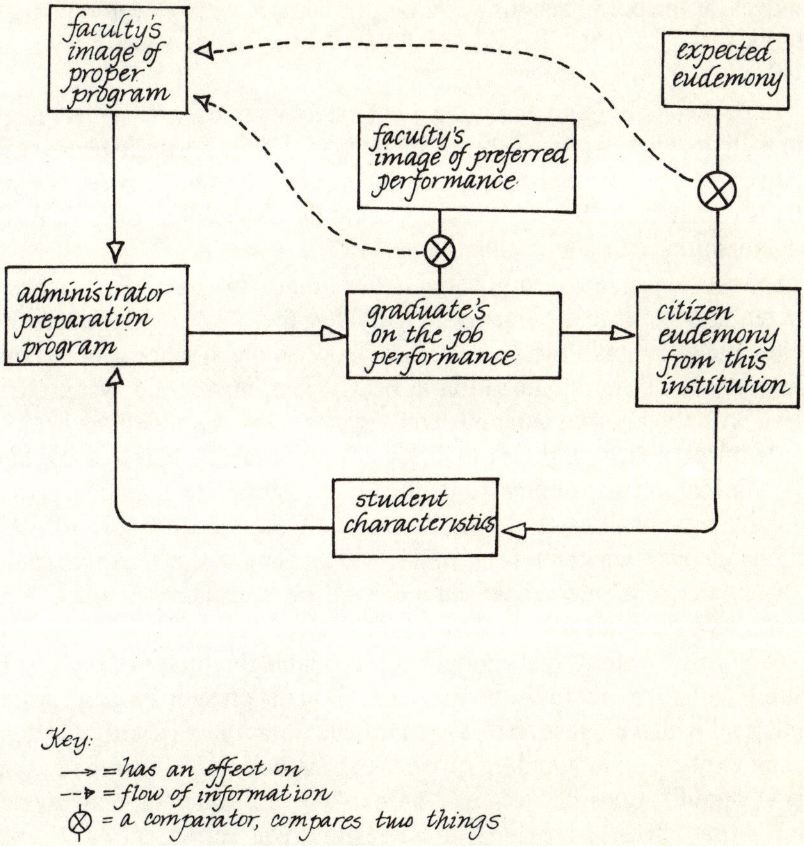

Figure 6.6. An initial model of the dynamics of an administrator training program.

selected precisely because he/she did a good job running some part of the organization or some part of a similar organization. So, typically, one's experience is with some part of the institution. Secondly, our training is typically in some one or two branches of knowledge and this tends to focus our attention upon particular sorts of phenomena and data. Thirdly, each of us has particular interests and predilections (e.g., toward the budget, or the political considerations, or technological developments, or public relations with clients). All of these factors get in the way of dealing with the enterprise holistically.

In the typical organization the most easily won research gains have to do with the overall picture for the institution. This is partly so because the above listed factors tend to obscure the big picture, but also because small improvements in the big picture frequently carry large payoffs to the organization.

Discussion of 'environments of decision' are, in effect, discussions of system four's role in the organization. System four's role was characterized a few pages ago as 'the organization in becoming' in contrast to system three's role of 'the organization in being'. Earlier we said system three dealt with the internal and now, while system four dealt with the external and future. In most organizations, if we set up a system four it would have as its initial job that of making explicit the organization's models of itself and its relationships to its environment. This is so because effective discharge of system three's role requires explicit models of the organization (e.g., synergy of the whole cannot even be considered if there is no agreement on what the whole is).

Similarly, system four cannot even consider the future of the organization without explicitly knowing what it is in the present. Nor can system four deal with the question of environmental relationships without having some explicit understanding of what the institution is. Therefore, since most organizations do not have an explicit self-understanding, system four's first job is to provide a focus for that self knowledge.

I painted a scenario for a system four ops room for a university and for a university department. In both cases these ops rooms included, 1) a viable system model, 2) models of system dynamics, 3) some sort of data bank, and 4) some sort of crisis monitoring system for the system's essential variables. The particular manifestation of the ops room must grow out of the nature of the organization for there is no simple formula that allows one to specify the ops room characteristics in advance of understanding the particular situation.

CONCLUSION

Decision making is a dynamic process of more or less continuously selecting particular actions (or non-actions) from some set of perceived alternatives. Chapter six has focused on the question of how to make the decision making process as effective as possible. The general approach taken was to describe an environment for decision making that facilitates the process.

The environment for decision making consists of an operations room with several types of capabilities:

1. A capability to simultaneously display several different levels of recursion of the viable system model. These displays should use size and motion to roughly indicate the relative sizes and speeds of the various parts of the model.
2. A capability, on a second wall, to display any of several models of the dynamic workings of the system. Something along the lines of Jay Forrester's system dynamics models are needed here.
3. A 'data bank' capability, especially including maps, photographs, and other visuals on the relevant system aspects.
4. A stability monitor that, essentially in real time, displays the time series for any of the essential variables that have changed in unexpected ways.

Obviously, the particulars of the operations room, including the sorts of technologies used, depends upon the particular organization it is designed for.

The main point about the operations room is that it is an attempt to bring together managers and models of the organization, in a mode that permits rapid learning. The models required are those which capture the key holistic dynamics of the system and its interactions with the problematic environment (i.e., the system dynamics models), the models that capture the key regulatory capabilities of the organization (i.e., the viable system models), and the models which provide an early warning system for unexpected changes in the system (i.e., the stability monitor). All of these capabilities represent an attempt to embody, in a managerially useful form, the implications of a number of the principles and laws of cybernetics, preeminently the law of requisite variety, the Conant-Ashby Law, and the feedback laws.

Notes

*The principles, theorems, and laws mentioned in this paragraph and the next are all discussed in chapter eight.

CHAPTER SIX REFERENCES

1. Richard M. Cyert and James G. March *A Behavioral Theory of The Firm* (Prentice Hall, Englewood Cliffs, New Jersey, 1963).
2. Herbert A. Simon *Administrative Behavior: A Study of Decision-Making Processes in Administrative Organization* 3rd Edition, New York: Free Press 1976; C. West Churchman *The Systems Approach* (Dell Publishing House, New York, 1968)
3. Russell L. Ackoff 'Management Misinformation Systems' *Management Science* 14.4 December 1967, 147-156.
4. Stafford Beer, *Brain of the Firm: A Development in Management Cybernetics* (Wiley, New York, 1981).
5. Simon, see especially chapter 14.
6. Figure 6.3 is adopted from Stafford Beer *Platform for Change* (Wiley, New York, 1979) p.440.

Chapter 7

ON GETTING STARTED

This book discusses a variety of topics: The role of the observer of systems (chapter one), the laws and principles of cybernetics (chapters two and eight), the basic questions the cybernetician brings to management situations (chapter three), the model building methods for managing production dynamics (chapter four), the viable system model or 'nervous system' (chapter five), and settings for decision making (chapter six). These other chapters, then, have spelled out the major aspects or tools of management cybernetics. The current chapter is out to do a different job: Rather than discussing some aspect or tool of management cybernetics, this chapter attempts to say something useful about the *process* of using management cybernetics. The other chapters have, in effect, explained hammers, saws and screwdrivers while this chapter explains the process of using the set of tools to actually build something. Just as the process of using carpentry tools depends upon the particular job to be done, so the process of using the tools of management cybernetics depends upon the particular situation.

INTRODUCTION

The book has articulated a number of tools that the manager can put to use. This section will briefly review these tools:

1. *Observer Effect*

Chapter one discussed the interaction between the observer and the reality observed. In particular, chapter one emphasized the extent to which any observer (including the manager) of a social system, affects that social system. This point is widely recognized as the phenomenon of the self-fulfilling prophecy. The manager's definition of the system (i.e., the particular aspects he/she selects to pay attention to, and the premises or beliefs about the way his/her system works) is a critical aspect of the 'observer structure' that affects the nature of that system. The wise manager consciously selects a system definition and premises about the system's workings, in the knowledge that this selection affects the behavior of the system and the possible futures for that system. The observer effect, when taken seriously, tends to humble one because certainties about organizations tend to evaporate. If carried to extremes, the observer effect can lead one into a paralysis of inaction while carrying out an endless series of alternative analyses. However, without an understanding of the observer effect, the manager can never achieve more than a very distorted view of his/her own role.

2. *Principles*

Chapter two discussed a number of 'laws' of cybernetics. These laws or principles are, in effect, rules of the game for all organizations. The laws of cybernetics are limits on what is and is not possible. They provide a connection between details of organizational structure and possible outcomes. These principles are therefore useful in diagnosing an organization and in designing improvements. Chapter eight provides many more principles that can be used in this way. Unfortunately, the laws do not solve the design problem, i.e., the laws provide limits on what is possible but they do not provide an answer to the question of how to structure an organization. For example, the laws of physics determine whether or not a house will fall down and how energy efficient it will be, but they do not solve the design problem for a 'good' house — the design of a 'good' house requires the science *and* art of the architect.

3. *Questions*

Chapter three discussed the sorts of questions the cybernetician typically asks about complex situations. These questions provide an orientation and direct attention to certain aspects of the organization. Self conscious attention to the most useful questions to ask, allows one to transform the given situation in various ways, and (usually!) to find a framework for thinking about the situation that permits effective action to be taken. This is quite critical because we are frequently confronted with a definition of a situation that simultaneously makes us extremely uncomfortable *and* prevents us from improving that situation. In such cases we can 1) endure being uncomfortable, 2) leave the situation, or 3) change our way of viewing the situation to something that can be improved upon. The latter is frequently, but not always possible. The questions of chapter three are important because they are often helpful in changing our definition (i.e., perceptions) of frustrating situations into something that we can actually change. The difficulty with this approach is that it is quite impossible to know in advance where one ought to start — one must simply dive in and muck about. Further, the various questions are inter-related, and thinking about one frequently changes our understanding of others. Thus, this approach typically leads one into a morass of shifting questions and insights. Nevertheless, the approach is important because it 1) typically deepens our understanding of the organization, and 2) sometimes works when nothing else will.

4. *Model Building*

We frequently have to manage organizations where our understanding of the production dynamics or 'how it works' is intuitive at best. The 'how it all works' question applies to the organization's relationship to its environment, to the relationships among the organization's various parts, and the relationship between what the organization does and what sorts of results are produced. Very often there are people in the organization who in fact have an excellent grasp on some or even all the parts of this complex 'how it works' question. Typically, however, the various people in the organization have radically different notions about how it works. Furthermore, it is quite common for everyone concerned to be mistaken. At best, even with the intuitive genius who basically understands the workings of the whole thing, there will always be big gaps and unclarities. Chapter four presented a model building method designed to permit rapid construction of models that attempt to explain 'how it works' for some aspects of the organization. It should be emphasized that this is an area in which an organization can always improve, but it is simply not possible to gain full knowledge. One of the major difficulties in this area is that the academic scientist and the practical manager have very different outlooks on appropriate methodologies and on what constitutes useful results. It is therefore very difficult to find people who can actually do the model building needed to manage an organization's production dynamics.

5. *Viable System Model*

Chapter five discussed the necessary conditions for an effective 'nervous system' for an organization. There are obviously alternative ways of discussing an effective nervous system, but the viable system model of chapter five presents a number of constraints and criteria that an effective system must meet. Just as the law of gravity specifies that apples will fall unless supported, the viable system model specifies a number of conditions that *must* be met if an organization is to simultaneously maintain internal stability and adapt to its environment. The viable system model provides a framework for structuring the organization and for channeling its communication/decision making processes. One of the difficulties in dealing with this area is that the viable system model is itself very complex. Despite the length of chapter five, there are important aspects of the model that were not even touched upon (e.g., algedonics, see *Brain of the Firm*).

6. *Environments of Decision*

Chapter six described a way of bringing all of the tools into play more or less simultaneously in an operations room that would facilitate decision making within the organization. There are perhaps two major difficulties in implementing an operations room: 1) our habitual approaches to the issues lead us astray (as has been discussed throughout the book), and 2) much of the necessary applied research remains to be done so that, for most organizations, the implementation of an operations room will be breaking new ground. This chapter deals with both of these difficulties.

Other chapters (i.e., observer effect, principles, basic questions, model building, viable system model, and environments of decisions) then, provide practical tools for the manager to use. Unfortunately, handing someone a set of tools doesn't make that person a skilled craftsman. The carpenter has to work with his/her hammers, saws and chisels for some years before achieving the title of 'journeyman'. The engineer spends several years in school getting the theory, and typically has several years practical experience before earning the chance to head up any significant projects. Similarly, the manager will not become a management cybernetician simply by reading this book. This chapter is aimed at helping the manager take the first few practice steps along the road to becoming a journeyman management cybernetician.

THE CONTEXT: MESS PERCEPTION

Describing a process to help you learn to perform that process is never easy — it is much easier to *show* you how to waltz or shoot a basketball than it is to tell you how to do it. Unfortunately for both of us, we don't have the option of my showing you — I either manage to *say* something useful or you have to figure it out on your own. This chapter attempts to say something about the process of using management cybernetics — in fact, it says several different somethings, each of which discusses a different aspect of the process. Neither singly nor altogether do these things add up to a neat recipe for using management cybernetics. In my opinion, any such recipe would do a great deal more harm than good. For instance, from Godel's incompleteness theorem, we can see the logic of the following argument:

- A recipe (any recipe, all recipes) constitutes a language for describing some particular aspects of reality.

- Godel's incompleteness theorem assures us that every language will include undecidable propositions.

- Therefore we can be assured that any recipe whatsoever will, under some conditions, put us into a posture that guarantees inability to deal with those conditions.

Cybernetics thus includes a built in awareness of its own limitations. And this book has no recipes, no neat little flow charts that lead one through the process. There are a number of process suggestions that have proven useful in the past and that may be useful to others. The chapter will discuss those suggestions.

Russell Ackoff[1] says that we have been preoccupied with problem solving, where a problem is implicitly defined as some difficulty that can be separated out from the rest of the organizational situation, and assigned to a junior manager or a consultant for 'solving'. Problem solving, in this sense, means that some particular action, set of actions, or policy will remove the difficulty. Ackoff argues that this whole way of thinking encourages us to focus attention upon bits and pieces of our organizations and thereby leads up to adopt policies and carry out actions that as often as not make the original situation worse. Ackoff suggests that we typically do not face discrete 'problems', we face interlocking sets of problems that can be separated only by artificially (and unhelpfully) carving the organization up into pieces. What managers typically face are these sets of complex, interlocked, interacting problematical situations — in short, managers confront 'messes'. Successful managers don't solve problems in the sense that something is dealt with and disposed of. Rather, successful managers perform a more or less continuous balancing, adjusting, steering, of very messy situations. In Ackoff's marvelous terminology this is 'mess management'. In cybernetic terminology this is 'regulation'. Ackoff argues that rather than 'problem solving' we should be focusing upon 'mess management'. Ackoff's argument then, is another way of describing the manager as a cybernetic regulator.

'So, practically, specifically, what does the manager do?' The answer, of course, is that it all depends upon the particular situation. More precisely, what to do depends upon the manager's *perception* of the situation. The manager's perception of the mess confronting him/her determines what ought to be done. This sounds like a truism, but it is important that we not only remind ourselves that it is our *perception* of the situation that counts, but that we also remind ourselves that the only possible perception is our somewhat subjective perception of the mess. By constantly remembering that our perception is necessarily subjective, we maximize the possibilities for learning about the situation and thereby maximize the extent to which our perceptions are 'true' or at least useful for our practical purposes.

THE CONTEXT: POLITICS & PSYCHOLOGY

Management cybernetics is an applied science, or, to be precise, management cybernetics is the application of the science of cybernetics to the practice of management. Management, inevitably, has to do with the politics of groups and the psychology of individuals. Indeed, many perceptive observers have argued that inspired management, i.e., leadership, involves more psychology and politics than anything else. The cybernetician is not terribly interested in arguments over the relative importance of politics/psychology as compared to, say, cybernetics: both are necessary, just as both food and water are necessary to human life.

This book has devoted almost all of its attention to cybernetics and has said almost nothing about the politics or the psychology of organizations. This indicates, not the relative importance of the two, but the role of this book — to introduce the reader to management cybernetics. However, at this point, in order to describe the *process* of using management cybernetics it is necessary to say a little about the politics/psychology of organizations.

The politics/psychology of organizations has been ably discussed by many others, beginning perhaps with Machiavelli[2] and continuing with scholars such as Herbert Simon[3] and Katz and Kahn[4]. The present author doesn't have anything to add to that rich literature except to affirm its importance in the process of using management cybernetics.

The problem of devising an appropriate process for using management cybernetics might be usefully conceptualized as involving several dimensions, each of which puts some constraints upon acceptable solutions. The dimensions mentioned above are:

- the science of management cybernetics;
- the politics of organizations; and
- the psychology of the individuals making up the organizations.

Another dimension that was mentioned earlier is the technology of the particular organization's productive processes. As Thompson[5] so ably points out, differences in technology require different sorts of boundary units and co-ordinative mechanisms. This book dealt with this point in terms of modelling the productive processes. Let us add, then, the dimension of:

- the technology of the productive processes.

These four dimensions (management cybernetics, the productive technologies, politics of the organization, and psychology of the individuals), must be considered in designing a process to use management cybernetics. The manager, if he/she is any good at all, has a pretty firm grasp on the politics and the psychology of the situation and these dimensions delimit what actions are, and are not, feasible to consider at a given point in time.

Similarly, the cybernetics of the organization and the technology of the organization's business delimit what actions are or are not *useful* to consider at a given point in time. For instance, the cybernetician may notice that the organization has lost its sense of purpose and identity — but the management may not be psychologically able to acknowledge this. Or the cybernetician may notice that the overall organization has no system four or system five — but the 'organization' may consist of a 'boss' presiding over numerous autonomous entities which are busily ensuring that there will be *no* overall system four or five. In such cases the cybernetician's analysis merely reveals that nothing much in the way of *cybernetics* can be done until the psychological or political issues are shifted.

The conclusion in the last paragraph is perhaps too weak. The cybernetician's analysis reveals that no cybernetics can be applied directly to the cases cited. However, the analysis also reveals something else that is very important: In both of the examples, the cybernetician's analysis reveals that the organization is in serious trouble and, in fact, *cannot* function effectively as constituted.

In order to use management cybernetics, then, one must devise strategies which simultaneously meet several criteria:

1) The strategies must be psychologically acceptable to the relevant

managers.

2) The strategies must be politically feasible given the existing groups and factions within the organization.

3) The strategies must be appropriate to the types of technologies employed within the organization.

4) The strategies must be appropriate to improve the cybernetics of the organization.

These criteria make clear the difficulty of devising an appropriate process.

One response to the last few paragraphs is to simply say 'it's all too difficult — I shall simply muddle through somehow'. But that response is too hasty. In a real sense, all that the last few paragraphs has done is to make explicit the task that the successful manager has always accomplished. Far seeing managers have always identified strategies that could be implemented only *after* difficulties in one or more of these areas have been solved.

In conclusion, the task is to design a strategy that is simultaneously acceptable from the separate standpoints of 1) psychology of the individual, 2) politics of the organization, 3) technology, and 4) the cybernetics of the organization. For each action taken or not taken, of course, the situation is changed to a greater or lesser degree, and the whole question of *process* thus unfolds over time within the organization.

GUIDELINES TO PROCESS

This section provides a number of general rules or suggestions about the desired results or the general directions that use of management cybernetics should provide. The order of presentation was chosen primarily for ease of explanation. Perhaps the best way to use the guidelines is as a set of possible strategies for organizational improvement from which a selection can be made to fit a given situation. For ease of reference, the guidelines are repeated as a list at the end of the chapter.

When there are particular defects or pathologies that seem localized but resistant to treatment, one is wise to suspect that basic laws or principles are being violated. More precisely, one should suspect that the formal, intended structure or procedures are attempting to violate basic laws. This distinction is important because the suggestion here is that the *formal* arrangements (as compared to the actual organization), are attempting to violate natural laws and therefore couldn't possibly work.

A first example is given with the relatively new university practice of the super dean, charged with 'co-ordinating' the activities of colleges on several different campuses, where each college has its own dean. The super dean typically has no faculty as such (the faculty all belong to one or the other of the campus based deans), but will have a small executive staff. The first cybernetic critique of this arrangement is to notice that the super dean lacks requisite variety by orders of magnitude. The regular dean typically is overwhelmed by trying to keep on top of the activities of between ten and two hundred radically individualistic faculty members. Further, the regular dean has very few areas in which he/she can order anyone about. The dean's role is more like that of a facilitator and (possibly) an inspirational leader than it is a 'boss'. The super dean, then, is cast in a role that primarily relates to the regular deans. The super dean then is attempting to regulate the activities of several geographically dispersed campuses through deans who are themselves barely able to keep on top of their respective campus activities. In such a situation the super dean has little chance of doing more than carrying on protracted conflict with the campus based deans.

The typical reaction of university personnel to the conflicts between deans and the super dean, is to deplore the personality traits or the incompetence of one or more of the people involved. This may be a problem, but from the standpoint of cybernetics is hardly the critical one. The variety inherent in the activities of a college is huge. If the super dean's role was carefully defined to be a system two role of co-ordinating some particular aspects of the college's activities, such as the regions from which they draw students, and the super dean was forbidden to deal with anything else, then the arrangement might work. At least then the formal arrangements would not attempt to violate the law of requisite variety.

Another very common sort of violation of basic principles is that of having ostensible objectives which are in conflict with the actual feedback loops in the organization. Numerous examples of this have been given earlier, including the ostensible objectives of good teaching at universities and in the schools, keeping people healthy in hospitals, and ensuring the public's security by the criminal justice system. In short, organizations *will* achieve those ends which have effective feedback loops on them and organizations will not achieve those ends which lack effective feedback loops.

A third example of violation of basic principles is given by the co-ordinating committee or task force charged with co-ordinating some process or units where the relevant changes happen more often than the committee meets. The structure can clearly *not* discharge its assigned responsibility.

The people in a situation where the formal arrangements are not working, typically work out informal arrangements to make things work. These informal arrangements are always necessary (the formal arrangements never, or almost never, have requisite variety). Thus, the informal arrangements are not, per se, a problem, but rather a necessity. The problem is that a formal arrangement that violates a basic principle makes the whole task enormously more difficult than it needs to be.

An unworkable formal arrangement has several bad consequences. A formal organizational arrangement means that some individual has been assigned a job which they will try to carry out. Trying to do a seemingly reasonable but actually impossible job is an excellent way to get oneself a nervous breakdown. The individual's alternative to mental illness is to blame the failure on other people and then either become cynically detached or paranoid and defensive.

The second bad effect of unworkable formal arrangements is that they generate red tape and procedures that get in the way of the informal arrangements that are actually doing the work. The person assigned to the formal role must at least be talked to, met with, and otherwise mollified. Usually, all concerned attempt to work things through the formal arrangements. The informal arrangements typically arise as people respond to particular difficulties or problems. At the very least, the formal arrangements take up the manager's time and effort. At the worst, the formal arrangements distract the manager and lead him/her into ignoring the crucial aspects of the situation.

In most cases, the unworkable formal arrangements are the direct cause of a great deal of unproductive conflict. This conflict is likely to be particularly severe if all concerned are truly committed to doing a good job. If the various managers are simply worried about their own careers, they will accommodate the formal arrangements and won't be too concerned about the fact that those arrangements interfere with their real mission. If, on the other hand, the people concerned are truly committed to their mission, they will resist the formal arrangements that they perceive as getting in the way. If the person responsible for those unworkable formal arrangements is also convinced of the moral necessity of their role, the stage is set for open warfare.

The guideline that rests upon these considerations is this:

- When localized difficulties persist despite attempts to improve, check to see if the formal arrangements attempt to violate one of the basic laws of chapters two or eight. If necessary, restructure the formal arrangements to comply with the basic laws.

The primary image of an organization that the management cybernetician holds is that of a system which is:

1. Exceedingly complex, i.e., there is more relevant detail than can possibly be dealt with.
2. Probabilistic, i.e., there are important aspects of system behavior that are at least partially randomly determined.
3. Dynamic, i.e., both system structures and behavior change over time.
4. Integral, i.e., the system is, in some important respects, a single coherent entity.
5. Vulnerable, i.e., the system is embedded in an environment which affects it and which the system acts upon.

This list of system properties makes clear that perfection and equilibrium are not attainable except, perhaps, for brief periods. Management then is about guiding an organization in a process of adaptation. The manager's job is overwhelmingly concerned with two constraints: 1) the organization's health (i.e., internal stability or homeostasis) must be continuously maintained, and 2) the organization must adapt to changing external conditions.

The first part of the manager's job, that of maintaining the organization's health, is the domain of systems 3-2-1. In traditional management theory, this includes considerations normally dealt with under questions of efficiency, financial solvency, labor relations, morale, inventory, etc.

The second part of the manager's job, that of adapting to changing conditions, is the purview of systems 3-4-5, in particular system four. This function includes what is normally thought of as R&D, planning, diversification, new technologies, organizational change, reorganization, forecasting, etc.

From the perspective of management cybernetics then, the manager's job is a process of 1) maintaining a balance on the multiple dimensions that make up internal homeostasis, and 2) maintaining an appropriate rate of change on selected dimensions as required to be adaptive. The process for using management cybernetics must facilitate the twin requirements of 1) maintaining internal homeostasis and 2) adaptation to meet changing conditions. The argument of the last few paragraphs leads to the following general guideline:

- use of management cybernetics should improve the organization in its ability to maintain internal homeostasis, or to adapt to changing conditions, or both.

The arguments of the last few paragraphs suggest another similar guideline. It was argued that the manager's role is to simultaneously maintain internal stability and facilitate adaptation. The viable system model (VSM) with its systems 1-2-3-4-5 and its rich interconnections, is designed to do precisely the same thing for an organization. It then makes sense to say that one of the key guidelines for using management cybernetics is:

- always move towards a closer approximation of the viable system model within your organization.

The two guidelines listed above are alternative ways of saying the same thing.

Perhaps the most common way of using the VSM is to begin by using it diagnostically, i.e., to describe the organization as it exists and to compare the existing arrangements with the model's prescriptions. In the majority of cases studied the following problems are obtrusive.

- The levels of recursion are muddled; therefore, it is impossible to specify appropriate degrees of autonomy and proper roles for people.

- The system fours are either non-existent or fragmented into ineffective pieces so that the organization typically has little capability for effective planning at any level.

- Since system four is ineffective, system five typically gets involved in system three's role with the result that no one pays attention to overall integration; no one seriously prepares for the future; and management spends its time interferring with the autonomy of the system ones who are trying to do the work of the organization.

- System two, in its co-ordinative function, is typically either not recognized or is organized in a way that couldn't possibly work. Therefore, system three resorts to laying down rules and/or ordering the system ones around. Because the system two role of providing a co-ordinating *service* to system one productive units is not recognized or fulfilled, system three becomes a dictator in this area (and the productive units then attempt to outwit system three's heavy handedness in order to do their job).

Since these four problems are so common, it is appropriate to check for them.

Thus, we have the following sub-points under the last guideline:

- Examine the levels of recursion. The system ones at each level should be integral, coherent, (relatively) autonomous entities capable of separate existence.

- Each level of recursion should have a robust and integrated system four.

- System five should be monitoring the system three - system four interactions. System five should not collapse into system three.

- System two should be adequate to provide co-ordinative service to the productive units of system one.

There is yet another problem that is almost universally found when using the VSM in a diagnostic mode: the communication channels linking a management and its managed system are generally very poorly designed (see illustration).

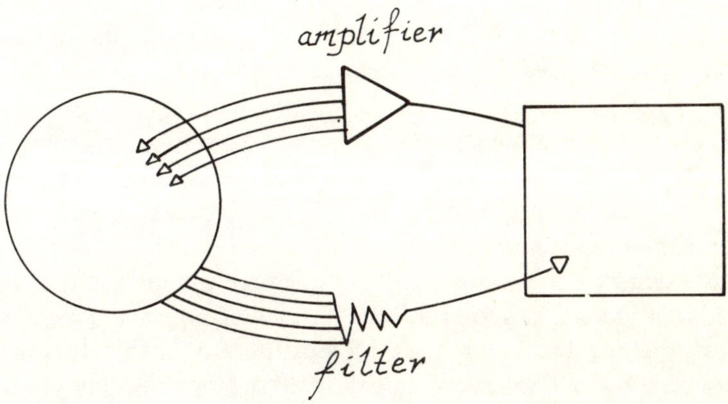

There are several related questions to the business of designing communication channels, including:

1. Is the system's massive variety filtered appropriately so that the manager gets the key information he/she needs without being overwhelmed with data?
2. Is the manager's relatively low variety adequately amplified to impact the system in the desired way?

3. Are the transducers that translate data from the system's language into the manager's language (and vice versa) adequate to the job?
4. Overall, are the filters, amplifiers, transducers, and channel capacity *matched* so that no one part of the network is a bottleneck or massively excessive compared to other parts?

These four points suggest a further sub-guideline for the VSM guideline:

- Examine the communication channels for the adequacy of the amplifiers, filters, and transducers and for the degree to which the various loops are balanced in their capabilities.

The VSM constitutes a nervous system designed to regulate the organization i.e., to integrate the various parts and their interactions. The VSM, however, doesn't help much in understanding what the organization *does*. For example, a lawyer, a carpenter and a boxer, all have (more or less) the same nervous system, but the products to be produced by the three are quite different and require different things from the nervous system. Similarly, a steel plant, a hospital, and a school, should have (more or less) the same nervous system, but the 'products' are quite different for the three. The question, then, is 'what are the dynamics of the organization's productive processes?' What, for example, are the dynamics of producing steel? What is involved in improving the health of a person? Or, how does a person become 'educated'?

The argument of the last paragraph leads to the conclusion that managers should continually seek to improve their understanding of the dynamics of their unit's productive processes. At one level, the last sentence is an empty truism, but in the context of management cybernetics there is more to say.

The productive processes we are concerned to manage are typically exceedingly complex, dynamic and fast changing, and probabilistic. Systems having these three characteristics are obviously not fully comprehensible. Thus we need models of those processes. The OR model building methods of chapter four can be employed to investigate the production dynamics of our system one units.

An argument that applies to the production dynamics of a system one unit at one level of recursion must also apply to system one units at *all* levels of recursion. We might then state the guideline something like this:

- Seek models of the essential dynamics of the productive processes for each level of recursion in the organization.

The methods of chapter four are, of course, not the only useful model building methods available. The quanitified flow chart models discussed in chapter six are also extremely useful and serve a similar purpose.

Management cybernetics focuses on several key dimensions of the organization.

- The nervous system, i.e., the VSM.
- The dynamics of the productive processes, i.e., models of the workings of system ones at each level of recursion.
- The purpose, i.e., the identity of each unit at each level of recursion.

The first two of these were discussed earlier in this section, but the last one has not yet been dealt with.

It is quite commonly the case in modern organizations, that 1) the organization is perceived by all concerned to be functioning poorly, and 2) the responsible managers are unable to improve the situation within the boundaries provided by the perceived constraints. In such a situation it is usually helpful to entertain some very basic questions about the organization, e.g., the questions on system definition, purpose, meta-language, etc., given in chapter three. The guideline might be stated thus:

- When dissatisfied with the existing situation *and* available alternatives, examine and attempt to re-formulate the system definition, language, and purpose.

This section has, so far, addressed the organizational situation in which, cybernetically speaking, the rudiments are missing, i.e., the organization has:

- formal arrangements in violation of natural laws;
- a poorly developed nervous system;
- poorly developed models of production dynamics;
- little commonality in purpose, i.e., a weak identity.

There are many organizations which have worked very hard to deal with all four of these problem areas.

For instance, many organizations have, in the nervous system dimension, highly refined (and frequently automated), information systems for financial information, personnel information, 'production' efficiency and quality control, resource/raw material availability, market analyses, etc. The problems that usually arise in this situation are basically two: 1) How to interpret the information on these various aspects of the organization in order to discern the state of the whole, and 2) how to find the significant information in the flood of data generated by the MIS?

The first problem, how to interpret the information, arises primarily because most of the information systems are providing information on aspects of the organization which 1) seem important, but 2) are not related in any understandable way to the overall state of the organization. The financial information system is an illuminating counter-example. The financial processes within an organization receive an enormous amount of attention from managers. And yet many thoughtful observers and many of our most spectacularly successful managers play down the importance of finances or speak of it as 'only' a constraint.

Why, then, does the economist/accountant viewpoint hold such power within our organizations? The common answer is that money provides a useful measuring rod, that focusing on money allows us to measure and compare and to thereby neatly summarize everything. The advantage of a measuring rod is clearly important, but there is another more fundamental point: money and the financial accounting system provides, in a sense, a comprehensive picture—it deals (in a more or less adequate way) with all of the bits and pieces of the organization. None of the other information systems available to a manager even comes close to matching the financial accounts' ability to tell him/her the overall state of the organization.

We should take a lesson from the utility of the financial accounting system: information provided to managers is useful precisely to the extent that it tells them something about the state of the organization they are managing. There are several guidelines that follow from this line of thinking:

- Design software packages that identify *changes* (as distinct from random fluctuation) to constitute filters that extract significant management information from mountains of data.

- The information system should monitor and report on *changes* in the dynamics of the VSM (i.e., on the significant changes in the behavior of the organization's nervous system).

- The models of system one production dynamics, taken as a group across all levels of recursion, represent everything the organization produces. The information system should provide managers at each level with notice of *changes* in their unit's production dynamics.

- Information systems should *not* provide data on aspects of the organization other than the VSM and the production dynamics models unless there are truly compelling reasons for doing so.

There are two further guidelines that can be extracted from the argument outlined above. The mechanics of the information system can be made very simple if all data is stored as a ratio between actuality and some ideal. This permits *one* statistical software package to examine *all* variables for significant changes over time. The guidelines are:

- Express all data as a ratio between actuality and the ideal.
- Move your data collection procedures as close as possible to a continuous, automated monitoring of the production dynamics and the VSM dynamics.

This last guideline means that data collection should be built into the normal operations of the system. For instance, hospitals and doctor's offices should be (and in fact are) moving toward instruments and recording systems so that data on patients is automatically entered into the proper computer files *as it is generated.* Schools have begun this process in that some computerized instructional systems keep track of the number of correct responses and variables such as the level of difficulty the student is working at.

The point is that it simply doesn't work to have separate processes for 1) the system's normal operations, 2) collecting data on those operations, and 3) entering the data into a computer. The first reason is that separating these processes introduces too much opportunity for error. The second reason is that the human work involved in collecting the data and entering it into the computer is terribly dull. The third reason is that separating the three processes makes it impossibly expensive.

Unfortunately, it is true that no one knows precisely how to implement this guideline in a school because no one has ever really done it. It has, however, largely been done in hospitals. And it could be done in schools — probably with large scale savings after the intitial development stage.*

There is one final notion that applies to management cybernetics as well as to any other attempt to assist managers: The managers must feel comfortable with a tool or they won't use it. Perhaps the most important implication of this point applies to the models of production dynamics. Cyberneticians and managers frequently disagree about the production dynamics for a given unit. In the limiting case, where the manager is both certain of his/her beliefs and seriously wrong, the scientist is unlikely to make any headway in developing a more adequate model. In such a case, an information system built upon a wrong model is very likely to reveal to the manager that the model and reality are contradictory. This provides a useful learning experience and a more adequate model can then be developed. Unfortunately this doesn't always work.

The reason the learning process described above doesn't always work is rooted in the notions of language and meta-language discussed in chapter three. Specifically, each framework or model focuses attention upon certain aspects of reality and away from others. For example, focusing upon the financial accounts will seldom if ever reveal problems with student learning or patient illnesses. Thus, it is possible for the cybernetician and the manager to be so far apart (as discussed in chapter three) that there is no reasonable way to bridge the gap and the 'faulty' model may be self-validating. In these cases the cybernetician needs to work elsewhere.

The guideline based upon this argument is:

> The management tools provided by management cybernetics must be friendly, i.e., they must meet the manager where he/she is, the manager must feel ownership, and the tools must be easy to use.

If this guideline is not met, the tools won't be used anyway.

BEGINNING IMPLEMENTATION: MINIMAL FIRST STEPS†

Much of Stafford Beer's writing has been concerned with spelling out the structure and processes required by the viable system. That is to say, Beer has described, under the general heading of the 'viable system model', the structure and nervous system required *if* the organization is to be capable of rapid learning and adaptation. An organization with capabilities for adaptation looks rather different than most existing organizations. Thus, when one looks at an existing organization from Beer's perspective, the first reaction is to think about redoing the organization from top to bottom. Now, obviously it is seldom, if ever, possible to redo an organization — it must continue to accomplish its mission without interruption and the staff must be retained and cared for, etc. People thinking about using management cybernetics seem to go through (implicitly or explicitly) a thought process something like this:

1. Management cybernetics offers enormous benefits. We really ought to try it.
2. Management cybernetics suggests radical changes in our organization.
3. We seem unable to muster the will or the political muscle necessary to make those radical changes.
4. Therefore, our particular conditions do not permit implementation of management cybernetics. We really need it, but our leadership is: (choose one) too conservative, too uninformed, too timid, etc.

Many enthusiasts of Stafford Beer, it seems, are caught in this thought block and are therefore unable to use management cybernetics.

The question we are left with is: How can an organization begin implementing management cybernetics in a way that:

- Is feasible, i.e., it doesn't require radical initial changes?
- Improves the organization's viability in the short run?
- Provides a base for further implementation of management cybernetics, thus improving the organization's viability in the long run?

This section intends to provide an answer to the above questions. More precisely, the intent is to describe a minimal possible starting point.

Rapid learning for an organization depends critically upon the organization knowing what its current state is. Much of the impetus for management information system (MIS) efforts is based, at least in part, upon this notion. Unfortunately, most MIS efforts have neither met short run expectations nor have they been flexible enough to meet new needs as conditions change.

The usual approach to building an MIS is to 'provide the right data in the right form to the right people at the right time'. Alternatively, the MIS may be designed to 'provide the data each manager needs to make the decisions he or she is confronted with'. These two approaches lead to approximately the same end result: the Universal Data Base MIS in which the MIS attempts to gather and store 'all the relevant facts'. Such a MIS typically:

- handles a large number of different kinds of data elements;
- processes and combines data elements in a large number of different ways;
- provides a large variety of reports for a large number of different people;
- provides detailed snapshots of the organization, each at one point in time;
- does not provide time series data;
- is not a real-time system;
- is very expensive;
- is difficult to keep up to date;
- is difficult to modify (primarily because the parts are richly interconnected so that change in one element requires corresponding changes in others);
- does not perform well.

All in all, these information systems have not lived up to expectations.

The management cybernetics starting point described herein is also a

MIS, but one which is radically different from the traditional MIS described above. The purpose of the MIS is to provide organizational self-knowledge to support organizational learning. This means information on homeostasis and production dynamics for the organization and each of its parts. The cybernetic information system, then, has these characteristics:

1. Units, sub-units, etc., and the environment relevant to each must be defined (these units and sub-units correspond to systems three and one). These units may or may nor correspond to elements of the standard organization chart.

2. Each unit and sub-unit must be characterized by a simple model of its production dynamics. These models can be extremely crude to begin with, but should attempt to reflect major transactions with the environment, chronic problems, if any, and major internal processes. The intent of the model is to provide an initial insight into intended homeostasis and performance for the unit.

3. The models of the various units provide the basis for selection of variables for continuous monitoring. Schwember [6] suggests that between five and twelve variables per unit is generally adequate to monitor homeostasis and performance. Each of these variables is made into a ratio by comparing the actual value to some ideal (if necessary, the ideal can be chosen quite arbitrarily). The point of using ratios is simply to make the data easy to handle.

4. Some sort of data processing routine must take the various ratios as input, must store them as time series, and must somehow check to see if any are changing in unexpected ways. Ideally, this function is carried out by a sophisticated computer program such as cyberstride[7]. If necessary, it could be started by a clerk with a pocket calculator and lots of graph paper.

5. If any of the time series seem to be changing, the relevant managers must be alerted. The cyberstride software does this automatically. If one can't afford the $100,000.00 or so that a cyberstride type program costs, it might be necessary to rely upon cruder methods (in the extreme case, eyeballing the graphs). However this is handled, managers need to be alerted to changes. The rest of the data should *not* be sent to them.

The information system described above is a system for monitoring the performance and state of homeostasis of an organization and its parts. In order for the system to support maximally effective learning, it must be essentially a real-time system. The major delays in traditional systems occur at the boundaries: getting data from the operational unit into the computer room and getting data from the computer room into the decision maker's hands. These are the areas where time, money, and talent should be focused to build a real-time system.

This section proposed, as an initial step towards implementing the viable system model, a particular type of MIS. It is important to make the differences between the proposed system and the traditional MIS explicit.

1. The traditional MIS takes as input large numbers of different sorts of data elements, e.g., teacher and student demographic data, student test scores, financial data, etc. The proposed MIS takes as input *only* pure number ratios between zero and one (these ratios might stand for nearly anything, but all data processing is done in terms of these pure numbers).

2. The traditional MIS processes the data in a large number of different ways to produce a huge variety of different kinds of outputs. The proposed MIS processes all data in essentially the same way: it performs a standard set of statistical routines on all data and assesses the probability that each time series has or has not changed.

3. The traditional MIS provides masses of data to administrators. The proposed MIS suppresses all information *unless* a time series has changed (e.g., its mean or slope may change).

4. Change in the data being processed or in the output, for the traditional MIS, requires reprogramming. Unless the system is *very* small, such reprogramming is difficult at best. Changes in the data being processed for the proposed MIS is trivial — time series are simply added or deleted with *no* reprogramming required. The data being processed and the computer program are de-coupled by the device of processing only ratios. Changes in either can be made without affecting the other. The traditional MIS couples the data elements and the program so that neither can be changed without affecting the other.

5. The traditional MIS inevitably destroys autonomy by centralizing control over all data. Properly done, the proposed MIS *could* protect the autonomy of sub-units. This is done by reporting changes in indices *only* to the responsible manager — at least for a time

period judged adequate to get the indicator back under control. The sub-units' autonomy can also be enhanced by permitting them to monitor any aspects of their operation they wish to — without even informing the center of the meaning of their ratios. In a traditional MIS, the problems of protecting autonomy and privacy are much more severe than in the proposed system.

6. The traditional MIS seeks to provide a snapshot of the organization at one point in time. Learning and adaptation, however, require knowledge of behavior over time. The proposed MIS provides time series data on many behavioral measures.

The proposed MIS is intended to provide a starting point toward a fully fledged viable system model application. The proposed system has the following characteristics:

1. It is very inexpensive.
2. It can be started with a minimal amount of analysis.
3. It requires very little in the way of computer capability or software.
4. It provides assistance to managers very soon after beginning implementation.
5. The various elements (models, data elements, software, and reports) are relatively independent and therefore easily modified.
6. It provides the necessary experience for increasingly sophisticated efforts.
7. Extension of the system to include sophisticated planning and simulation capabilities is fairly straightforward.

The obstacles to implementation of management cybernetics are primarily conceptual blocks within the would be implementor. The resources required to begin a useful management cybernetics MIS are trivial compared to those required for beginning a traditional MIS.

QUESTIONS OF METRIC

One of the major conceptual blocks standing in the way of using management cybernetics has to do with measurement of the relevant variables. The MIS proposed in the last section is effective because it monitors, in more or less real-time, the state of the organization and its various parts. In order to actually *do* this, the organisation's performance and processes must be *measured* in some way. The social sciences have expended enormous energy and resources in devising and testing measures of various phenomena. This effort has been directed by the twin criteria of validity and reliability. We have, quite properly, sought measures which objectively describe the phenomena studied. Most of this work has been designed to describe the state of the phenomena at some particular point in time. This is the 'snapshot' approach. In it, a detailed picture of the phenomena, at one point in time, emerges.

For purposes of regulation and control a different sort of picture is needed. There are really only two basic judgments needed: Is the system (more or less) doing what it's supposed to and is it (more or less) healthy? The first question is the question of production, of output, of performance. The second question is the question of viability, of internal homeostasis, of process. For the regulator of a complex system made up of many parts (e.g., a teacher regulating 30 students, a superintendent regulating 100 schools, a president regulating 50 factories, or a government official regulating who knows how many offices, bureaus, divisions, etc.), a detailed snapshot of a particular system is not generally helpful — the regulator doesn't usually have time to comprehend it and, if comprehended, it doesn't provide the most useful information anyway. The regulator of a complex system made up of many parts needs, for each part, to be alerted to significant changes in: 1) the level of performance, and 2) the state of health. It is more useful to know that something is changing and to have some idea of how it's changing than to have a detailed but static picture.

What, after all, can the regulator do? The regulator can never actually deal with the details of the parts of the individual operations. The regulator can (through rewards and punishments mainly) influence the general direction of performance and some general dimensions of the process. The regulator can also increase or decrease the level of resources and can, in the short run, expedite raw material allocations. The actual, detailed operations of the various parts, of necessity, must be left to those parts. The regulator, therefore, needs information that will help in deciding whether a given part is producing more or less well, whether it is more or less healthy, and whether it has resource or logistics requirements that can be expedited by the central administration.

We are then left with the question of measures of performance and process. This opens up a yawning chasm in the sense that we are not accustomed to dealing with the required measures. We are accustomed, through long usage, to dealing with, for instance, standardized test scores of ability and achievement, questionnaire data of all sorts and 'census data' on everything from daily attendance to the supply of paper on hand and finished products in the warehouse. We 'know' what such data means, more or less, because we have used it over a long period of time and are accustomed to interpreting it. Unfortunately, all such data is expensive to gather and is time consuming to process (and therefore out of date when available).

What is needed is not necessarily an 'objective' measure at all. What is needed is a measure (or realistically, measures) which reflect *changes* in system performance or health. Let me make the point by using, as examples, measures which everyone knows are radically subjective and, even worse, loaded with systematic biases.

My first example is the normal grade given periodically by the public school teacher. Every twelve weeks or so, the teacher enters on the student's report card, grades for performance, effort, and behavior. These grades reflect some mixture of objective performance by the student, performance of classmates, how well the teacher likes the student, the teacher's level of expectations and standards for the class, and (not infrequently) parent characteristics such as status or inclination to demand good grades for Johnny regardless of Johnny's performance. There is, in addition, good reason to expect that some teachers discriminate for or against particular ethnic groups, particular SES classes, or particular types of students. In summary, grades are a thoroughly subjective, biased, unreliable and probably non-valid measure of student performance. I want to argue in spite of all these problems, that grades *as currently given* could provide us with meaningful indications of important system characteristics:

- In combination with performance tests, grades reveal anomalies in standards (e.g., if a 7th grader who reads and writes at a 3rd grade level received A's in 4th, 5th, and 6th grade reading classes, there is something radically wrong with this student's elementary school).

- Low grades clearly indicate a mismatch between the student and the system and probably should *always* be treated as a signal requiring immediate attention.

Unfortunately, given the current structure of the schools, it is difficult to act on either of these kinds of data.

Other, simple measures of classroom health might be devised. A simple 'noise-meter' which electronically monitors noise levels and 'groans' if the decibels exceed a pre-set threshhold has been effective in reducing classroom noise[8]. Experiments have also been done with a 'satisfaction meter' which provides a way for members of a class or work group to register their level of satisfaction essentially whenever they wish[9]. The 'satisfaction meter' consists of, for instance, individual dials which can be adjusted to any desired setting along a continuum from 'awful' to 'wonderful' and a way of electrically summing the individual settings. The satisfaction meter thus provides instantaneous feedback.

No one knows if classroom noise or 'satisfaction' meters will be useful indicators or not — the research has not been done. The noise meter was suggested because of the amount of time and energy teachers spend trying to control noise. 'Satisfaction' is an attempt to get at the individual's effective relationship to his/her situation. Regardless of the utility of these particular examples, they are examples of variables that are monitored automatically as part of the ongoing process (as advocated in the last section) and illustrate the sort of approach to measurement that is needed.

The utility of any measurement always depends upon a context for interpreting it. The most useful context for a manager is some sort of framework that describes the workings of his/her operation, i.e., a model of that operation. Without at least an implicit model of an organization, no measure whatsoever would provide any information because there would be no way to interpret it. Conversely, a good model makes even crude measures useful.

Consider the following example: Teachers and principals are required to maintain a smooth, quiet operation‡ within their classrooms and school buildings, respectively. Failure to maintain smooth operations is much more likely to get an educator into trouble (or even fired) than is failure to maintain good conditions for learning. Furthermore, many of the simplest strategies available for maintaining smooth operations in the short run (e.g., an authoritarian style of leadership or a comprehensive set of policies) are virtually guaranteed to drive down the staff's motivation to produce — and without high motivation to produce, the organization cannot be long effective. These arguments suggest the model given in figure 7.1

We can look at the actors in this system with the feedback laws articulated in Chapter two, e.g., See figure 7.2:

The feedback laws tell us that, within wide variations of input, the output is dominated by the feedback. Thus, a principal who focuses his/her attention on 'smoothness' will end up with a staff who: 1) achieves smooth classes, 2) has low motivation and therefore low levels of effort, and 3)

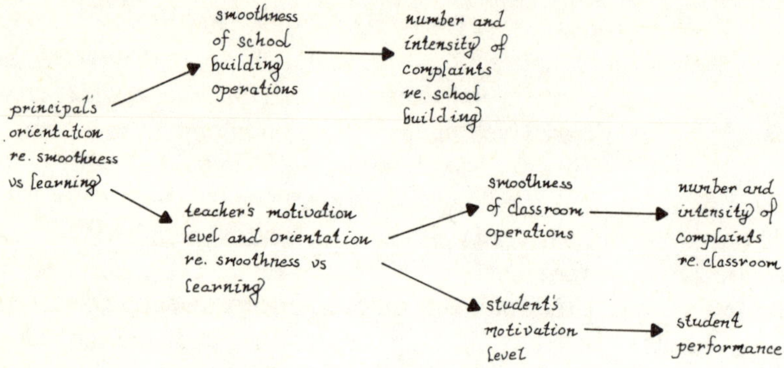

Figure 7.1. The dynamics of emphasizing smoothness of operations vs. emphasizing the conditions for learning.

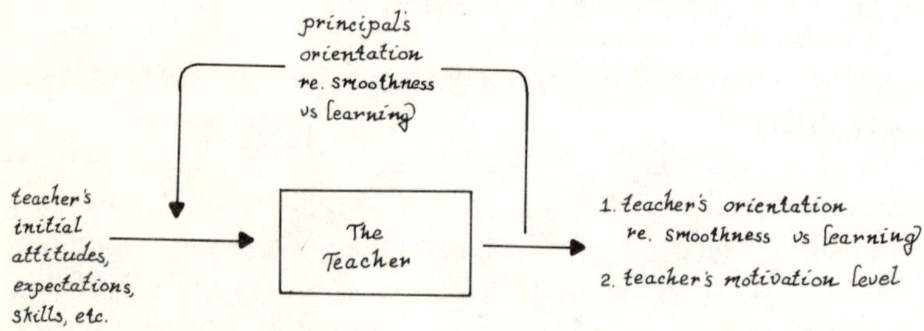

Figure 7.2. The principal as a feedback loop on teacher behavior.

probably achieves little in the way of student learning. Alternatively, a principal who focuses on motivating his/her staff will achieve 1) a high level of effort by the staff, 2) smooth classes, and 3) high levels of student learning.

The same model applies to the principal, e.g., See figure 7.3:

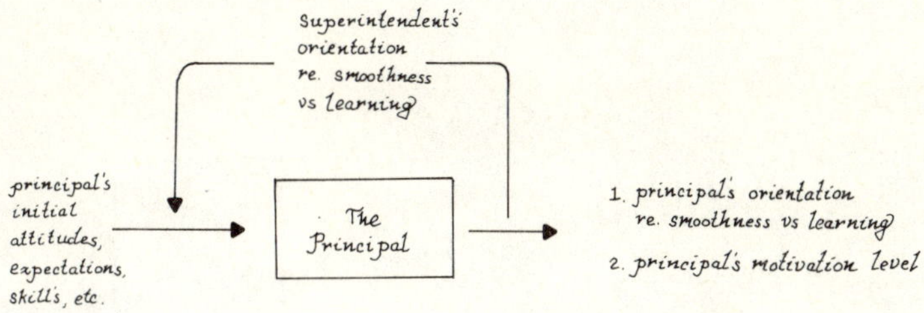

Figure 7.3. The superintendent as a feedback loop on principals' behavior.

Overall, then, we see that the superintendent, in the long run, largely determines the staff's level of effort and whether they focus on 'smoothness' or on a balance between 'smoothness' and learning.

It might well be argued that the model just developed is so well known and so simple that it is trivial. Trivial or not, however, there are very few superintendents or school systems which have taken its lessons to heart. Lets see what it would mean for a school system to monitor its operations, using this simple model (see figure 7.4)

For the principal, we need to measure: 1) level of motivation to produce, and 2) orientation relative to smoothness versus motivating the staff. It is important to remember that we don't need absolute values for these measures. Rather, measures of *changes due to the superintendent's actions* are needed because that's what the superintendent needs in order to act intelligently. Some variation of the satisfaction meter mentioned earlier should work for these measures. Further, each person's response could be anonymous, the results can be summed automatically, and anytime there is a significant change, the superintendent could be automatically alerted.

For the teachers, the same two variables (i.e., level of motivation and orientation relative to smoothness versus motivating students) need to be measured. However, it would probably be useful to measure the impact of the principal and the superintendent separately as they affect teachers.

In addition, student motivation and performance need to be monitored carefully. Some combination of yearly achievement tests and teacher assessments are probably adequate to monitor performance. However, the school needs to address the issues of 1) how to use teacher

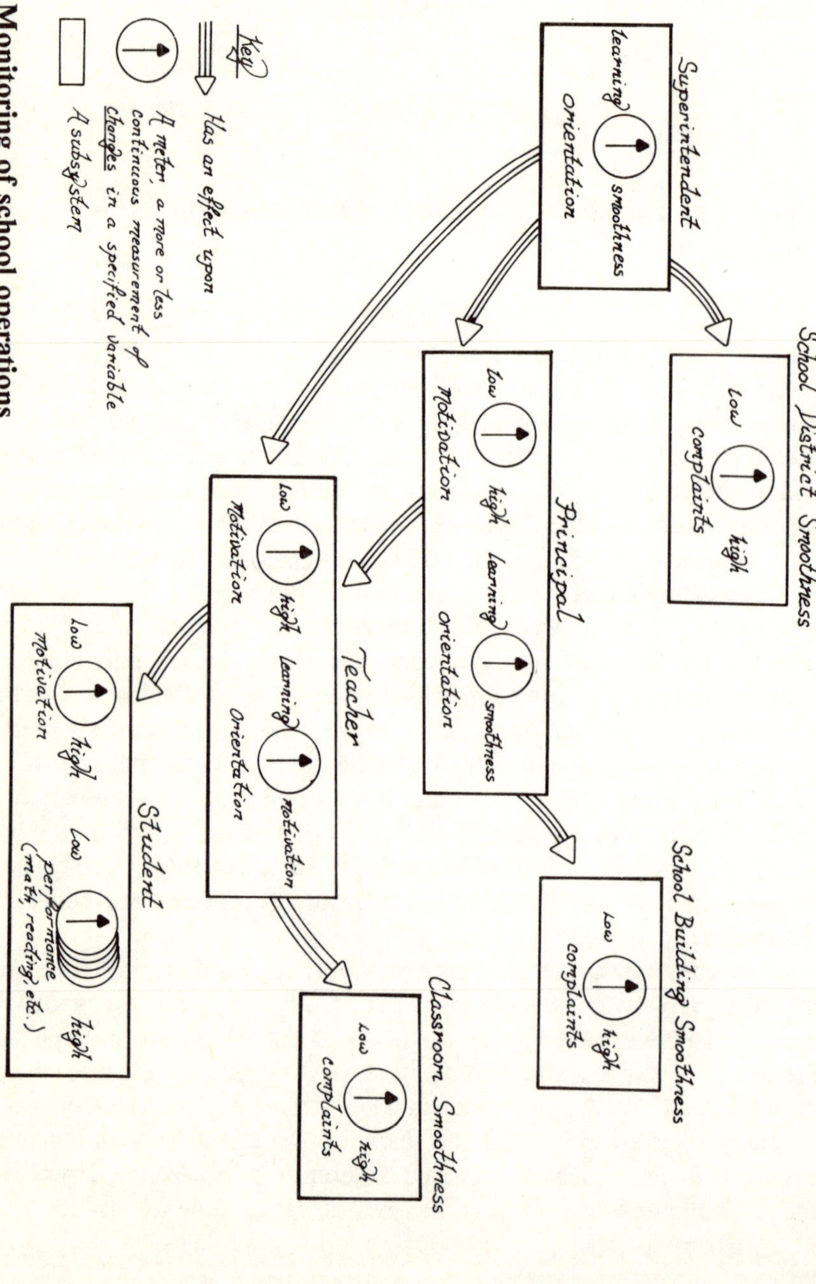

Figure 7.4. Monitoring of school operations

assessments of students to know when changes are necessary, and 2) how to structure the organization so that a reasonable range of strategies for dealing with problem learners is available. Student motivation could be monitored with some variation on the 'satisfaction meter' used for teachers and principals.

The final variables are those of smoothness for buildings and classes. The primary measure of these in most districts is parental complaints.

The results from this simple model are fairly startling. The results include:

1. All concerned, including students and parents, have an understandable model of the way the district works.

2. The model is fully 'quantifiable' in the sense that *changes* in all of the important variables are easily monitored and observed.

3. Monitors of roughly a dozen variables (three at the level of the building, five at the level of the class, two to six on the student depending on how many measures of performance are desired) is all that is required to actually begin using the model.

4. Teachers, principals, and superintendents know *immediately* when their actions cause important changes in levels of motivation or in orientation of their subordinates.

The point of this extended example is not that the model is 'right' in any fundamental sense, but rather that it illustrates the sort of model that the approach of management cybernetics uses. It should also be noted that the combination of 1) a model of system dynamics, 2) monitoring the variables in the model, and 3) essentially real-time reporting to managers, provides a very potent management tool.

CONCLUSION

This chapter has articulated a number of general guidelines for the process of using management cybernetics. The guidelines that were specified are:

1. When localized difficulties persist despite attempts to improve, check to see if the formal arrangements violate one of the basic laws of chapters two or eight. If necessary, restructure the formal arrangements to comply with the basic laws.

2. Use of management cybernetics should improve the organization in

its ability to maintain internal homeostasis, or to adapt to changing conditions, or both. An alternative statement of this guideline is: Always move toward a closer approximation of the viable system model within your organization.

a. Examine the levels of recursion. The system ones at each level of recursion should be integral, coherent, (relatively) autonomous entities capable of separate existence.

b. Each level of recursion should have a robust and integrated system four.

c. System five should be monitoring the system three-system four interactions. System five should not collapse into system three.

d. System two should be adequate to provide co-ordinative service to the productive units of system one.

e. Examine the communication channels for the adequacy of the amplifiers, filters, and transducers and for the degree to which the various loops are balanced in their capabilities.

3. Seek models of the essential dynamics of the productive processes for each level of recursion in the organization.

4. When dissatisfied with the existing situation *and* available alternatives, examine and seek to re-formulate the system definition, language, and purpose.

5. Design software packages that identify *changes* (as distinct from random fluctuations) to constitute filters that extract significant management information from mountains of data.

6. The information system should monitor and report on *changes* in the dynamics of the VSM (i.e., on the significant changes in the behavior of the organization's nervous system).

7. The models of system one production dynamics, taken as a group across all levels of recursion, represent everything the organization produces. The information system should provide managers at each level with notice of *changes* in their unit's production dynamics.

8. Information systems should *not* provide data on aspects of the organization other than the VSM and the production dynamics models unless there are truly compelling reasons for doing so.

9. Express all data as a ratio between actuality and the ideal.

10. Move your data collection procedures as close as possible to a continuous, automated monitoring of the production dynamics and the VSM dynamics.

11. The management tools provided by management cybernetics must be friendly, i.e., they must meet the manager where he/she is, the manager must feel ownership, and the tools must be easy to use.

These eleven guidelines provide a checklist of frequently helpful considerations in using management cybernetics.

The second major section of chapter seven dealt with the minimal first step in implementing the VSM in an organization. The argument in this section was, essentially, that you begin by doing two things: 1) mapping the organization into the framework of the VSM, and 2) inventing models of the various system one production dynamics. The critical point is that, no matter how (initially) crude and inaccurate these two efforts may be, they provide a starting point for a learning process. However, the organization will actually undergo a learning process *only* if the managers use the models and the managers will use the models only if the models are their own and if the information system meets *their* perception of utility. The chapter concludes with examples of production dynamic models and associated measures from a school system. The school system example is used, not because the model is 'right' in any ultimate sense, but rather as an example of the utility of even very poor measures when they are embedded in an appropriate framework.

Notes

* Lest there be misunderstandings, this argument should *not* be construed to mean that schools ought to be turned over to computers or that teachers can be replaced by computers. The argument is simply that we need to *invent* ways of automatically monitoring key system variables.

† Portions of this section are from an earlier paper, 'An Injection of Cybernetics', *Proceedings of the Annual Meeting of the Society for General System Research*, ed Richard Ericson (SGSR, Washington, DC, 1977).

‡ The precise definition of 'smooth operation' depends somewhat upon the norms of the particular community. Deviations from 'smoothness' are recognized primarily through someone complaining.

CHAPTER SEVEN REFERENCES

1. Russell L. Ackoff, 'Beyond Problem Solving' *General Systems* **XIX**, 237-239 (1974).

2. Niccolo Machiavelli, *The Prince and the Discourses*, (Modern Library, New York, 1950).
3. Herbert A. Simon, *Administrative Behavior: A Study of Decision-Making Processes in Administrative Organization* 3rd edition, (Free Press, New York, 1976).
4. Daniel Katz and Robert L. Kahn, *The Social Psychology of Organizations* (John Wiley and Sons, New York, 1966).
5. James D. Thompson, *Organizations in Action: Social Science Bases of Administrative Action*, (McGraw Hill, New York, 1967).
6. Herman Schwember, 'Project Cybersin: An Experience with New Tools for Management in Chile: 1971-1973,' in Hartmut Bossel (ed.) *Computer Assisted Policy Analysis*, (Birkhauser Verlag, Basel, Switzerland, 1977).

   Stafford Beer, *Platform for Change*, London, John Wiley & Sons, Ltd., 1975 final chapter.
8. Harold R. Strang, 'Clowning Around to Stop Clowning Around: A Brief Technical Report on an Automated Approach to Monitor, Record, and Control Classroom Noise' *J. Appl. Behav. Anal.* **8**, 4 (Winter 1975) pp 471-474.
9. Stafford Beer, 'Cybernetics of National Development Evolved from Work in Chile' The Zaheer Lecture (Zaheer Science Foundation, New Delhi, 5 December 1974).

Chapter 8
Technical Notes on Cybernetics
by Allena Leonard and Barry Clemson

PART ONE: LAWS, PRINCIPLES, THEOREMS

INTRODUCTION

The previous seven chapters provided an overview of the major aspects of management cybernetics. However, only a handful of concepts and laws have been explicitly presented so far. This chapter presents a number of the 'laws' of cybernetics and an extensive glossary of the major terms. As far as possible, the laws and concepts are presented as quotes from the major scholars responsible for their articulation.* Thus, the chapter consists of many quotes and a few additional comments.

The first part of the chapter presents a number of laws, theorems, and principles. The distinctions among these three are somewhat arbitrary. Roughly speaking, we use the terms to mean the following:

> Theorem:
> a generalization which has been proven in a formal mathematical or logical sense.
>
> Law:
> a generalization, based upon empirical evidence, which is well established, widely accepted, and which has considerable history behind it.
>
> Principle:
> a generalization, based upon empirical evidence, but which does not yet enjoy the status of law.

The theorem, then, is a matter of a formal argument in logic or mathematics and owes little to experience or 'evidence'. Laws and principles, on the other hand, derive from experience and evidence. The boundary between laws and principles is fuzzy and has partly to do with how long the principle has been recognized and how fundamental it is considered to be.

The chapter is divided into two major parts. The first part gives the laws, principles and theorems. The second part provides a glossary of major terms. A list of the laws, principles and theorems is followed by a list of the concepts treated in the glossary. The laws, principles, and theorems are:

1. SYSTEM HOLISM PRINCIPLE: A system has holistic properties possessed by none of its parts. Each of the system parts has properties not possessed by the system as a whole.
2. DARKNESS PRINCIPLE: No system can be known completely.
3. EIGHTY-TWENTY PRINCIPLE: In any large, complex system, eighty percent of the output will be produced by only twenty percent of the system.
4. COMPLEMENTARITY LAW: Any two different perspectives (or models) about a system will reveal truths about that system that are neither entirely independent nor entirely compatible.
5. HIERARCHY PRINCIPLE: Complex natural phenomena are organized in hierarchies with each level made up of several integral systems.
6. GODEL'S INCOMPLETENESS THEOREM: All consistent axiomatic foundations of number theory include undecidable propositions.
7. ENTROPY: THE SECOND LAW OF THERMODYNAMICS: In any closed system the differences in energy can only stay the same or decrease over time; or, in any closed system, the amount of order (or organization) can never increase and must eventually decrease.
8. REDUNDANCY OF INFORMATION THEOREM: Errors in information transmission can be protected against (to any level of confidence required) by increasing the redundancy in the messages.
9. REDUNDANCY OF RESOURCES PRINCIPLE: Maintenance of stability under conditions of disturbance requires redundancy of critical resources.
10. REDUNDANCY OF POTENTIAL COMMAND PRINCIPLE: In any complex decision network, the potential to act effectively is conferred by an adequate concatenation of information.

11. RELAXATION TIME PRINCIPLE: System stability is possible only if the system's relaxation time is shorter than the mean time between disturbances.

12. CIRCULAR CAUSALITY PRINCIPLE ONE: Given positive feedback (i.e., a two-part system in which each stimulates any initial change in the other), radically different end states are possible from the same initial conditions.

13. CIRCULAR CAUSALITY PRINCIPLE TWO: Given negative feedback (i.e., a two-part system in which each part tends to offset any change in the other), the equilibrial state is invariant over a wide range of initial conditions.

14. FEEDBACK DOMINANCE THEOREM: For high gain amplifiers, the feedback dominates the output over wide variations in input.

15. HOMEOSTASIS PRINCIPLE: A system survives only so long as all essential variables are maintained within their physiological limits.

16. STEADY STATE PRINCIPLE: If a system is in a state of equilibrium (a steady state), then all sub-systems must be in equilibrium. If all sub-systems are in a state of equilibrium, then the system must be in equilibrium.

17. REQUISITE VARIETY LAW: The control achievable by a given regulatory sub-system over a given system is limited by 1) the variety of the regulator, and 2) the channel capacity between the regulator and the system.

    An alternate statement of the law is that the upper limit on the amount of regulation achievable is given by the variety of the regulatory system divided by the variety of the regulated system.

18. CONANT-ASHBY THEOREM: Every good regulator of a system must be a model of that system.

19. SELF ORGANIZING SYSTEMS PRINCIPLE: Complex systems organize themselves; the characteristic structural and behavioral patterns in a complex system are primarily a result of the interactions among the system parts.

20. BASINS OF STABILITY PRINCIPLE: Complex systems have basins of stability separated by threshholds of instability. A

system 'parked' on a ridge will 'roll downhill'.

21. VIABILITY PRINCIPLE: Viability is a function of the balance maintained along two dimensions: 1) autonomy of sub-systems versus integration of the system as a whole, 2) stability versus adaptation.

22. RECURSIVE SYSTEM THEOREM: If a viable system contains a viable system, then the organizational structure must be recursive, or, in a recursive organizational structure, any viable system contains, and is contained in, a viable system.

The glossary treats the following concepts:

adaptation	level
algorithm	meta-language and meta-system
autonomy	model
black box	observer
boundary	output
change	physiological limits
channel capacity	recursive
circular causality (or feedback)	redundancy
complementarity	regulation
current information	requisite variety
cybernetics	second order cybernetics
environment	self-organization
equifinality	stability
essential variables	sub-system
feedback	synergy
heuristic	system
high gain amplifier	threshhold
holon	transducer
homeostasis	variety
information	viability
input	

1. **SYSTEM HOLISM PRINCIPLE** A system has holistic properties possessed by none of its parts. Each of the system parts has properties not possessed by the system as a whole.

Russell L. Ackoff, 'Towards a System of System Concepts'[1]

MANAGERIAL IMPLICATION. A formal organization has holistic properties possessed by none of its parts. Each of the units of the organization has properties not possessed by the organization as a whole. Understanding of the organization and successful decision making about the organization requires that the holistic properties and the properties of the parts are both clearly recognized.

NOTES

Synergy means behavior of integral, aggregate, whole systems, unpredicted by behaviors of any of their components or subassemblies of their components taken separately from the whole.

R. Buckminster Fuller, *Synergetics*[2]

Very often the ability of a system to carry out its function is a property of the system as a whole and not any particular element. Examples: the ability of a service organization to provide standardized services at many locations, the financial strength of a life insurance company as a whole, the reputation of a university, training opportunities, the ability to employ high calibre and highly paid experts, etc. When a system as a whole is reduced to its parts the qualities of the whole are likely to disappear.

Sub optimization is a direct result of managing sub-system properties at the expense of system properties.

The structure of the system to be managed (i.e., the system, subsystems, sub-sub-systems, etc.) must determine the structure of the management.

Further, the systems, sub-systems, etc. and their relevant environments and boundaries must be explicitly identified and share in a corporate understanding of the organization. Otherwise there can be:

- no clear role definitions or divisions of responsibilities;
- no clear communications about the nature of the organization.

Deciding what the system is and which properties belong to the system and which to the various sub-systems (or sub-subsystems) is the foundation upon which all management must rest. In most formal organizations this has not been explicitly done and this lack is the source of enormous trouble.

2. DARKNESS PRINCIPLE No system can be known completely.
W. Ross Ashby. *An Introduction to Cybernetics*[3]

MANAGERIAL IMPLICATION. The organization must be managed effectively without full knowledge of the parts by the top managers.

NOTES

Any material thing can be characterized by an effectively infinite number of variables. The potential knowledge about that thing is therefore effectively infinite.

Since full knowledge is impossible, the question becomes 'what should we try to know as managers?'. The answer clearly depends upon where we sit and on what is happening in the business. What I need to know is different from what my boss or my subordinates need to know (i.e., each of us needs to know about the systemic, holistic properties of the systems we are respectively responsible for). Further, we need to know if something unusual or dangerous is happening within our respective systems (and again, 'unusual or dangerous' means different things for each of us because we are dealing with different systems and different system levels).

'In cybernetic terminology, we note that a box within which all possible states are observable, is transparent. If this is not the case, the box is opaque. Most of the boxes with which managers deal are not completely transparent and not completely opaque either. Let us call them MUDDY BOXES. This distinguishes them from the truly opaque boxes that are known to cybernetic theory as black boxes. Managers, especially as they rise in seniority, find their muddy boxes becoming more opaque. Obviously this is because they are more distant and there are more boxes to be considered'.

Stafford Beer, *The Heart of Enterprise*

Managers of effective, survival worthy systems make no attempt to know all about those systems. Rather, strategies are developed to know about crucial aspects of the system and to actually avoid knowing about (hopefully) irrelevant detail.

3. EIGHTY-TWENTY 'LAW' In any large, complex system eighty percent of the output will be produced by only twenty percent of the system.

Stafford Beer, *The Heart of Enterprise*[5]

MANAGERIAL IMPLICATION. In any large organization eighty percent of the benefit will result from twenty percent of the effort (e.g., teachers, machines, units, etc.).

NOTES

'Given accepted conventions, any system has an effort applied to make it work. This effort produces a pay-off from the system (otherwise the system would soon be abolished). Except in exceptionally simple systems, the pay-off is NON-LINEAR in relation to the effort put into the operation. The non-linear curve typically looks like this (see figure). Engineers, economists, psychologists, et al know about this curve too, and especially recognize the point marked with a circle — where 20% of the effort achieves 80% of the result. They speak of an 80-20 Law. In round terms, this so-called law usually works — which is why people have noticed it. Twenty percent of the fighter pilots shoot

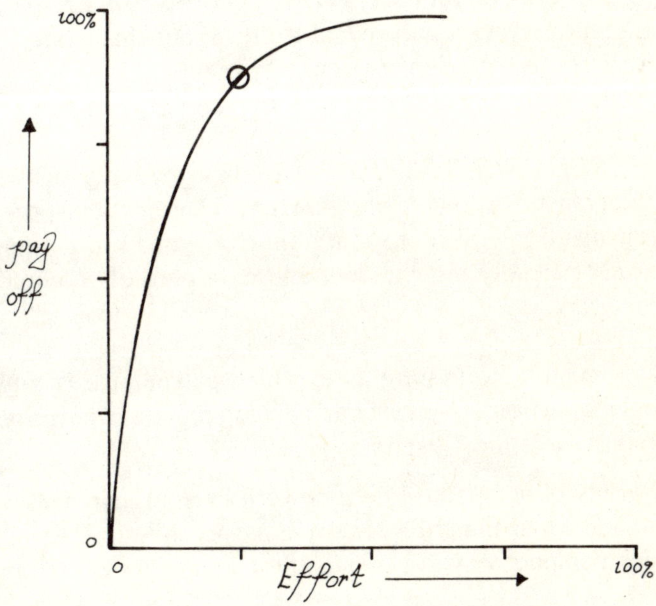

down eighty percent of the shot-down bombers. .... the obvious management strategy is the CHOP OFF the uneconomic tail of the curve. Too much effort in the final eighty percent is expended trying to raise the pay-off through its final 20%. If the relationship between effort and payoff tends to stabilize itself on a highly convex curve, typically running through an 80-20 point, then it will do so again AFTER we have chopped off the original tail'.

Stafford Beer, *The Heart of Enterprise*[6]

The eighty-twenty law seems to be a result of the inherent messiness of the world and the organization's attempt to regulate itself vis a vis its environment. Strategies to shift the point of inflection in the curve to be overall more profitable, must not interfere with the organization's ability to flexibly respond to its environment or they will make the situation worse.

The 'metabolic' processes (i.e., the causal inter-relationships) within a large system are extremely complex, richly interconnected, and in most cases poorly understood. Attempts to increase productivity (i.e., more of some desired output) are frequently counter productive. Successful increase in productivity requires considerable understanding of the system.

4. COMPLEMENTARITY LAW Any two different perspectives (or models) about a system will reveal truths about that system that are neither entirely independent nor entirely compatible.

Gerald Weinberg, *Introduction to General Systems Thinking*[7]

MANAGERIAL IMPLICATION. Any management group will hold a variety of perspectives on the organization. These various perspectives on the organization will reveal different truths about the organization that are only partially independent and only partially compatible.

NOTES

It is a mistake to inquire as to which perspective is 'right'. The proper question is 'given our current practical purpose, which perspective is most useful?'.

A variety of perspectives is a powerful resource in dealing with a dynamic environment because it is not possible to anticipate which perspective will be needed for some new set of conditions.

A variety of perspectives can lead to mass confusion if the perspectives are not reasonably explicit and understood by all concerned. An effective management team should be able to self-consciously adopt a particular perspective as the need arises.

5. HIERARCHY PRINCIPLE Complex natural phenomena are organized in hierarchies with each level made up of several integral systems.

Herbert Simon, *The Organization of Complex Systems*[8]

MANAGERIAL IMPLICATION. Large organizations become organized into hierarchies with each level made up of several integral systems.

NOTES

We are already accustomed to the hierarchy of the organization chart. However, when we look to natural systems, there is more to be said. Nature has a strong tendency to evolve sets of semi-autonomous systems nested within larger systems which are in turn nested within larger systems. In such hierarchies, each system typically has several semi-autonomous sub-systems, so that the whole is structured like a set of Chinese boxes each of which has boxes inside, each of which has boxes inside, etc.

'And nature is organized in levels because hierarchic structures — systems of Chinese boxes — provide the most viable form for any system of even moderate complexity.'

Herbert Simon, '*The Organization of Complex Systems*'[9]

6. GODEL'S INCOMPLETENESS THEOREM All consistent axiomatic foundations of number theory include undecidable propositions.

Kurt Godel, *On Formally Undecidable Propositions*[10]

MANAGERIAL IMPLICATION. The language framework of a given organization is always incomplete in the sense that decision situations arise that can't be adequately expressed within that framework and therefore cannot be resolved within that framework.

NOTES

'Godel's discovery involves the translation of an ancient paradox (the paradox of the liar) into mathematical terms.'

Douglas Hofstadter, *Godel, Escher, Bach: An Eternal Golden Braid* [11]

'*What this sentence says cannot be proved*. If this proposition can be proved, then it is impossible to prove it; but, if the proposition can be disproved, then it follows that it can after all be proved...The conclusion to be drawn from this ridiculous situation is that a sentence of this sort can neither be proved nor refuted within the limits of its own language. ..But if this verbal account of the way in which a proposition can turn out to be undecidable is followed...then the conclusion may not be too surpising. It is that in most formal languages, of which mathematics is an example, there will be regions which are undecidable. Certainly no ordinary language can be complete and self-sufficient. This is known as Godel's Incompleteness Theorem.'

Stafford Beer, *Cybernetics and Management* [12]

Paradox is not a nasty trick but a regular feature of the human landscape which may lead us into the equivalent of a Mobius strip treadmill. If a disturbance (to a system with a formal control system) of a type that was not foreseen arises, the control system may find itself in an undecidable situation.

Undecidability is perhaps most common when the organization faces a situation that is in some sense unprecedented. The critical aspects of the new situation may not be expressible in the traditional terms of discourse. For instance, how is a buggy whip manufacturer to consider the proposition that rather than improving his technology, he needs to become a totally different sort of business.

Repeated failures to solve a problem or a persistently frustrating situation should be viewed as evidence of undecidability.

Each organization and organizational unit develops its own language framework, including a more or less specialized vocabulary, set of assumptions, and a general outlook on the world and itself. Godel's Theorem shows that undecidable propositions will arise within this framework. One of the major functions of the next higher level in the organization (i.e., the next bigger system) should be the construction and use of a meta-language adequate to deal with the undecidable issues that arose in the original system.

The Hierarchy Law section discussed the Chinese boxes within Chinese boxes structure of nature. This hierarchy of levels of boxes stretches from the level of the universe to the level of sub atomic particles. The system holism section spoke of systems made up of parts (i.e., sub-systems) which were themselves systems. In turn, those sub-systems are made of parts which are also systems. For instance, a school system is made up of school buildings made up of classrooms made up of people made up of cells made up of atoms — all of which can be treated as systems or sub-systems depending upon our interests.

Godel's Theorem shows that the language used at any given level in the hierarchy of levels must be incomplete. In logic, this requires an infinite progression of meta-meta-meta-systems. In practice we humans provide closure by standing outside (i.e.,transcending our immediate circumstances). This, of course, requires a certain amount of detachment and typically requires examination and revision of some of the basic assumptions out of which the system operates.

Normal operations require official use of a shared language framework, but that same shared framework causes decision-making paralysis when confronted with an undecidable situation. Resolution of the undecidable situation is only possible by violating (i.e., going outside of) the shared bounds of the language framework. Thus, the organization faces an inherent, unavoidable dichotomy between the need for a shared language for communicating and the need for a meta-language to resolve undecidability.

7. ENTROPY: THE SECOND LAW OF THERMODYNAMICS

In any closed system the differences in energy can only stay the same or decrease over time; or, in any closed system, the amount of order (or organization) can never increase and must eventually decrease.

MANAGERIAL IMPLICATION. Any organizational unit closed to its environment can never increase in order and must eventually decrease in order. Openness to the environment is the first requirement for survival, growth, learning, or change.

NOTES

'The physicist believes entropy to be somehow in or of physical systems. It may or must increase with time. But it is neither material nor efficient, in fact, it is a number; namely, the logarithm of the probability of the state. It is, therefore, a measure of the disorder of an ensemble — or collection of systems. Now Norbert Wiener has proposed that information is orderliness and suggests that we measure it by negative entropy....Ideas are then to be construed as information. Sensation becomes entropic coupling between us and the physical world, and our interchange of ideas, entropic coupling among ourselves. Our knowledge of the world, our conversation — yes, even our inventive thought — are then limited by the law that information may not increase on going through brains, or computing machines.'

Warren McCulloch *Embodiments of Mind*[13]

'We measure 'disorder' by the number of ways that the insides can be arranged, so that from the outside it looks the same. *The logarithm of that number of ways is the entropy*. The number of ways in the separated case is less, so the entropy is less, or the 'disorder' is less.

So with the above technical definition of disorder we can understand the proposition. First, the entropy measures the disorder. Second, the universe always goes from 'order' to 'disorder', so entropy always increases. Order is not order in the sense that we like the arrangement, but in the sense that the number of different ways we can hook it up, and still have it look the same from the outside, is relatively restricted.'

Richard P. Feynman, Robert B. Leighton, and Mathew Sands, *The Feynman Lectures on Physics: Mainly Mechanics, Radiation and Heat*[14]

'If a closed system is not in a state of statistical equilibrium, then its macroscopic state will vary with time until the system eventually reaches total equilibrium. We may specify every macroscopic state of the system by the distribution of its energy between its various sub-systems; we can then say that successive states through which the system passes correspond to energy distributions of successively greater probabilities. This increase in probability is, in general, extremely important owing to its exponential nature which was demonstrated in the last section. As we have seen, the probability is given by the expression whose exponent is an additive quantity (the entropy of the system). We can hence say that processes taking place in a closed system which is not in equilibrium, occur in such a manner that the system steadily passes from states of lower entropy to those of higher entropy until finally the entropy attains its maximum possible value, corresponding to total statistical equilibrium.

Thus, if a closed system is at some instant of time in a macroscopic state not in equilibrium, then the most probable consequence will be that the entropy of the system will increase monotonically in successive instants of time. This is the so-called law of increase of entropy or the 'second law of thermodynamics'. It was discovered by R. Clausius and its statistical foundation was given by L. Boltizmann.

When we talk about the "most probable consequence' we must bear in mind the fact that in reality the probability of a change to a state of higher entropy is so overwhelmingly large compared with the probability of any appreciable decrease that the latter cannot in fact be observed in nature.

L.D. Landau & E.M. Lifshitz, *Statistical Physics*[15]

8. REDUNDANCY OF INFORMATION THEOREM Errors in information transmission can be protected against (to any level of confidence required) by increasing the redundancy in the messages.

Claude Shannon & Warren Weaver,
The Mathematical Theory of Communication[16]

MANAGERIAL IMPLICATION. Errors in communication can be avoided by making the messages redundant.

NOTES

Remember the old prescription for effective public speaking: tell them what you're going to say, say it, then tell them what you said.

Redundancy is expensive in that it requires extra channel capacity, and humans get bored with excessive redundancy.

A balance between tolerable levels of error and tolerable amounts of redundancy is required.

9. REDUNDANCY OF RESOURCES PRINCIPLE Maintenance of stability under conditions of disturbance requires redundancy of critical resources.

Ludwig von Bertalanffy, *General System Theory*[17]

MANAGERIAL IMPLICATION. Maintenance of smooth internal operations and continuous progress toward overall objectives under conditions of disturbance requires redundancy of critical human and material resources.

NOTES

The process or organization that has optimum efficiency under perfect conditions will suffer near continuous difficulties because real world conditions are seldom perfect.

Stability relative to overall objectives may require considerable change in short term objectives, in ways of operating, and in technology utilized. These changes all require extra resources.

New opportunities can be seized only if there exists some *extra* managerial and resource capabilities.

10. REDUNDANCY OF POTENTIAL COMMAND PRINCIPLE In any complex decision network, the potential to act effectively is conferred by an adequate concatenation of information.

Warren McCulloch, *Embodiments of Mind*[18]

MANAGERIAL IMPLICATION. In a management structure, the potential to act effectively belongs to that subset of the management that first acquires the proper information.

NOTES

Information confers power.

Any problematical situation can potentially be resolved in numerous ways by numerous subsets of the managers.

Failure to recognize this potential (or over zealous adherence to the chain of command) robs the organization of creative solutions; the ability to recognize crucial facts, trends, and events; and, in general, a large fraction of its overall decision making capability.

A management that encourages utilization of the redundancy of potential command will increase its speed of response; ability to detect novel events, information, trends, threats, and opportunities; creativity of decision-making; and comprehensiveness of decision-making.

11. RELAXATION TIME PRINCIPLE System stability is possible only if the system's relaxation time is shorter than the mean time between disturbances.

Arthur Iberal, *Toward a General Science of Viable Systems*[19]

MANAGERIAL IMPLICATION. An organizational unit can maintain smooth functioning, routine operation, and efficient production only if its recovery time from disturbances is shorter than the mean time between disturbances.

NOTES

Think of a still pond disturbed by a pebble tossed into the middle. The time it takes for the pattern of expanding circular ripples to die out is the pond's relaxation time. If a second pebble is tossed in a few seconds after the first, the wave patterns from the two pebbles interact with each other and generate a very complicated pattern. If many pebbles are thrown *very* rapidly, the pond surface will appear chaotic and will have no discernible pattern of expanding circular ripples — the systems ability to respond is destroyed by a too rapid series of disturbances.

'It is characteristic of our society that its institutions...have a longer relaxation time on average than the mean interval between massive external perturbations.'

Stafford Beer, *Platform for Change*[20]

Proper structuring of the unit's regulatory system can reduce the relaxation time so that it can maintain stability under a higher rate of disturbances.

Sometimes the rate of disturbances can be influenced by influencing the environment.

An organization has only a limited capability to absorb changes. Too many changes at the same time can and often do destroy organizations, although each individual change may be perfectly justified.

Crisis management, when it becomes a dominant or even important mode for an organization, is a sympton that the organization is being disturbed at a rate with a mean interval that is less than its relaxation time.

The relaxation time law shows that there is a critical relationship between the organization's speed of responses and the rate at which disturbances arrive. This relationship determines whether or not it is possible for the organization to maintain its internal stability.

12. CIRCULAR CAUSALITY PRINCIPLE ONE Given positive feedback (i.e., a two part system in which each stimulates any initial change in the other), radically different end states are possible from the same initial conditions.

W. Ross Ashby, *An Introduction to Cybernetics*[21]

MANAGERIAL IMPLICATION. An organizational unit or process with a positive feedback loop will be unstable and prone to catastrophic change.

13. CIRCULAR CAUSALITY PRINCIPLE TWO Given negative feedback (i.e., a two part system in which each part tends to offset any change in the other), the equilibrial state is invariant over a wide range of initial conditions.

W. Ross Ashby, *An Introduction to Cybernetics*[22]

MANAGERIAL IMPLICATION. An organizational unit with a negative feedback loop will return to the same equilibrial state despite a variety of attempts to change it.

W. Ross Ashby, *An Introduction to Cybernetics*[23]

14. FEEDBACK DOMINANCE THEOREM For high gain amplifiers, the feedback dominates the output over wide variations in input.

Stafford Beer, *Brain of the Firm*[24]

MANAGERIAL IMPLICATION. The results produced by an organizational unit are determined by the feedback loops, regardless of wide variations in the input.

NOTES

Large instabilities, particularly in alternating directions, are evidence for positive feedbacks.

Periodic failure of apparently sound regulatory systems suggests an undetected positive feedback.

Several failures in attempting to change some pattern of behavior is evidence for the existence of a negative feedback loop.

An 'innovation' which tends to disappear as soon as efforts are relaxed is probably disturbing the equilibrial state of a negative feedback loop.

A unit's operational goals (as distinct from the *intended* goals) are determined by the actual feedbacks on that unit.

A gap between rhetorical goals and operational goals is evidence of improper feedback loops.

Every operational goal will have an associated feedback loop.

Any 'goal' that does not have a feedback loop will not be consistently achieved (and probably won't be achieved at all).

15. HOMEOSTASIS PRINCIPLE A system survives only so long as all essential variables are maintained within their physiological limits.

Walter Cannon, *The Wisdom of the Body* [25]

MANAGERIAL IMPLICATION. An organization is healthy only so long as essential variables are maintained within their critical limits.

NOTES

Essential variables for a business include such things as cash flow, availability of capital, availability of labor, market share, etc.

Identification of essential variables typically involves choosing about seven variables for each operational unit.

Essential variables should be continuously monitored so that serious departures from stability can be detected and corrected immediately. An organization that has not done this could well be in a catastrophic difficulty before any warnings of trouble were recognized.

16. STEADY STATE PRINCIPLE If a system is in a state of equilibrium (a steady state), then all sub-systems must be in equilibrium. If all sub-systems are in a state of equilibrium, then the system must be in equilibrium.

W. Ross Ashby, *Design for a Brain*[26]

MANAGERIAL IMPLICATION. If an organization is in a state of equilibrium, then all units of that organization must be in equilibrium. If all units of the organization are in equilibrium, then the organization must be in equilibrium.

NOTES

'That a whole dynamic system should be in equilibrium at a particular state it is necessary and sufficient that each part should be in equilibrium at that state, in the conditions given to it by the other parts ... We can say (metaphorically) that every part has a power of veto over the states of equilibrium of the whole'.

W. Ross Ashby, *Design for a Brain*[27]

An organization that is not changing (i.e., is in equilibrium) is either asleep or dead. Change in this respect doesn't necessarily mean growth or decline in size or material measures, it could mean change in the people's capabilities, for instance.

Since each unit affects the others, there is a danger that after some critical fraction of the units fall asleep, they may put the rest to sleep.

If none of the units are asleep, the organization's management is likely to be unable to regulate the unit interactions well enough to maintain overall cohesion and synergy.

Organizations, particularly if they have a history of successful performance, are very likely to *not* recognize a change in environmental conditions nor a need for change in themselves.

17. REQUISITE VARIETY LAW The control achievable by a given regulatory sub-system over a given system is limited by 1) the variety of the regulator, and 2) the channel capacity between the regulator and the system. An alternate statement of the law is that the upper limit on the amount of regulation achievable is given by the variety of the regulatory system divided by the variety of the regulated system.

W. Ross Ashby, *Introduction to Cybernetics*[28]

MANAGERIAL IMPLICATION. The degree to which an organization can be regulated is limited by the variety of the organization's regulatory systems, including the management itself and all of the management systems and regulatory procedures utilized.

NOTES

Total regulation of a subordinate can be achieved by devoting all of one's time to it or reducing the subordinate's variety of behaviors to a very small set. Both strategies obviously involve huge costs.

Total regulation of a situation more complex than one person is achievable only if the variety of that situation is artifically restrained, e.g., through the use of rigid rules.

As a practical matter, it is almost never worthwhile to attempt to achieve total regulation. This is because much of the potential variety doesn't concern the regulator one way or the other.

A certain amount of lack of control is necessary if the regulated system is to have any capability for adaptation or growth.

Successful systems usually have a mixed strategy for regulation: 1. Those events/disturbances that are potentially lethal are controlled as completely as possible, and 2. Those events/disturbances that are less immediately lethal are typically controlled only in terms of their *effects* on the system, not in terms of their causes. (See 'homeostasis' discussion).

The variety of a system to be regulated can be assessed by deciding how many meaningfully different states, behaviors, and disturbances the system has.

The variety of a regulator can be assessed by counting the number of meaningfully different responses the regulator is capable of.

The upper bound on the regulation achievable can be calculated by taking the ratio of the two numbers above. In practice, no regulator is 100% efficient so that the actual regulation achieved will be somewhat less (and possibly much less if the regulator is badly designed).

In complex managerial situations it may not be feasible to actually count the variety of either the regulator or the system. In such cases intuitive 'guesstimates' are very helpful.

Many large organizations are attempting to operate with regulatory systems that clearly do not have the variety to match those aspects of the situation that the management itself is concerned with. These regulatory systems could be redesigned at low cost and with enormous savings for the organization.

18. CONANT-ASHBY THEOREM Every good regulator of a system must be a model of that system.

Roger Conant and W. Ross Ashby,
'Every Good Regulator of a System must be a Model of That System'[29]

MANAGERIAL IMPLICATION. The management of an organizational unit is able to regulate only those aspects of the unit that it has in some sense modelled. The model may be an implicit one, carried in someone's head, but the management has no way of even noticing (much less managing) those aspects that are not included in their models.

NOTES

Decision making (other than flipping a coin) involves a model of the way things work, i.e., 'if I do this, such and so will likely result'.

Regulation involves the selection of one choice from some set of possible alternatives, based on the anticipated consequences of the choice. The set of alternatives and the assessment of the consequences both require a model of the situation.

Managers with defective models are in fact not managing their units. This situation may go unrecognized for long periods of time if the unit is not in a highly competitive environment. In such cases the activity of the management is irrelevant or damaging to the unit.

Explicit models, even when they are very simple, are much more effective than are implicit models. This is partly because a) it is impossible to share implicit models, b) implicit models shape our perception in ways we are unaware of, c) explicit models force us to be aware of our assumptions (which are often wrong), and d) explicit models can be easily falsified and this teaches us about the situation and the model is usually improved.

'The first effect of this theorem is to change the status of model making from optional to compulsory. As we said earlier, model-making has hitherto largely been suggested as a possibility for regulating complex dynamic systems. The theorem shows that, in a very wide class (specified in the proof of the theorem), success in regulation implies that a sufficiently similar model must have been built, whether it was done explicitly, or simply developed as the regulator was improved'.

Roger Conant and W. Ross Ashby,
'Every Good Regulator of a System must be a Model of That System'[30]

19. SELF ORGANIZING SYSTEM PRINCIPAL Complex systems organize themselves; the characteristic structural and behavioral patterns in a complex system are primarily a result of the interactions among the system parts.

W. Ross Ashby, Principles of Self-Organizing Systems [31]

MANAGERIAL IMPLICATION. Most of the structural and behavioral patterns in an organization are a result of interactions among the parts of the organization; they are not primarily the result of the management's deliberate decisions.

NOTES

Managers are most aware of those aspects that they design, but some of the aspects that are not intentionally designed include:

- the culture of the organization
- the informal communication network
- the operational goals

Even the organization chart is at least as much a result of tradition as of design.

The law of self-organization shows that the business largely organizes itself — the manager's task is to use the system's self organizing tendencies to achieve the holistic purpose he/she is charged with. This requires that the manager's purposes and the system elements' purposes must at least overlap.

20. BASINS OF STABILITY PRINCIPLE Complex systems have basins of stability separated by threshholds of instability. A system 'parked' on a ridge will 'roll downhill'.

G. Nicholis & Ilya Prigogine,
Self-Organization in Non-Equilibrium Systems[32]

MANAGERIAL IMPLICATION. Organizations have a limited number of stable configurations. An organization that is shifted out of a stable configuration will, seemingly by itself, gravitate toward one of the stable configurations.

NOTES

A marble on a hilly surface provides a good analogy; the marble is stable only at the bottom of a hollow.

Some configurations of, for instance, staff performance and organizational reward system are stable and others are not.

Basins of stability are separated by ridges that represent changes in energy potential. Thus, moving from one basin of stability to another requires work, even when the new basin is at a lower potential than the old.

The ridges separating basins represent threshholds. Thus, while it may be very difficult to push a system 'up' a ridge, the moment it crosses the threshhold it will continue without further external effort.

In a human being, addictions (e.g., to heroin, cigarettes, alcohol) represent basins of stability that are generally considered undesirable. A life style without drug addiction is generally considered a 'better' basin of stability. Addictions are so troublesome precisely because they are surrounded by high ridges that are difficult to climb.

Successful 'mutations' represent a shift in the landscape. A system state that was, for instance, stable at the bottom of a hollow may, after the mutation, be perched on a ridge or on the side of a hill.

Bateson points out that society, by practicing agriculture that is heavily dependent upon insecticides and large scale machinery, settles into a basin of stability that has very different consequences for both the natural and societal environment than would an agriculture based upon small sçale firms and non-chemical control of pests.

Gregory Bateson, *Steps to an Ecology of Mind*[33]

An investment in one type of building (or in one technology or in one location) puts an organization in one basin of stability as compared to other possible plants, technologies, or locations.

21. VIABILITY PRINCIPLE Viability is a function of the balance maintained along two dimensions:
1. Autonomy of sub-systems versus integration of the system as a whole.
2. Stability versus adaptation.

Stafford Beer, *The Heart of Enterprise* and *Brain of the Firm*[34]

MANAGERIAL IMPLICATION. Organizational effectiveness is a function of the balance maintained along two dimensions:
1. Autonomy of organizational units versus integration of the business as a whole.
2. Stability of operations versus adaptation to changing conditions.

NOTES

Too much autonomy of organizational units results in lack of overall purpose, loss of cohesion and synergy, loss of identity, and typically generates a demand for 'centralization'.

Too much integration results in loss of flexibility and initiative by the units, much red tape, loss of morale in the units, and typically generates a demand for 'decentralization'.

Too much stability results in an organization that is increasingly obsolete.

Too rapid a pace of adaptation results in chaos and massive inefficiency.

22. RECURSIVE SYSTEM THEOREM If a viable system contains a viable system, then the organizational structure must be recursive, or, in a recursive organizational structure, any viable system contains, and is contained in a viable system.

Stafford Beer, *The Heart of Enterprise* and *Brain of the Firm*[35]

MANAGERIAL IMPLICATION. The deep structure that is responsible for organizational viability (i.e., health and effectiveness) is repeated at each level in the organization. The viable organization has a structure like chinese boxes, i.e., each unit is filled with smaller units which are each in turn filled with smaller units, and each of these units (of whatever size) has the deep structure of the viable system.

NOTES

Every system of whatever size must maintain its own structure and must deal with a dynamic environment, i.e., the system must strike a proper balance between stability and change. The cybernetic mechanisms for stability (i.e., homeostasis, negative feedback, autopoiesis, equifinality) and change (i.e., positive feedback, algedonodes, self-organization) are found in all viable systems.

Failure to recognize and respect the distinct levels results in:

1. A top management that experiences a loss of cohesion and integration and feels the organization is too decentralized.
2. Unit managers that experience a loss of independence and autonomy and feel the organization is too centralized.

And both these contradictory feelings exist at once *because* no one is clear on who should be doing what!

Effective integration at one level in the organization requires that information on lower levels accurately and concisely reflect the *holistic* system aspects of those lower levels.

Effective autonomy requires that managers should be required to routinely report upward *only* on the holistic system aspects of their own operations.

Failure to recognize the recursive nature of organizations leads to confusion in managerial roles, which leads to high level managers dabbling in details of a lower level unit's operations, which leads to an absence of anyone managing the overall system and causes endless conflict between the managers at the various levels.

Effective management requires that operational units be defined and that the operational units be given autonomy limited only by the requirements of system cohesion/integration. This requires that each level of management focus on the holistic aspects of their system (e.g., the interaction and synergy among their sub-units) and that they then not meddle in the details of those unit's operations.

Higher level managers who have been drawn into the details of their sub-units' operations will have no time for planning, exploring the environment or generally preparing for the future. This typically causes the unit to fall into a pervasive style of crisis management.

NOTES: Laws, Principles, Theorems

1. Russell L. Ackoff, 'Towards a System of System Concepts' *Management Science* **17**, 11, 661-669 (July 1971).
2. R. Buckminster Fuller, *Synergetics* (Macmillan Co., New York and London 1975) p.3.
3. W. Ross Ashby, *An Introduction to Cybernetics* (Chapman & Hall and University Paperbacks, London, 1964).
4. Stafford Beer, *The Heart of Enterprise* (Wiley, New York, 1979) p.40.
5. *Ibid.*, chapter one.
6. *Ibid.*, pp.15-16.
7. Gerald Weinberg, *Introduction to General Systems Thinking* (Wiley-Interscience, New York and London, 1975).
8. Herbert Simon 'The Organization of Complex Systems' in Howard Pattee (ed) *Hierarchy Theory* (Braziller, New York, 1973).
9. *Ibid.*, p.27.
10. Kurt Godel *On Formally Undecidable Propositions* (Basic Books, New York, 1962).
11. Douglas Hofstadter, Godel, Escher, Bach: An Eternal Golden Braid (Basic Books, New York, 1979) p.17.
12. Stafford Beer, *Cybernetics and Management* (Wiley, New York, 1959) pp.71-72.
13. Warren McCulloch, *Embodiments of Mind* (M.I.T. Press, Cambridge, Mass., 1965) p.73.
14. Richard P. Feynman, Robert B. Leighton, and Mathew Sands, *The Feynman Lectures on Physics: Mainly Mechanics, Radiation and Heat*, (Addison Wesley, Reading, Massachusetts, 1963) pp.46-7, emphasis in original.

15. Lev D. Landau and E. M. Lifshitz, *Statistical Physics*, (Pergamon Press, London, 1955) p.28.
16. Claude Shannon and Warren Weaver, *The Mathematical Theory of Communication* (The University of Illinois Press, Urbana, Illinois, 1959).
17. Ludwig von Bertalanffy, *General System Theory:* revised edition (Braziller, New York, 1968).
18. Warren McCulloch, *Embodiments of Mind* (ref.13).
19. Arthur Iberall, *Toward a General Science of Viable Systems* (McGraw-Hill, New York, 1972).
20. Stafford Beer, *Platform for Change* (Wiley, New York, 1978) p.404.
21. W. Ross Ashby, *An Introduction to Cybernetics* (ref.3).
22. *Ibid.*
23. *Ibid.*
24. Stafford Beer, *Brain of the Firm*, second edition (Wiley, Chichester, 1981) chapter three.
25. Walter Cannon, *The Wisdom of the Body* (W.W. Norton, New York, 1932).
26. W. Ross Ashby, *Design for a Brain* (Chapman and Hall and Science Paperbacks, London, 1965).
27. *Ibid.*,p.79.
28. W. Ross Ashby, *An Introduction to Cybernetics* (ref.3).
29. Roger Conant and W. Ross Ashby, 'Every Good Regulator of a System Must be a Model of That System' *Intern. J. Systems Sciences'* **1**, 2, 89-97. (1970).
30. *Ibid page 97.*
31. W. Ross Ashby, 'Principles of Self Organizing Systems' in Heinz von Foerster and George Zopf (editors) *Principles of Self Organization*, (Pergamon Press, New York, 1962).
32. G. Nicolis and Ilya Prigogine *Self-Organization in Non Equilibrium Systems* (Wiley, New York, 1975).
33. Gregory Bateson, *Steps to an Ecology of Mind* (Ballantine Books, New York, 1972) part VI.
34. Stafford Beer, *The Heart of Enterprise* (Wiley, New York, 1979) and *Brain of the Firm* (Wiley, New York, 1980).
35. *Ibid.*

PART TWO: GLOSSARY OF KEY TERMS

The most important terms used in the book are defined and/or discussed below. Where possible quotes from one or more of the key authors are used. The terms treated in this glossary are listed at the beginning for easy reference.

adaptation
algorithm
autonomy
black box
boundary
change
channel capacity
circular causality (or feedback)
complementarity
current information
cybernetics
environment
equifinality
essential variable
feedback
heuristic
high gain amplifier
holon
homeostasis
information
input
level
meta-language & meta- system
model
observer
output
physiological limits
recursive
redundancy
regulation
requisite variety
second order cybernetics
self-organization
stability
steady state
sub-system
synergy
system
threshhold
transducer
variety
viability

ADAPTATION

'...a form of behavior is adaptive if it maintains the essential variables within physiological limits.'

(W. Ross Ashby, *Design for a Brain*)[1]

'...Just what are adaptation's salient features? We can see at once that adaptation, whatever its context, involves a progressive modification of some structure or structures. These structures constitute the grist of the adaptive process, being largely determined by the field of study. Careful observation of successive structural modifications generally reveals a basic set of structural modifiers or operators: repeated action of these operators yields the observed modification sequences. ...all variations of the problem give rise to the same fundamental questions:

- To what parts of its environment is the organism (system, organization) adapting?
- How does the environment act upon the adapting organism (system, organization)?
- What structures are undergoing adaptation?
- What are the mechanisms of adaptation?
- What part of the history of its interaction with the environment does the organism (system, organization) retain?
- What limits are there to the adaptive process?
- How are different (hypotheses about) adaptive processes to be compared?

Moreover, as we attempt to answer these questions in different contexts, essentially the same obstacles to adaptation appear again and again. They appear with different guises and names, but they have the same basic structure. for example, ...

1. The set of attainable structures is large so that there are many alternatives to be tested.
2. The structures in the set of attainable structures are complicated so that it is difficult to determine which sub-structures or components (if any) are responsible for good performance.
3. The performance measure is a complicated function with many interdependent parameters (e.g., it has many dimensions and is non-linear, exhibiting local optima, discontinuities, etc.).
4. The performance measure varies over time and space so that given adaptations are only advantageous at certain places and times.
5 The environment presents...a great flux of information (including performances) which must be filtered and sorted for relevance.

(John Holland, *Adaptation in Natural and Artificial Systems*)[2]

ALGORITHM

'...a comprehensive set of instructions for reaching a known goal.'

(Stafford Beer, *Brain of the Firm*)[3]

A computer program is a good example of an algorithm.

See also HEURISTIC.

AUTONOMY

Autonomy refers to a system that is able to act as an independent or free agent, without constraint from a higher level system.

'Autonomy — literally control of the self, from the Greek autos (self) and nomos (a law) — is provided (to the mind) by the recursive nature of the system. Whether or not a simple machine with a governor can control or be controlled by itself, can be disputed, but imagine more loops of information and effect added on top of the simple circuit. What will be the content of the signal material carried by these loops? The answer, of course, is that these loops will carry messages about the behavior of the whole system. In a sense, the original simple circuit already contained such information ('it's going too fast'; it's going too slow'), but the next level will carry such information as 'the correction of' it's going too fast' is not fast enough', or 'the correction of' it's going too fast' is excessive'. That is, the messages become messages about the previous lower level. From this to autonomy is a very short step.'

(Gregory Bateson, *Steps to an Ecology of Mind*)[4]

'Autonomous systems are mechanistic (dynamic) systems defined as a unity by their organization. We shall say that autonomous systems are organizationally closed, that is their organization is characterized by processes such that 1) the processes are related as a network, so that they recursively depend on each other in the generation and realization of the processes themselves, and 2) they constitute the system as a unity recognizable in the space (domain) in which the processes exist.'

(Francisco Varela, *Principles of Biological Autonomy*)[5]

BLACK BOX

'The problem of the Black Box arose in electrical engineering. The engineer is given a sealed box that has terminals for input, to which he may bring any voltages, shocks, or other disturbances he pleases, and terminals for output from which he may observe what he can. He is to deduce what he can of its contents... In our daily lives we are confronted at every turn with systems whose internal mechanisms are not fully open to inspection, and which must be treated by the methods appropriate to the Black Box...the primary data of any investigation of a Black Box (of given input and output) consists of a sequence of values of the vector with two components: (input state, output state)....from this there follows the fundamental deduction that all knowledge obtainable from a Black Box (of given input and output) is such as can be obtained by recording the protocol; all that and nothing more.'

(W. Ross Ashby, *An Introduction to Cybernetics*)[6]

A 'black box' is a system whose internal workings are not open to inspection or study. The brain is a black box that cannot be taken apart for study. Similarly, a manager cannot dissect his/her unit for analysis except in the imagination.

BOUNDARY

A boundary separates a system and its environment. Just as there is a subjective element in defining a system, there is a subjective element in choosing a boundary. Defining a boundary is tantamount to defining the thing that is to be considered as a 'system' and those other things that are to be considered as the system's 'environment'.

CHANGE

The notions of 'stability' and 'change' complement each other: a firm grasp of one illuminates the other. Stability is discussed as meaning that some variable of interest has no meaningful differences over time. Change, then, has the corresponding meaning that some variable of interest shows a difference over time. Thus, whether we perceive 'change' or 'stability' depends entirely on our selection of variables to observe and our ability to detect differences in those variables over time.

CHANNEL CAPACITY

The capacity of a communication channel is equal to the number of bits per second which can be transmitted by means of the channel. The maximum possible rate of transmission for the channel is called the channel capacity.

'Theorem II. Let a discrete channel have the capacity C and a discrete source the entropy per second H. If $H < C$ there is a coding system such that the output of the source can be transmitted over the channel with an arbitrarily small frequency of errors (or an arbitrarily small equivocation). If $H > C$ it is possible to encode the source so that the equivocation is less than $H - C + \varepsilon$ where ε is arbitrarily small. There is no method for encoding, which gives an equivocation less than H-C. ...one is not surprised that the capacity of a channel is to be described not in terms of the number of symbols it can transmit, but rather in terms of the information it transmits. Or better, since the last phrase lends itself particularly well to a misinterpretation of the word information, the capacity of a channel is to be described in terms of its ability to transmit what is produced out of a given source of information.'

(Claude Shannon and Warren Weaver, *The Mathematical Theory of Communication*)[7]

CIRCULAR CAUSALITY

See FEEDBACK.

COMPLEMENTARITY

'Within the scope of classical physics, all characteristic properties of a given object can in principle be ascertained by a single experimental arrangement,...in quantum physics, however, evidence about atomic objects obtained by different experimental arrangements exhibits a novel kind of complementary relationship....the notion of 'complementarity' simply characterizes the answers we can receive by such inquiry, whenever the interaction between the measuring instruments and the objects forms an integral part of the phenomena.'

(Neils Bohr, *Essays*, 1958-1962)[8]

'These are the essential ingredients in our idea of complementarity: two mutually irreducible points of view that are not entirely independent....If, for whatever reason, observers do not make infinitely refined observations, then between any two points of view there will generally be complementarity.'

(Gerald Weinberg,
An Introduction to General Systems Thinking)[9]

CURRENT INFORMATION

'Current', in this context, means timely relative to the decision needs of the situation. If the variable to be controlled is the position of a steel rod moving at 70 miles per hour through a set of machinery, 'current' must be measured in milliseconds. If the variable to be controlled is the number of engineers with advanced degrees, 'current' probably means one year old. 'Current information' must be defined in terms of the characteristic frequencies of the system to be regulated. The term can have no meaning outside of the context of the rapidity (or slowness) with which events occur in the system to be regulated.

CYBERNETICS

'Cybernetics...is a 'theory of machines' but it treats not things but ways of behaving. It does not ask 'what is this thing?' but 'what does it do?'...It is thus essentially functional and behavioristic...Cybernetics deals with all forms of behavior in so far as they are regular or determinate, or reproducible. The materiality is irrelevant, and so is the holding or not of the ordinary laws of physics.'

(W. Ross Ashby, *An Introduction to Cybernetics*)[10]

'Cybernetics or Control and Communication in the Animal and the Machine'.

(Norbert Wiener, *Cybernetics*)[11]

'Cybernetics is precisely about organization — for this is the medium through which control is exercised. Therefore, cybernetics may also be defined, as it has been by certain Russian writers, as the science of effective organization.'

(Stafford Beer, *The Heart of Enterprise*)[12]

ENVIRONMENT

'Given an organism, its environment is defined as those variables whose changes affect the organism, and those variables which are changed by the organism's behavior. It is thus defined in a purely functional, not a material sense.'

(W. Ross Ashby, *Design for a Brain*)[13]

'A set of elements and their relative properties, which elements are not part of the system but a change in any of which can produce a change in the state of the system. Thus a system's environment consists of all variables which can affect its state. External elements which affect irrelevant properties of a system are not part of its environment.... although concrete systems and their environments are objective things, they are also subjective insofar as the particular configuration of elements that form both is dictated by the interests of the researcher. Different observers of the same phenomena may conceptualize them into different systems and environments. For example, an architect may consider a house with its electrical, heating, and water systems as one large system. But a mechanical engineer may consider the heating system as a system and the house as its environment.'

(Russell Ackoff, *Towards a System of System Concepts*)[14]

The problematic environment consists of those things outside of a system that are important to it. Understanding or management of the system's behavior and/or survival usually requires some understanding of the environment.

Although we generally think of the environment as given, it is not usually so. The critical aspects of the environment are usually characteristics of some micro-environment rather than characteristics of some ill-defined general miiieu. For instance, insects do not adapt to the Pennsylvania climate, they adapt to climates such as those under rocks in moist soil, under the bark of pine trees or on the surface of still water. Similarly, organizations choose particular micro-climates such as particular markets, legal frameworks (i.e., choice of country or state for corporate headquarters), particular suppliers, and so on.

Organizations have a great deal of control over their environment in two respects: They can choose particular micro-environments; and they can set out to mold their environments to fit their needs. Successful organizations have always done this through choice of product lines, market segments, corporate image, lobbying, and public relations.

EQUIFINALITY

'In any closed system, the final state is unequivocally determined by the initial conditions: e.g., the motion in a planetary system where the positions of the planets at time t are unequivocally determined by their positions at a time t_o. Or in a chemical equilibrium, the final concentrations of the reactants naturally depend on the initial concentrations. If either the initial conditions or the process is altered, the final state will also be changed. This is not so in open systems. Here, the same final state may be reached from different initial conditions and in different ways...'

(Ludwig von Bertalanffy, *General System Theory*)[15]

'...the same final state, the same 'goal', may be reached from different initial conditions and in different pathways in the organismic process. Examples are the development of a normal organism from a whole, a divided, or a fused ova, or from any pieces as in hydroids or planarians, or of the reaching of a definite final size from different initial sizes and after a different course of growth, etc.'

(Ludwig von Bertalanffy, *General System Theory*)[16]

ESSENTIAL VARIABLES

'...variables which are closely related to survival and which are closely linked dynamically so that marked changes in any one leads sooner or later to marked changes in the others.'

(W. Ross Ashby, *Design for a Brain*)[17]

Identification of essential variables in an organization might well start by simply making a list of those factors that the management attempts to maintain in a stable state. If these variables were explicitly identified, along with their causal inter-relationships, the management would have a model of its essential variables that would, at a minimum, provide a basis for rapid learning.

FEEDBACK

'...an extremely important factor in voluntary activity is what the control engineers term 'feedback'...when we desire a motion to follow a given pattern the difference between this pattern and the actually performed motion is used as a new input to cause the part regulated to move in such a way as to bring its motion closer to that given by the pattern. For example, one form of steering engine of a ship carries the reading of the wheel to an offset from the tiller, which so regulates the valves of the steering engine as to move the tiller in such a way as to turn these valves off....clearly any friction or other delaying force which hampers the motion of the tiller will increase admission of steam to the valves on one side and will decrease it on the other in such a way as to increase the torque tending to bring the tiller to the desired position. Thus the feedback system tends to make the performance of the steering engine relatively independent of the load. ...on the other hand under certain conditions of delay, etc. a feedback that is too brusque will make the rudder overshoot, and will be followed by a feedback in the other direction, which makes the rudder overshoot still more, until the steering mechanism goes into a wild oscillation, or hunting, and breaks down completely.'

(Norbert Wiener, *Cybernetics*)[18]

'Cybernetics is, however, specially interested in the case where each affects the other, a relation that may be represented by

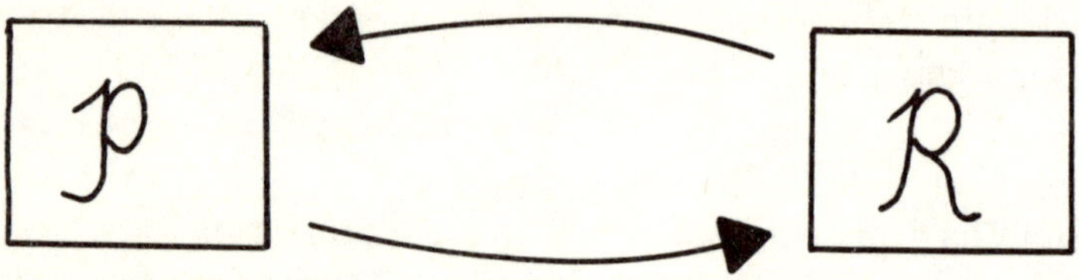

When this circularity of action exists between the parts of a dynamic system, feedback may be said to be present....the fact is that the concept of 'feedback', so simple and natural in certain elementary cases, becomes artificial and of little use when the interconnections between the parts become more complex. When there are only two parts joined so that each affects the other, the properties of the feedback give important and useful information about the properties of the whole. But when the parts rise to even as few as four, if every one affects the other three, then twenty circuits can be traced through them; and knowing the properties of all the twenty circuits does not give complete information about the system. Such complex systems cannot be treated as an interlaced set of more or less independent feedback circuits, but only as a whole.

For understanding the general principles of dynamic systems, therefore, the concept of feedback is inadequate in itself. What is important is that complex systems, richly cross-connected internally, have complex behaviors, and that these behaviors can be goal-seeking in complex patterns.'

Ex. 1. Trace twenty circuits in the diagram of Fig. 4/11/1

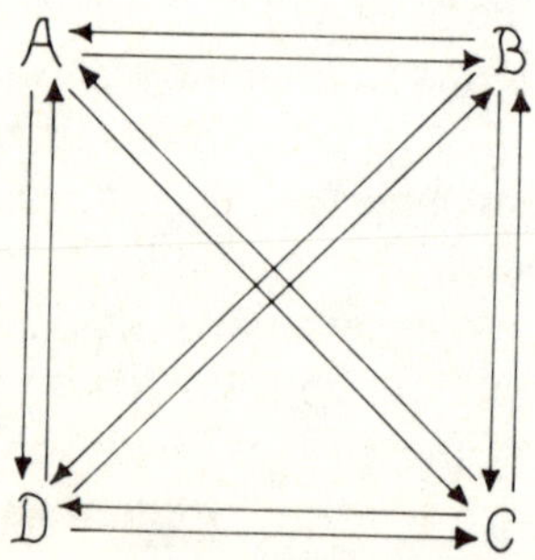

(W. Ross Ashby, *An Introduction to Cybernetics*)[19]

Feedback refers to all phenomena in which there is circularity of causality. This circularity makes the phenomenon both very complex and rather strange from the point of view of traditional science. For convenience, feedback can be divided into two types: Negative feedback which actively seeks to maintain stability and positive feedback which actively seeks change. To understand feedback, consider two parts of a system, say A and B, connected so that each affects the other. In general, if a change in one causes a change in the other in the *same* direction, the feedback is positive because any initial small change gets bigger and bigger as it goes around the loop. If a change in one causes a change in the other in the *opposite* direction, the feedback is negative because the overall effect is to cancel out or eliminate the effect of changes introduced into either. As a practical matter there are a lot of technicalities having to do with the timing of the effects and the relative size of one part's effect on the other so that rather subtle changes can transform a positive feedback into a negative feedback and vice versa.

The managerial implications of feedback are fairly startling. To begin with, if a manager is able to set up an appropriate feedback loop on some desired result, he/she can then go away in confidence that the system will competently achieve that result. A manager can achieve a desired result starting from a large number of different configurations, *if* appropriate negative feedback loops are designed in.

When we examine actual organizations, we discover that there are many, many feedback loops that no one actually designed, but that 'grew like topsy'. These 'accidental' feedback loops are often positive in nature (i.e., they promote instability) or they are negative feedback on results that the organization really doesn't want. These 'accidental' feedback loops go a long way toward explaining the organization's seeming resistance to managerial plans.

Our culture is dominated by a notion of causality that says in effect 'how much I put in determines how much I get out'. This is not at all true for most organizational situations. Rather the output is determined by the feedback. The amount put in is unimportant as long as it is between some minimum that is the physiological equivalent of dehydration and some maximum that is the equivalent of drowning.

HEURISTIC

'...a set of instructions for searching out an unknown goal by exploration, which continuously or repeatedly evaluates progress according to some known criterion.'

(Stafford Beer, *Brain of the Firm*)[20]

'An heuristic specifies a method of behaving which will tend towards a goal which cannot be precisely specified because we know *what* it is but not *where* it is...Heuristics prescribe general rules for reaching general goals, then, and do not typically prescribe an exact route to a located goal as does an algorithm.'

(Stafford Beer, *Brain of the Firm*)[21]

See also ALGORITHM

HIGH GAIN AMPLIFIER

A high gain amplifier is a process which makes a large change in the input.

HOLON

'The members of a hierarchy, like the Roman god Janus, all have two faces looking in opposite directions: the face turned toward the subordinate levels is that of a self-contained whole; the face turned upward toward the apex, that of a dependent part. But there is no satisfactory word in our vocabulary to refer to these Janus like entities...It seems preferable to coin a new term to designate these nodes on the hierarchic tree which behave partly as wholes or wholly as parts, according to the way you look at them. The term I would propose is 'holon' from the Greek holos whole, with the suffix 'on' which, as in proton or neutron, suggests a particle or part'.

(Arthur Koestler, *The Ghost in the Machine*)[22]

HOMEOSTASIS

'The constant conditions which are maintained in the body might be called equilibria. That word, however, has come to have fairly exact meaning as applied to relatively simple physico-chemical states, in closed systems, where known forces are balanced. The co-ordinated physiological processes which maintain most of the steady states in the organism are so complex and so peculiar to living beings involving, as they may, the brain and nerves, the heart, lungs, kidneys and spleen, all working co-operatively — that I have suggested a special designation for these states, HOMEOSTASIS.'

(Walter Cannon, *The Wisdom of the Body*)[23]

Homeostasis is a dynamic process of regulation in which a set of essential variables regulate each other via the mechanism of a complex set of interlocking feedback loops. The 'essential variables' are those which give a particular system its distinctive characteristics. They are typically closely linked in that they regulate each other, if one is driven out of its normal bounds the others sooner or later go out of regulation also, and if any one of the essential variables remains outside of its normal bounds for long, the system is typically destroyed. Systems characterized by homeostatic regulation have the following characteristics:

1. There are numerous environmental variables, internal variables, and system behaviors that show no correlation over the range of the variables normally encountered.
2. If the environmental or internal variables are forced to extreme values, step function relationships (i.e., sudden, drastic effects) become important between environmental, internal, and system behavior variables.
3. The essential variables (i.e., the critical internal variables) all stay essentially constant or all change radically. The point at which they all change radically corresponds to system destruction.
4. There are some internal variables (e.g., hunger, sex drive, fatigue) which are highly correlated with both environmental variables and system behavior.

Regulation in homeostatic systems is achieved through the dynamic effect of the essential variables upon each other. It is difficult to determine the limits at which such a system breaks down because while it will generally show enormous resiliency and ruggedness, there are typically an enormous number of ways in which it can quite suddenly and catastrophically fail. One quite surprising way to make the system fail is to artifically fix one of the variables. Fixing a variable (i.e., freezing it at one value) that is part of a regulatory network will sometimes make the rest of the network quite unstable.

Organizations maintain internal stability through homeostasis. As every manager knows, a critical part of his/her job is to maintain the stability of the organization and, in cybernetic terms, this means to make sure that the homeostatic mechanisms are in good health. Homeostasis means that the whole and each of its parts are maintaining a dynamic equilibrium in which each part has, in Ashby's poetic terms, a power of veto over the state of equilibrium of the others. The critical managerial task in this regard is to be alert to incipient instability. The managerial tool to accomplish this is some sort of model that identifies the essential variables and some system to monitor those variables and set off an alerting signal if the variables diverge from their normal limits. One type of model that has been used to good effect in this regard is a simple flow model that represents the major dynamics of the process to be controlled. Time series data on the major variables from the flow model then provide a monitoring device for organizational homeostasis.

INFORMATION

'...this word information in communication theory relates not so much to what you do say as what you could say. That is, information is a measure of one's freedom of choice when one selects a message.... To be somewhat more definite, the amount of information is defined, in the simplest cases, to be measured by the logarithm of the number of available choices. It being convenient to use logarithms to the base 2...the information, when there are only two choices, is proportional to the logarithm of 2 to the base 2. But, this is unity; so that a two choice situation is characterized by information of unity, as has already been stated above.'

(Claude Shannon & Warren Weaver,
The Mathematical Theory of Communication)[24]

'When we have an information source which is producing a message by successively selecting discrete symbols (letters, words..) the probability of choice of the various symbols at one stage of the process being dependent on the previous choices (i.e., a Markov process), what about the information associated with this procedure? The quantity which uniquely meets the natural requirements that one sets up for 'information' turns out to be exactly what is known in thermodynamics as entropy.'

(Claude Shannon & Warren Weaver,
The Mathematical Theory of Communication)[25]

Norbert Wiener, Claude Shannon, Warren Weaver, and R.F. Fisher were all working on a statistical theory of information during the 1940s. Toward the end of the decade of the 40s, Weaver[26] commented on this work by drawing a distinction among 3 different levels of communication:

'*Level A* How accurately can the symbols of communication be transmitted? (The technical problem).

Level B How precisely do the transmitted symbols convey the desired meaning? (The semantic problem).

Level C How effectively does the received meaning affect conduct in the desired way? (The effectiveness problem).'

The statistical theory of information dealt with level A (the technical problem of transmission), but those findings illuminate a number of issues at levels B and C. For example, Miller[26] said: 'The amount of information is exactly the same concept we have talked about for years under the name of 'variance'. The equations are different, but if we hold tight to the idea that anything that increases the variance also increases the information, we cannot go far astray. The similarity of variance and the amount of information might be explained this way: when we have a large variance, we are very ignorant about what is going to happen. If we are very ignorant, then when we make the observation it gives us a lot of information. ...on the other hand, if the variance is very small...we get little information from making the observation'.

The practical significance of 'information' in this technical sense is that it gives us a measure of the 'stuff' that flows in and around management situations. Since management is almost entirely taken up with communicating, we need some way of looking at the ebb and flow, at the dynamics, at the process of all this communicating in the statistical sense to give us a handle on this stuff of communication. Information as a technical term lets us measure, channel, and regulate the dynamics of communication without getting overwhelmed with the content of that communication.

INPUT

'The input consists of all those things the environment provides for or does to the system. Generally, explicit acknowledgement is made of only those inputs which potentially affect the outputs we are interested in.

LEVEL

A level consists of a set of systems that all have the same status within a hierarchy. Within the hierarchy consisting of school district — buildings — classrooms — individuals, each of those four defines a level.

Every level within a hierarchy has the character of a holon (i.e., from one perspective it is an holistic system and from another perspective it is a particle within a system).

If levels are properly defined, then every organizational unit, at whatever level, has the same three tasks: 1) to maintain its own stability; 2) to provide the outputs required by the next level up; and 3) to adapt to changes in its environment (where the environment consists of the rest of the organization plus relevant aspects of the outside world).

META-LANGUAGE AND META-SYSTEM

A meta-language is one used to discuss propositions that are undecidable in a language.

'...we shall adopt an omniscient attitude and look externally upon the observer and his black box. We are now talking about the observer rather than seeing the world through his eyes, and of course, we talk in different terms. Since we shall use this gambit and others like it a good deal, I shall call the observer's language an object language (with words that refer to states in his reference frame) and our language (in terms we talk about an observer) the meta-language.

(Gordon Pask, *An Approach to Cybernetics*)[27]

A meta-system is defined as one which speaks a meta-language. It is impossible to identify a meta-system without identifying the system (and its language) referred to.

MODEL

'Some people think of a model as a mathematical equation, others think of it as a theory, still others as an hypothesis, and yet others as a physical thing. The last group looks the least sophisticated, and yet these people have understood best. We talk about a model ship or a model railway; especially we talk about a working model. In these expressions four key notions are embedded. There is a *scaling down* in both size and complexity — a model of Shakespeare's birthplace, for instance, could stand on a table and would not be expected to incorporate miniature bricks in equivalent numbers to the building in Stratford upon Avon. There is *transfer across* whereby actual parts of things are represented again in their relative positions, and arising from this there is *workability*, by which I mean that the model can, in principle anyway, operate like the original. Thus a model train actually runs around a model railway and it looks so much like the thing modelled that cine films of models can be substituted for film of actual trains and successfully pretend to be real. That this can be so, although the engine may be driven by clockwork, (and no real railway engine was ever so driven) introduces the fourth point. The model is a good model if it is appropriate. Someone watching the film just mentioned is not in the least concerned with how the engine is powered; but an engineering student who dismantled a model railway engine in a technical college would not be impressed.'

(Stafford Beer, *Brain of the Firm*)[28]

'We can now see much more clearly what is meant by 'model'. The subject was touched on in S.6/8, where three systems were found to be isomorphic and therefore capable of being used as representations of each other. The subject is of some importance to those who work with biological systems, for in many cases, the use of a model is helpful, either to help the worker think about the subject or to act as a form of analogue computer.

The model will seldom be isomorphic with the biological system: usually it will be an homomorphism of it. But the model itself is seldom regarded in all its practical detail: usually it is only some aspect of the model that is related to the biological system; thus the tin mouse may be a satisfactory model of a living mouse provided one ignores the tinniness of the one and the proteinness of the other. Thus what usually happens is that the two systems, biological and model are so related that an homomorphism of the one is isomorphic with an homomorphism of the other. (This relation is symetric, so either may justifiably be said to be a 'model' of the other.)'

(W. Ross Ashby, *Introduction to Cybernetics*)[29]

'A symbolic model of a problem has two parts. The first is an equation that relates a measure of system performance to those aspects of the problem situation, both controlled and uncontrolled, that can affect it. The performance equation has the following form: performance of a system = a specified relationship between controlled variables and uncontrolled variables. ....the second part of the model expresses the limits within which each of the controlled variables can be manipulated. For example, suppose that a specified sum of money is available and it must be allocated to several activities. Then the sum of the amounts cannot exceed the amount available, and the amount allocated to each cannot be less than zero. Such constraints can also be expressed in symbolic form.

The solution to a modelled problem consists of those values of the controlled variables that, within the specified constraints and under the relevant uncontrolled conditions yield the best performance of the system. A solution that does so is said to be optimal.'

(Russell Ackoff, *Redesigning the Future*)[30]

A model is a representation of the essential features of a system from the perspective of the observer or participant in that system. It can be as simple as a mental picture or as complex as the computer models of the world produced under the auspices of the Club of Rome.

OBSERVER

'The 'observer' is that which imputes purpose to a system. To go even further, the observer is that which *invents* the system by *perceiving* a purposive unity.

'Any theory starts off with an observer or an experimenter...now, in order to establish the identification and to form a predictive theory (indeed, in order to select one model from the set of possibilities) the

observer needs to know the purpose for or the purpose of the system with which the model is identified. Lacking such a purpose, the observer would be at a loss to know what constitutes a sensible interpretation of the model or what properties of the world are relevant. In essence, of course, the purpose for or the purpose of the system is invented by the observer himself and it is stated in an observer's meta-language for talking about the system.'
(Gordon Pask, *Meaning of Cybernetics in the Behavioral Sciences*)[31]

There are two aspects to this business of the observer influencing the nature of reality. The first has to do with the inherent limitations of the observer in apprehending what reality consists of. The second has to do with the observer's process of observation disturbing (and thereby changing) the reality being observed.

We humans have in fact changed our 'sensory organs' as science has developed. Psychological profiles, attitude surveys, lie detectors, the balance sheet and many others are in effect 'sense organs' that help us detect certain aspects of the organization. Thus our own inventions are changing us as observing systems and thereby changing our perceptions of the organizational reality that we manage.

The activity of observing some phenomenon, in general, changes that phenomenon. The extent of the change depends upon both the phenomenon and the methods of observation. The problem is very severe in the realm of the subatomic and in the realm of social phenomena. It is apparently not at all a problem in the realm of astronomy.

OUTPUT

Outputs include everything sent into the environment from the system that we care to pay any attention to. It may be difficult to identify as outputs all those things that we ought to be concerned about, because the connections between our activities (through the environment) and our success or failure may be obscure. Pollution provides a good example of an output that was unrecognized until recently.

OPERATIONAL ELEMENT

An operational element is a sub-system of the organization that meets two criteria: 1) it produces at least one of the goods or services (or an identifiable piece of one of the goods or services) that the organization is intending to produce, and 2) it is one of the nested Chinese boxes discussed under 'hierarchies'.

An operational element should have its own management and be charged with responsibility for an identifiable sub-set of the organizations objectives.

PHYSIOLOGICAL LIMITS

In all systems, the essential variables have some normal values or some normal range of values. If one or more essential variables are driven to increasingly extreme values, at some point the system becomes 'sick' and/or is destroyed. The point at which the essential variable begins to make the system 'sick' is the physiological limit.

RECURSIVE

Recursive means to repeat the same operation(s) or structure or for something to refer back to itself.

the number seven can be defined by saying 7=6+1. If you then ask what six is, 6=5+1. And 5? 5=4+1. If we continue this game until we get to 2=1+1 we have recursively defined 7 in terms of 'adding'. To sum up,

$$7=6+1=(5+1)+1=(4+1)+1+1=(3+1)+1+1+1=(2+1)+1+1+1+1$$
$$=(1+1)+1+1+1+1+1$$

This set of arithmetic statements gives a recursive definition of the number 7.

In mathematics or computer programming, a recursive function is one which doubles back upon itself or, in other words, refers to itself. For example, suppose a function

$$f(n) = n+1 \text{ then,}$$
$$f(f(fn)) = (n+1)+1$$
$$f(f(f(n))) = ((n+1)+1)+1$$

The statement $f(f(f(n)))$ recursively refers to $f(n)$.

REDUNDANCY

Dd y knw tht mst ppl cn rd nglsh wtht vwls? Tht sntnc dmnstrts th rdndncy f th nglsh lngge.

Redundancy means, quite simply, that more than the logically required minimum is included, that there are elements which are in some sense repetitious to other elements.

REGULATION

'The act of regulation is the selection of an appropriate response such that essential variables are maintained within narrower limits than they would otherwise attain under some disturbance.'

(Barry Clemson, A General Systems Theory of Educational Organizations and Accountability)[32]

'In general, then, an essential feature of the good regulator is that *it blocks the flow of variety from disturbances to essential variables.*'(W. Ross Ashby, *An Introduction to Cybernetics*)[33]

REQUISITE VARIETY

The Law of Requisite Variety shows that regulation can be measured and that the maximum possible effectiveness of a regulator will be directly measurable by a comparison between the variety of the regulator and that of the reguland.

Ashby gives a trivial example of a press photographer who has twenty subjects, each with a distinct distance and exposure. If the photographs are to be of uniform density and sharpness, the camera must have at least twenty settings. Ashby says, 'in its elementary forms, the law is intuitively obvious and hardly deserving statement. Where the law, in its quantitative form, develops it's power is when we consider the system in which these matters are not so obvious, and particularily when it is very large...thus the law, though trite in simple cases, can give real guidance in those cases that are much too complex to be handled by unaided intuition'.

(W. Ross Ashby, *An Introduction to Cybernetics*)[34]

Only variety can absorb variety. The law is described as follows: '...we are watching two players, R and D, who are engaged in a game. We shall follow the fortune of R. who is atempting to score on D...If R's move is unvarying, so that he produces the same move, whatever D's move, then the variety in the outcomes will be as large as the variety in D's moves. D now is...exerting full control over the outcomes. If R uses, or has available, two moves, then the variety of the outcome can be reduced to a half (but not lower). If R has three moves, it can be reduced to a third (but not lower); and so on. Thus, if the variety in the outcomes is to be reduced to some assigned number, or assigned fraction of D's variety, R's variety must be increased to at least the appropriate minimum. *Only variety in R's moves can force down the variety in the outcomes.*'

(W. Ross Ashby, *An Introduction to Cybernetics*)[35]

'To maintain regulation — equilibrium between antithetical subsystems, or stability in the whole — there is a certain variety REQUIRED in the regulator; and this cannot be less than the variety the black box of our concern itself proliferates...I consider this law stands in the same relation to management as the law of gravity stands to Newtonian physics. It is equally central to an understanding of why things are as they are. ...by variety engineering, requisite variety can be pumped into a management system that does not...have it inherently,...this is done at a price — in the expenditure of information.'

(Stafford Beer, *The Heart of Enterprise*)[36]

Management must find ways to either increase (amplify) the variety in the regulator or decrease (attenuate) the variety in the reguland, or both simultaneously, if the outcome is to be effective regulation. Because the real world proliferates so much variety, models must be made which reduce this variety and present the decision-maker with the appropriate information.

SECOND ORDER CYBERNETICS

'I submit that the cybernetics of observed systems we may consider to be first order cybernetics; while second order cybernetics is the cybernetics of observing systems...From this it appears to be clear that social cybernetics must be a second order cybernetics — a cybernetics of cybernetics in order that the observer who enters the system shall be allowed to stipulate his own purpose: he is autonomous.'

(Heinz von Foerster, *Cybernetics of Cybernetics*)[37]

'The key issue in the new epistemology is interaction between the theory and the system the theory describes or between observations and the observer who makes them. The classical scientific method assumes that such interactions do not exist. The new epistemology recognizes that observations are always a function of the observers that make them and the observer's cultural experiences. However, effects due to the observer can often be neglected, particularly when steps are taken to minimize the significance of the effects. Agreement that these effects can be neglected is most easily obtained when dealing with inanimate objects. When dealing with human subjects in laboratory conditions, similar agreement can usually be achieved by carefully controlling experiments. However, when dealing with communities and people's lives, agreement is often less easily achieved. Therefore the new epistemology or a new scientific method will reduce to the earlier epistemology and scientific method when interaction between an observer and his observations or between a theory and the system being studied can be assumed to be insignificant. This situation is revealed by agreement in the observations of numerous observers.'

(Stuart Umpleby, 'Second Order Cybernetics and the Design of Large Scale Social Experiments)[38]

SELF-ORGANIZATION

'To say a system is 'self-organizing' leaves open two quite different meanings. There is first a meaning that is simple and unobjectionable. This refers to the system that starts with its parts separate (so that the behavior of each is independent of the others' states) and whose parts then act so that they change towards forming connections of some type. Such a system is 'self-organizing' in the sense that it changes from 'parts separated' to 'parts joined.' An example is the embryo nervous system which starts with cells having little or no effect on one another, and changes, by the growth of dendrites and formation of synapses, to one in which each part's behavior is very much affected by the other parts. In general such systems can be more simply characterized as 'self-connecting'....Here, then, is a perfectly straightforward form of self-organizing system,; but I must emphasize there can be no assumption at this point that the organization developed will be a 'good' one. If we wish it to be a 'good' one, we must first provide a criterion for distinguishing between the bad and the good, and then we must ensure that an appropriate selection is made.

We are here approaching the second meaning of 'self-organizing.' Self-organizing may have the first meaning, just discussed, of changing from 'unorganized' to 'organized'. But it may also mean 'changing from a bad organization to a good one... (For example) if an automatic pilot and a plane were so coupled by mistake, that positive feedback made the whole error aggravating rather than error correcting. Here the organization is bad. The system would be 'self-organizing' if a change were automatically made to the feedback changing it from positive to negative; then the whole would have changed from a bad organization to a good one.'

(W. Ross Ashby, *Principles of the Self-organizing Systems*)[39]

'A non-stationary system becomes 'self organizing' when there is uncertainty about the criteria for macroscopic similarity....An observer is compelled to change his criteria of similarity (hence, also his reference frame) in order to make sense of the self-organizing systems' behavior and he changes it on the basis of what he has already learned (by his interaction with the system)....Hence the phrase 'self-organizing system', entails a relationship between an observer and an assembly. It also entails the observer's objective (an assembly may be a self-organizing system for one observer but not another, or for one objective, but not another).'

(Gordon Pask, *An Approach to Cybernetics*)[40]

Prigogine and his colleagues discuss self-organization in physics and biology. He uses the terms 'order through fluctuation' and 'dissipative structures' to refer to the result of self-organizing processes: 'The principle of order through fluctuation applies to systems through which energy and matter flow and whose macroscopic variables obey non-linear equations. An ecosystem described by the equations or population dynamics corresponds to just such a situation, and it may now be proposed that biological evolution through mutation and selective advantage is yet another example of the principle of order through fluctuation.'

(Peter Allen, 'Appendix: Population, Dynamics and Evolution')[41]

'The result of this work is to show that dissipative structures form by a nucleation process. Fluctuations on a sufficiently small scale are always damped by the medium. Conversely, once a fluctuation attains a size beyond a critical dimension, it triggers an instability.'

(Ilya Prigogine, 'Order Through Fluctuation: Self Organization and Social Systems')[42]

STABILITY

'Through all the meanings runs the basic idea of an 'invariant': that although the system is passing through a series of changes, there is some aspect that is unchanging; so some statement can be made that, in spite of the incessant changing, is true unchangingly. Thus, if we take a cube that is resting on one face and tilt it by 5 degrees and let it go, a whole series of changes of position follow. A statement such as 'it's tilt is 1 degree' may be true at one moment but it is false at the next. On the other hand, the statement 'it's tilt does not exceed 6 degrees' remains true permanently. This truth is invariant for the system.'

(W. Ross Ashby, *An Introduction to Cybernetics*)[43]

'Stability was defined...as some variable of interest remaining within specified limits (i.e., within a given basin in a field). Our discussion has progressed from stability through ultrastability to evolution. We can speak of 'stability' in all these contexts, but the variables of interest change type. Stability in the first sense, what we may call ordinary stability, usually refers to motion, chemical/physical state, or outward appearance. Stability in the second sense, in the ultrastable self-vetoing homeostat, refers to the maintenance or survivial of a given multi-part system. Stability in the third sense, in the context of evolution, is more elusive. Stability here means that there is an uninterrupted succession of ultrastable forms. Any given stable form (in the ordinary sense) may or may not endure. Any given ultrastable homeostat may or may not evolve. The variable which is stable in the context of evolution is that a species of homeostat continues to exist.'

(Barry Clemson, 'Approaching Adaptive Information Systems')[44]

STEADY STATE

A steady state is a condition of dynamic equilibrium in which a system maintains its structure as invariant despite fluctuations in input.

SUB-SYSTEM

A sub-system is a part of a system. If we care to change our perspective, a sub-system may be considered as a system in its own right. Thus, everything that was said about systems, environments, and boundaries applies to sub-systems also.

SYNERGY

Synergy is the act of working together so that the combination of the separate parts is more effective than if each acted alone; with synergy the whole is greater than the sum of its parts. Examples of synergy include the combined interaction of muscles in the body, the effects of certain drugs taken together and the increased strength of metal alloys. Examples may also be found in human interaction as when members of a team complement and extend one another's strengths and compensate for their individual weaknesses.

Synergy may be expected to occur whenever system elements or systems themselves interact. The effects of synergy may impel the system along the intended direction or they may cause it to move in another direction altogether. Both its unpredictability and its amplification may lead to results requiring additional planning or action, and may lead also to problems or opportunities of a greater magnitude.

(R. Buckminster Fuller, *Synergetics*)[45]

SYSTEM

'A system is a set of inter-related elements. Thus, a system is an entity which is composed of at least two elements and a relation that holds between each of its elements and at least one other element in the set.'

(Russell Ackoff, *Towards a System of System Concepts*)[46]

'Faced with such a (large) system, the observer must be cautious in referring to 'the system', for the term will probably be ambiguous, perhaps highly so...The meaning can itself be ambiguous if the particular observer is not specified, for the system may be any one of the many sub-machines provided by homomorphism. Why all these meanings should be distinguished is because different sub-machines have different properties; so that although both sub-machines may be abstracted from the real 'thing' a statement that is true of one may be false of another.'

(W. Ross Ashby, *An Introduction to Cybernetics*)[47]

'When a general pattern of relatedness is detected, we call the set of relationships systemic. Even then, the collection is not dignified by the unitary notion of a system until some unifying purpose is devised for it. ...we select, from an infinite number of relations between things, a set, which, because of coherence and pattern and purpose, permits an interpretation of what might otherwise be a meaningless cavalcade of arbitrary events. It follows that the detection of a system in the world outside ourselves is a subjective matter.'

(Stafford Beer, *Decision and Control*)[48]

Most definitions seem to stress three attributes of a system: a) it has a set of components; b) it has a structure that determines the connectivity of the components for a purpose; and c) it is a subjective concept.

We might almost define science as the process of discovering or inventing systems whose behavior makes sense or is manipulatable to our own ends. Another way of saying the same thing is to note that the arguments that rage between different schools of thought within a discipline (or within, say, the social sciences generally) are usually based on the various protagonists focusing their attention on different systems. Thus a sociologist, economist, psychologist, and political scientist see very different things when they look at a factory or a work group.

THRESHOLD

A threshold is a point at which something suddenly changes. A threshold represents a discontinuity as compared to a smooth or continuous variable.

The amount of change (or adaptation) possible for a system is of two sorts:

1. Within a given basin of stability there is always a certain variety of alternative possibilities.
2. For systems such as organizations, there are always several possible basins of stability.

The adaptations that lie within the current basin of stability are generally easily achieved. The adaptations that lie within some other basin of stability are difficult to achieve precisely because some threshold must be crossed between the basins.

Achievement of an adaptation that requires changing to a new basin of stability is typically so difficult that it requires some coercion of at least some units of the organization.

The operational definition of 'sudden change' 'discontinuity' and 'continuous variable' depends upon the observing system. For instance, in psychology a threshold represents the level of, say, noise or light that is just noticeable to a human subject. The level that represents a threshold to the human subject is merely one of many points on a continuous scale for the physicist's instruments.

TRANSDUCER

'A machine, device, protocol or rule by which information is changed to an appropriate form and introduced into a system.'

(Stafford Beer, *Brain of the Firm*)[49]

'...all the inter connections entail the crossing of boundaries. Because the 'language' of each sub-system is unique to it, messages have to be 'translated' when a boundary is crossed. To be more precise, there has to be a mechanism at the boundary capable of coding or decoding these messages as they pass. This mechanism is called a transducer, because it 'leads across'....Whenever the information carried on a channel capable of distinguishing a given variety crosses a boundary, it undergoes transduction; and the variety of the transducer must be at least equivalent to the variety of the channel.'

(Stafford Beer, *The Heart of Enterprise*)[50]

VARIETY

Variety is 'the total number of possible states of a system, or of an element of a system.'

(Stafford Beer, *Brain of the Firm*)[51]

Variety is a measure of the complexity of a system: The variety is the total number of distinguishable states of the system. Thus, the variety depends upon the observational powers of the given observer.

If two observers wish to develop a mutually useful measure of the variety for a system, they must establish a set of conventions for observing the system. This requirement for a set of agreed upon conventions applies to any measurement whatsoever.

Variety is a peculiarly useful managerial measure because, as a measure of complexity, it specifies directly the amount of regulation required for a given system.

VIABILITY

'What are the essential characteristics of a viable system? ...viable systems have the ability to make a response to a stimulus which was not included in the list of anticipated stimuli when the system was designed. They can learn from repeated experience what is the optimal response to that stimulus. Viable systems grow. They renew themselves — by, for example, self reproduction. They are robust against internal breakdown and error. Above all they continuously adapt to a changing environment, and by this means survive quite possibly in conditions which had not been entirely foreseen by their designer...'

(Stafford Beer, *Decision and Control*)[52]

'Now the systems that must be handled in the economic, social and industrial worlds are indeed systems of such viable characteristics, which tend to have (when they are successful) the properties just listed. Cybernetics has demonstrated that they have these properties only if they have higher complexity; they must exist beyond a certain 'complexity barrier' to be viable. Therefore, to insist on treating them through concepts, models and controls that are deliberately of low complexity is to rob these systems of their viability.'

Stafford Beer, *Decision and Control*)[53]

'There are a great many ways of characterizing an enterprise. The law has one way, economics another, the financial press a third, and so on. From a cybernetic standpoint, I think the most useful characterization of the enterprise is as a viable system...The ability of a system to maintain a separate existence, which we call viability, depends on a number of necessary conditions which, in sum, will also be sufficient.... In order to discuss the organization of vast institutions as well as small ones, the principle of recursiveness was invoked. We should depict the organization as a set of viable systems within a set of viable systems, and so on. From this point, it certainly was a logical necessity to identify the operational elements of the viable system that are themselves viable systems and to understand how they work in cybernetic terms.

(Stafford Beer, *The Heart of Enterprise*)[54]

Viable systems are characterized by:

- a highly complex structure.
- complexity of internal connectivity and interaction among parts.
- complexity of interactions with the environment.

A viable system robbed of its complexity in any of these dimensions soon loses its viability.

Notes

*This chapter was possible because of a project funded by Paul Rubinyi. The project provided an opportunity for extended discussion among Paul, Stafford Beer, Barry Clemson, and Allena Leonard. The chapter grew out of those discussions.

Notes: Glossary

1. W. Ross Ashby, *Design for a Brain*, second edition, (Chapman and Hall, London, 1960) p.58.

2. John Holland, *Adaptation in Natural and Artificial Systems* (University of Michigan Press, Ann Arbor, Michigan, 1975) pp.2-4.
3. Stafford Beer, *Brain of the Firm*, first edition (Herder and Herder, New York, 1972) p.305.
4. Gregory Bateson, *Steps to an Ecology of Mind* (Bantam Books, New York, 1980) p.141.
5. Francisco Varela, *Principles of Biological Autonomy* (North Holland, New York, 1979) p.55.
6. W. Ross Ashby, *An Introduction to Cybernetics* (*Methuen* and Co., London, 1956) pp.86-89.
7. Claude Shannon and Warren Weaver, *The Mathematical Theory of Communication* (University of Illinois Press, Urbana, Illinois, 1959) pp.39-40, 106.
8. Niels Bohr, *Essays, 1958-1962* (Wiley-Interscience, New York, 1963) p.4.
9. Gerald Weinberg, *An Introduction to General Systems Thinking* (Wiley-Interscience, New York, 1975) pp.119-120.
10. W. Ross Ashby *An Introduction to Cybernetics* (ref. 6) p.1.
11. Norbert Wiener *Cybernetics or Control and Communication in the Animal and the Machine* (Wiley, New York, 1948).
12. Stafford Beer, *Decision and Control* (Wiley, London, 1966) p.425.
13. W. Ross Ashby, *Design for a Brain* (ref. l) p.36.
14. Russell L. Ackoff, 'Towards a System of System Concepts' *Management Science* **17**, 11, 662. (July 1971).
15. Ludwig von Bertalanffy, *General System Theory*; revised edition (Braziller, New York, 1968) p.40.
16. *Ibid.* p.142.
17. W. Ross Ashby *Design for a Brain* (ref. 1) p.42.
18. Norbert Wiener, *Cybernetics* (ref. 11) pp.6-7.
19. W. Ross Ashby *An Introduction to Cybernetics* (ref. 6) pp.53-54.
20. Stafford Beer, *Brain of the Firm*, first edition, (ref. 3) p.306, emphasis in original.
21. *Ibid.* p.69.
22. Arthur Koestler *The Ghost in the Machine* (Macmillan Co., New York, 1967) p.48.
23. Walter Cannon *The Wisdom of the Body* (W. W. Norton, New York, *1932)* p.24.
24. Claude Shannon and Warren Weaver *The Mathematical Theory*

of Communication (ref. 7) p.100.

25. *Ibid.* p.102.
26. Warren Weaver in *The Mathematical Theory of Communication* by Claude Shannon and Warren Weaver (University of Illinois Press, Urbana, Illinois, 1959) p.96.; George A. Miller, *Psychology of Communication* (New York, Basic Books, 1967) p.15.
27. Gordon Pask *An approach to Cybernetics* (Hutchinson and Co., London, 1961) p.33.
28. Stafford Beer *Brain of the Firm,* second edition, p.110-111.
29. W. Ross Ashby *An Introduction to Cybernetics* (ref. 3) p.109.
30. Russell L. Ackoff *Redesigning the Future* (Wiley, New York, 1974) p.233.
31. Gordon Pask 'Meaning of Cybernetics in the Behavorial Sciences' in John Rose (editor) *Progress of Cybernetics* (Gordon and Breach, London, 1970) p.23.
32. Barry Clemson, A General Systems Theory of Educational Organization and Accountability, (Unpublished dissertation, the Pennsylvania State University, 1976) p.32.
33. W. Ross Ashby *An Introduction to Cybernetics* (ref. 6) p.201, emphasis in original.
34. *Ibid.* pp.212-213.
35. *Ibid.* p.206, emphasis in original.
36. Stafford Beer *The Heart of Enterprise* (Wiley, New York, 1979) p.89.
37. Heinz von Foerster 'Cybernetics of Cybernetics' in Klaus Krippendorf *Communication and Control in Society* (Gordon and Breach, New York, 1979) pp.7-8.
38. Stuart Umpleby 'Second Order Cybernetics and the Design of Large Scale Social Experiments' *Proceedings of the Annual Meeting of the Society for General Systems Research* (Washington D.C., SGSR, 1976) p.6.
39. W. Ross Ashby, 'Principles of Self-Organizing Systems' in Heinz von Foerster and George Zopf (editors) *Principles of Self Organization* (Pergamon Press, New York, 1962) pp.267-268.
40. Gordon Pask *An Approach to Cybernetics* (ref. 27) p.47.
41. Peter Allen 'Appendix: Population, Dynamics and Evolution' in *Evolution and Consciousness* (eds). Erich Jantsch and Conrad Waddington (Addison Wesley, London, 1976) p.127.
42. Ilya Prigogine, 'Order Through Fluctuation: Self Organization and Social Systems' in *Evolution and Consciousness* (eds) Erich

Jantsch and Conrad Waddington (Addison Wesley, London, 1976) p.119.
43. W. Ross Ashby *An Introduction to Cybernetics* (ref. 6) p.73.
44. Barry Clemson 'Approaching Adaptive Information Systems' Luncheon address to the Symposium on Advanced Information Systems Technology, University of Maryland (April 12, 1977) pp.9-10.
45. Paraphrased from R. Buckminster Fuller *Synergetics* (MacMillan Co., New York and London, 1975) pp.12-13.
46. Russell L. Ackoff 'Towards a System of System Concepts' (ref. 14) p.662.
47. W. Ross Ashby *An Introduction to Cybernetics* (ref. 3) p.106.
48. Stafford Beer *Decision and Control* (Ref. 12 pp.242-243.
49. Stafford Beer *Brain of the Firm*, first edition (ref. 3) p.306.
50. Stafford Beer *The Heart of Enterprise* (ref. 36) p.101.
51. Stafford Beer *Brain of the Firm*, first edition (ref. 3) p.307.
52. Stafford Beer *Decision and Control* (ref. 12) p.256.
53. *Ibid.* pp.256-7.
54. Stafford Beer *The Heart of Enterprise* (ref. 31) pp.113, 199.

INDEX